D0687911

House and Household in Elizabethan England

House and Household in Elizabethan England

Wollaton Hall and the Willoughby Family

ALICE T. FRIEDMAN

The University of Chicago Press ♦ Chicago and London

Publication of this book has been aided by a grant from The Millard Meiss Publication Fund of the College Art Association of America.

ALICE T. FRIEDMAN is associate professor of art and codirector of the architecture program at Wellesley College.

The University of Chicago Press, Chicago 60637
The University of Chicago Press, Ltd., London
© 1989 by The University of Chicago
All rights reserved. Published 1989
Printed in the United States of America
98 97 96 95 94 93 92 91 90 89   5 4 3 2 1

Library of Congress Cataloging-in-Publication Data

Friedman, Alice T.
    House and household in Elizabethan England: Wollaton Hall and the
    Willoughby family / Alice T. Friedman.
        p.   cm.
    Bibliography: p. 215
    Includes index.
    ISBN 0-226-26329-0
        1. Wollaton Hall (Wollaton, Nottingham, England)   2. Willoughby
    family.   3. Nottingham (England)—History.   4. Households—England—
    Nottingham—History—16th century.   5. England—Social life and
    customs—16th century.   6. Architecture, Domestic—England—
    Nottingham.   7. Wollaton (Nottingham, England)—History.   I. Title.
    DA690.N92F75 1988
    942.5'27—dc 19   88–14224
                                                                    CIP

This book is printed on acid-free paper.

For my parents
who taught me to love old houses and the people who live in them

Contents

List of Illustrations ix

Acknowledgments xv

Introduction 1

1. The Making of an Elizabethan Patron 12

2. The Manor House and Its Household 38

3. A House Divided 53

4. Smythson, Wollaton, and the Elizabethan
   Building World 71

5. Life at the New Hall: 1587–1610 135

6. Fame and Changing Fortunes 155

Conclusion 179

Appendix A:
The Willoughby Household Orders of 1572 185

Appendix B:
Building Accounts and Related Documents 187

Notes 189

Selected Bibliography 215

Index 223

Illustrations

Color Plates (following p. 48)

1.   Wollaton Hall, Nottinghamshire
2.   George Gower, *Sir Francis Willoughby*
3.   George Gower, *Lady Elizabeth Willoughby*
4.   Anonymous, *Sir Percival Willoughby*
5.   Anonymous, *Lady Bridget Willoughby*
6.   Anonymous, *Dr. John Banister Delivering the Visceral Lecture to the Barber Surgeons in 1581*
7.   John Griffier (attributed to), *Wollaton Hall*
8.   Jan Siberechts, *Wollaton Hall From the Village*

Maps

1.1.   Southern England and the Midlands   16

Figures

1.1.   Sir Godfrey Kneller, *Cassandra Willoughby, Duchess of Chandos*   2
4.1.   Andrea Palladio, *Site and Plan Project for Villa Pagliarino, Lanzè(?) and for Villa Poiana, Poiana Maggiore*   74
4.2.   Andrea Palladio, *Sketch Plan for Villa Caldogno, Caldogno*   74
4.3.   Andrea Palladio, *Villa Thiene*, from *I Quattro libri dell'architettura*   75
4.4.   Sebastiano Serlio, *Villa Design*, from *Tutte l'opere d'architettura*   78
4.5.   Sebastiano Serlio, *Villa Design*, from *Tutte l'opere d'architettura*   78
4.6.   Villa Guistinian, Roncade   79
4.7.   Sebastiano Serlio, *Villa For a Noble Gentleman*   79

4.8.	J. A. Du Cerceau, *Design for a Chateau,* from *Livre d'architecture*	80
4.9.	Robert Smythson, *A Sketch Plan for a House in the Shape of a Greek Cross*	80
4.10.	Robert Smythson, *Variant Plan for Hardwick*	82
4.11.	Robert Smythson, *Three Designs for Screens*	83
4.12.	Robert Smythson, *Entrance Front of a Large House*	83
4.13.	Robert Smythson, *Wollaton Hall: Plan*	86
4.14.	Robert Smythson, *Wollaton Hall: Elevation of a Corner Tower*	86
4.15.	Robert Smythson, *A Screen Design for Wollaton Hall*	87
4.16.	Robert Smythson, *Decorative Panels (after Vredeman de Vries)*	87
4.17.	Jan Vredeman de Vries, *Gable Designs,* from *Architectura oder Bautung*	88
4.18.	Anonymous, *Sketch Plan for a Country House (after Du Cerceau)*	88
4.19.	Sebastiano Serlio, *Plan of Poggio Reale* from *Tutte l'opere d'architettura*	89
4.20.	Herstmonceaux Castle (1440)	89
4.21.	Henry Winstanley, *Wimbledon House,* built in 1588	91
4.22.	Wollaton Hall: Ground Floor Plan	92
4.23.	Wollaton Hall: Second Floor Plan	92
4.24.	Wollaton Hall: Plans of the Mezzanine Levels in the Southeast Tower: (1) Above the Ground Floor (2) Above the Second Floor (3) Tower Room	93
4.25.	Hardwick Hall, Derbyshire, 1596: Plans of the Three Principal Floors	94
4.26.	John Thorpe, *Design for a House Based on Palladio's Villa Pisani*	96
4.27.	John Thorpe, *House of Sir John Danvers*	96
4.28.	John Thorpe, *Plan and Elevation of Campden House*	97
4.29.	Wollaton Hall: North Front	98
4.30.	Anonymous, *View of Old Wardour Castle, Wiltshire*	98
4.31.	J. A. Du Cerceau, *Chateau of Chenonceaux*	99
4.32.	Sebastiano Serlio, *House For a Citizen or Merchant*	100
4.33.	Sebastiano Serlio, *House For a Citizen or Merchant . . . in the French Manner*	100
4.34.	Wollaton Hall: The Prospect Tower from the West	101
4.35.	Wollaton Hall: A Bartizan on the Prospect Tower	101
4.36.	Wollaton Hall: The Southeast Tower	105
4.37.	Hardwick Hall	105

4.38. Plasterwork Ceiling from Henry Shaw, *Details of Elizabethan Architecture*   107

4.39. Garret Johnson, *Tomb of the 4th Earl of Rutland* at Bottesford, Leicestershire   110

4.40. J. A. Du Cerceau, *Design for a Chimney-piece,* from *Livre d'architecture*   110

4.41. Hieronymous Cock, *Cartouche Designs,* from *Compertimentorum*   111

4.42. Wollaton Hall: Strapwork Gable   113

4.43. Jan Vredeman de Vries, *Gable Designs,* from *Architectura oder Bautung*   113

4.44. Wollaton Hall: The South Entrance (detail)   114

4.45. Jan Vredeman de Vries, *Doric Order,* from *Variae Architecturae Formae*   114

4.46. Diana, Wollaton Hall   115

4.47. Jan Vredeman de Vries, *Designs for Ornament,* from *Differents portraicts de menuiserie*   115

4.48. Wollaton Hall: Bust of a Roman Emperor in a Strapwork Frame, Second Floor   116

4.49. Wollaton Hall: Strapwork Frame on a Corner Tower   116

4.50. Old Wardour Castle: Inscription Plaque Over the Entrance   117

4.51. Old Wardour Castle: Detail of Sculpture Over the Entrance   117

4.52. Old Wardour Castle: Principal Entrance   118

4.53. Old Wardour Castle: Door Frame by Smythson in the Inner Court   118

4.54. Robert Smythson, *Ornamental Panel* (after Vredeman de Vries, *Variae Architecturae Formae*)   118

4.55. Old Wardour Castle: Detail of Door Frame in the Inner Court   119

4.56. Old Wardour Castle: Detail of Door Frame in the Inner Court   119

4.57. Wollaton Hall: Detail of Ornament on a Corner Tower   120

4.58. Wollaton Hall: Detail of Ornament on a Corner Tower   120

4.59. Wollaton Hall: Detail of Ornamental Sculpture on the Facade   120

4.60. Wollaton Hall: North Facade   121

4.61. Wollaton Hall: Detail of Ornament over the North Door   121

4.62.	Richard and Gabriel Royley, *Tomb of Thomas Fermor and Wife*	123
4.63.	Detail of the Fermor Tomb	123
4.64.	Nicholas Johnson, Isaac James and Nicholas Stone, *Tomb of Thomas Sutton*	124
4.65.	Richard Stevens (?), *Tomb of John Lord Russell*	124
4.66.	Bust of Virgil, Wollaton Hall	126
4.67.	Bust of Aristotle, Wollaton Hall	126
4.68.	Bust of Plato, Wollaton Hall	126
4.69.	Bust of Cato, Wollaton Hall	127
4.70.	Minerva, Wollaton Hall	127
4.71.	Lion's Head, Wollaton Hall: South Front	127
4.72.	Wenceslaus Hollar, *Wollaton Hall*, from Thoroton, *Nottinghamshire*	128
4.73.	Portrait of Charles I (after Lesueur)	128
4.74.	The Samian Sibyl	129
4.75.	Crispin van de Passe, *Samian Sibyl*	129
4.76.	The Egyptian Sibyl	129
4.77.	Crispin van de Passe, *Egyptian Sibyl*	129
4.78.	Flora, Wollaton Hall	130
4.79.	Mercury, Wollaton Hall	130
4.80.	Hercules, Wollaton Hall	131
4.81.	Bust of a Roman Soldier, Wollaton Hall	131
4.82.	Wollaton Hall: The Screen	132
4.83.	Wollaton Hall: The Screen (detail)	132
4.84.	Wollaton Hall: The Chimney-piece in the Hall	133
4.85.	Serlio, *Doric Chimney-piece*, from *Tutte l'opere d'architettura*	133
4.86.	Richard Stevens (?), *Design for a Wall Monument to Sir Henry Willoughby et al.*	133
5.1.	John Thorpe, *Wollaton Hall: Facade*	140
5.2.	John Thorpe, *Wollaton Hall: Sketch Plan*	140
5.3.	Hardwick Hall: The Gallery	144
5.4.	The Prospect Room (in the course of renovation)	145
5.5.	The Windows in the Prospect Room (in the course of renovation)	145
5.6.	Robert Smythson, *Design for a Closet or Office*	146
5.7.	Wollaton Hall: Entrance to a Tower Room from the Roof Terrace	150
5.8.	Wollaton Hall: Looking Across the Roof of the Prospect Tower	150
5.9.	Wollaton Hall: *The Hall*, from John Britton, *Architectural Antiquities of Great Britain*	152

5.10.   Hardwick Hall: The Screen in the Hall   152
5.11.   Charlton House, Greenwich, 1607: Plan   153
5.12.   John Smythson, *Plan of Worksop Manor*   153
6.1.   Jan Siberechts, *Wollaton Hall*, 1697   161
6.2.   J. Kip and L. Knyff, *Wollaton Hall*, from *Brittania
        Illustrata*   162
6.3.   *Wollaton Hall*, from John Throsby, *Thoroton's Antiq-
        uities of Nottinghamshire*   169
6.4.   Wollaton Hall: Plan of the Ground Floor, from John
        Britton, *Architectural Antiquities of Great Britain*   169
6.5.   Wollaton Hall: West Facade and Service Wing   170
6.6.   Aerial View of Wollaton Hall and Stables   170
6.7.   J. Wyatville, *Design for Wainscot*   171
6.8.   P. K. Allen, *Wollaton Hall, Plan and Section*, from
        The Builder   171
6.9.   J. Wyatville, *Wollaton Hall: East Front*   172
6.10.   J. Wyatville, *Wollaton Hall: South Front*   172
6.11.   Wollaton Hall: The Ceiling in the Prospect Room   173
6.12.   Wollaton Hall: Wall Niche in the Prospect Room   173
6.13.   The Gate Lodge   174
6.14.   The Camellia House, Wollaton Hall   174
6.15.   Wollaton Hall: The Hall, ca. 1902   175
6.16.   Wollaton Hall: The Drawing Room (North Great
        Chamber), ca. 1902   175
6.17.   Ladies at the Grand Fancy Bazaar, Wollaton Hall,
        1884   176
6.18.   Wollaton Hall: Early Museum Displays in the Hall   176

Acknowledgments

I have been helped and supported by many people in the course of writing this book. When I began the project as a Ph.D. dissertation in the Department of Fine Arts at Harvard, James Ackerman acted as my advisor and mentor; John Coolidge also taught me a great deal about architectural history and I am grateful to both of them. A number of other people read the text at various stages and offered advice: my colleagues in the Art Department at Wellesley College were an invaluable resource during the process of revising the manuscript, especially Margaret Carroll, Lilian Armstrong, James O'Gorman, and Peter Fergusson; Katharine Park served as both reader and editor, and I have benefited greatly from our discussions of many of the historical issues dealt with in this study; Alan Cameron, formerly of the Manuscripts Department at the University of Nottingham Library, helped me make sense out of the documents, and Mark Girouard made a number of thoughtful suggestions at significant points in my research and writing.

Many others have helped overcome the myriad problems that this sort of project entails. I am grateful to Lord Middleton for his enthusiasm about the book and for providing me with photographs, documents, and information about his family's history. Clive Wainwright introduced me to two research collections which I would not otherwise have been able to use, the archives of the Department of Furniture and Interior Design at the Victoria and Albert Museum and the library of the Society of Antiquaries; I am also indebted to him and to Jane Wainwright for their hospitality during my years in London. In Nottingham, Brian Playle, Assistant Arts Director, gave me full access to Wollaton Hall, now the Natural History Museum, and graciously provided plans, photographs, and valuable information at many times over the course of the last ten years. Graham Walley, Senior Keeper at Wollaton, has also been most generous, as has the staff of the museum, many of whom gave their time and shared their knowledge of the house with me during my visits. My research in the Manuscripts Department at the University of Nottingham Library has been made easier and more pleasant because of its knowledgeable and efficient staff—Mary Welch, the former Keeper, Alan Cameron,

Linda Shaw, and the present Keeper Dorothy Johnston. I owe much to them and to the staffs of many other archives and libraries where I conducted my research: the Warburg Institute, the Institute of Historical Research, the British Library, the Public Record Office, the Huntington Library and, at Harvard, the Widener, Houghton and Fine Arts Libraries.

A number of institutions generously provided financial assistance. My dissertation was supported by a travel fellowship from the Department of Fine Arts at Harvard University and by a Huber Fellowship from Wellesley College. Faculty Research Grants from Wellesley also provided funds for summer travel and for an important research leave in 1983–84. I am very grateful to the Huntington Library for a fellowship that enabled me to consult their manuscript collection. Finally, the Millard Meiss Publication Fund of the College Art Association has generously helped cover the costs of producing this book in its present form.

Many friends and colleagues also provided assistance and support of various kinds: among others too numerous to mention individually are Valerie Fraser, Virginia Carabine, Keith Carabine, Marie Companion, Joyce Kauffman, David Fixler, Dana Kubick, and David Stang. My parents, Edward and Winifred Friedman, not only introduced me to the joys of art history but also provided me with many years of financial support so that I could study and travel; this book is dedicated to them in loving recognition of their shared interest. Finally, I wish to acknowledge my debt to Lena Sorensen, who has never failed to provide the intellectual, emotional, and logistical supports that were needed along the way. This book could not have been completed without her.

Introduction

By 1720, or thereabouts, Cassandra Willoughby, Duchess of Chandos, (fig. 1.1) was nearing the end of the family history on which she had been working for the past thirty years. As her story drew to a close, she turned her attention to the events of her own life, describing the circumstances that had brought her to Wollaton Hall, her family's Nottinghamshire country seat, as a young woman of seventeen:

> My brother [Francis Willoughby] after spending some time in this unsettled way between London and Wollaton, made a short viset to France, only just to see that country, and soon after his return from thence to London began to think of settling at Wollaton, and taking me to live with him there, and help him to manage his household affairs. This proposall I was much delighted with, thinking it would be no small pleasure for me to be Mrs. of Wollaton, and to doe whatever I had a mind to, believing that such a government must make me perfectly happy.[1]

The years had proved her right: Cassandra's life was indeed a happy one, not least of all because, more often than not, she had had the freedom to "doe whatever" she "had a mind to." In 1687, Cassandra Willoughby became the mistress of Wollaton and made herself a part of it, remaining in charge after her brother's death in 1688 and the arrival of a younger brother Thomas as the new heir and master of the household. At his side, she oversaw the complete renovation of the Elizabethan house and the restoration of its gardens, transforming the rambling estate into a fashionable country seat. She lived at Wollaton until 1713, when she married her cousin James Brydges at the age of forty-three, running the household even after Thomas's marriage and the birth of his children, ever solicitous about their schooling and ever watchful over domestic affairs. Despite her duties, she found ample time to maintain an extensive correspondence and to spend hours each day in the library poring over the books and manuscripts left there by her ancestors. She filled her notebooks with scraps of letters, inventories, and household accounts from the Elizabethan age, and used these to form the basis for a work of history, entitled—with characteristic attention to detail—*The Account of the Willughby's [sic] of Wollaton taken out of the Pedigree, old Letters, and old*

1.1. Sir Godfrey Kneller, *Cassandra Willoughby, Duchess of Chandos.* ca. 1713. Collection of Lord Middleton.

*Books of Accounts in my Brother Sir Thomas Willoughby's study, Dec.
A.D. 1702.*[2]

Although her *Account* begins in the Middle Ages, it was the sixteenth and seventeenth centuries which captured Cassandra Willoughby's interest. In part this was the result of circumstances over
which she had no control: the family archive, a collection of thou-
sands of documents, was richest in papers dating from the Elizabethan
period and, in particular, contained an extensive collection of personal letters exchanged by Sir Francis Willoughby, the builder of
Wollaton Hall, and his wife Elizabeth. Yet it is also true that Cassandra was particularly fascinated by the sort of details contained in
these letters: as the new mistress of Wollaton, she was curious about
its builders and the way they lived, focusing her attention on domestic affairs, on household organization, and on the ups and downs of
her ancestors' private lives.

Cassandra Willoughby's presence—both as a historian and as the
restorer of her family's country house—will be felt throughout this
book. To begin with, we are indebted to her for the careful and
detailed transcriptions which fill the pages of the *Account* and the
notebooks in which she wrote her early drafts. These are especially
valuable to us because only a handful of the original Elizabethan
letters have survived. Happily, these include one which bears witness
to Cassandra's accuracy as a copyist since it is closely paralleled by
a transcription in the *Account*.[3] Moreover, because her working
method was to go through the letters one by one and make notes on
them, rather than to simply create her own narrative from the information contained in the documents, Cassandra's *Account* forms a
richly textured history in which the original language and feeling for
detail remain strong.

But Cassandra's activities at Wollaton are relevant to the concerns
of this study in another way as well. As a historian, and perhaps even
more as a woman who lived in a house which she rebuilt to accommodate the tastes and customs of her own time, Cassandra was aware
of the gulf which separated her way of life from that of its earliest
inhabitants. This consciousness of history and of her own place in
it—although amateur and largely unarticulated—fills the pages of
the *Account*, reminding us, as we look on Cassandra's efforts from our
own vantage point in the twentieth century, of the changes which
each new generation brought to the great house. This in turn helps us
to see the planning and construction of Wollaton Hall as the product
of a particular constellation of social, intellectual, economic and artistic forces that combined to give the house its distinctive form. These
forces were not only highly personal and localized but also in con-

stant flux, producing very different houses elsewhere for other patrons and at other moments, even within a relatively short span of time.

To put it another way, anyone who tries to write the social history of architecture must eventually confront the fact that the lives of buildings and the lives of human beings are timed by different clocks. The form of a building embodies a contradiction: it is the actualization of the social relationships, material resources, needs, and talents of a particular patron, architect, household, or group of builders at a fixed point in time, but it is expected to outlive them and to remain useful and meaningful long after they are gone. Buildings are expected to last. Men and women are relatively short-lived by comparison, yet—unlike buildings—they are continually changing. The passage of time for human beings is fast, bringing with it new ideas, new relationships, new ways of behaving. These shifts are not only experienced from one generation to the next, but also in the daily lives of individuals as experience unfolds and consciousness evolves. Thus each generation both changes the buildings that it inherits and builds new ones of its own, expressing and accommodating the relationships, habits of mind and beliefs which are all part of their distinctive culture.[4]

The primary goal of this book is to describe the planning and construction of Wollaton Hall, Nottinghamshire (plate 1), a country house designed by Robert Smythson and built in the 1580s. Intertwined with this narrative and, indeed, integral to it, is the history of the Willoughby family and of the men and women who lived and worked in the house and on the surrounding estate. Particular attention is focused here both on the years immediately preceding the construction of the country house and on those immediately following it. A short postscript brings the story up to the twentieth century. In a way, this study is an attempt to write the biography of a building. It describes how the house came to be planned and constructed, thus focusing attention on the patron, on his life in the years preceding the project, and on his motives as a builder, and it details the artistic development of the architect and his place in the Elizabethan building world. It then examines the ways in which the building was used over time. Changes on the relatively slow timetable of built form (that is, the tangible evidence of architectural history) are presented here in relation to, and as the result of, developments in the relatively fast-paced world of human interactions.

A large and complex country house like Wollaton can be analyzed in two ways: first, as a newly built structure which, in replacing an older one, bears witness either to a shift in the social or economic status of its builder, to the talents of its architect, or to changes in the day-to-day activities of its inhabitants (and perhaps to all of these);

and second, it can be treated as a repository of evidence, a living record of human relationships which in itself reflects the ebb and flow of culture. Here another image comes to mind: by outliving its original occupants and accommodating new ones over successive generations, a house becomes a sort of palimpsest on which successive texts are written, some more boldly than others. Each text represents a shift in cultural norms and mental habits, expressing values and aesthetic conventions that can also be found, often much more clearly presented, in the newly constructed buildings of each period.

Wollaton Hall is not only a splendid monument to its time and its builders, but also a major work in the history of English architecture. But whereas the Elizabethan period has always been one of particular interest to economic and social historians, marked as it is by important shifts in business, trade, and family structure, buildings in "The Age of Shakespeare" have never received much attention.[5] Indeed, Elizabethan and Jacobean country houses have traditionally been shunned as uncouth and somewhat demented distant cousins of the villas and palaces of the Italian Renaissance. Until recently, little serious attention had been paid to the formation of English architectural style in the generation before Inigo Jones. His designs for the court of James I are treated as evidence of a new age of classicism which shines forth from the darkness of English architecture with the axial plans, symmetrical elevations, and classicized details of seventeenth-century architecture.[6] Yet there is now ample documentary and visual evidence on which to base a new approach to the architecture of the early period, as well as a rich literature in other fields on which to draw.[7]

The Middleton Collection at the University of Nottingham contains a wide range of documents which, together with Cassandra's *Account,* provide us with detailed evidence relating not only to the history of Wollaton Hall but also to the design and use of the medieval manor house nearby which preceded it as the family's principal Nottinghamshire residence.[8] Building accounts, household ledger books, legal papers, and personal letters shed light on many aspects of the history of the period; these, in conjunction with documents in other collections, allow us to construct a fairly detailed picture of the day-to-day activities, attitudes, and social customs which underlay decisions about the planning of Wollaton Hall and buildings like it. There are gaps, to be sure, and many questions which cannot be answered, but the richness and diversity of surviving documents permits us to go quite far in looking for answers to the questions raised here. In addition, the Drawings Collection at the Royal Institute of British Architects contains a large number of plans and drawings by Robert Smythson, including several projects for Wollaton Hall. These make it possible to study the range of his portfolio and to assess the importance of his designs for Wollaton and other country houses, notably Hardwick Hall, built for the Countess of Shrewsbury in the 1590s. Smythson emerges through his drawings as both a committed student of Renaissance planning and an innovative practitioner of country-house design.

The research of Sir John Summerson, Eric Mercer, and Mark Girouard, among others, has established the framework of events in architectural history during the Elizabethan and Jacobean periods, and they have laid the foundations for further discussions of stylistic change.[9] In Mercer's fundamental study of "The Houses of the Gentry," for example, he casts the discussion of country-house planning in terms of social status and function, suggesting that the treatment of great halls, galleries, and courtyards could be used as indices of the differing tastes and values of courtiers and gentry patrons during the reigns of Elizabeth and James I.[10] Mercer makes it clear that money was not the sole determining factor in decisions controlling design; the evidence he focuses on is, on the contrary, cultural rather than economic.

The publication of Mark Girouard's *Life in the English Country House* in 1978 introduced the general reader to the method of studying the architecture of country houses in relation to the patterns of social behavior which they accommodated. Using household regulations, inventories, diaries, and letters, Girouard described the patterns of architectural change from the Middle Ages to the middle of the twentieth century in terms of power relationships and changing cultural values. Thus, domestic planning was shown to reflect new methods of estate management, shifting political alliances, and changing fashions in personal display.[11]

This book takes its overall methodological direction from the questions raised by these studies over the past twenty years. But by focusing on a single building, its household, and the surrounding estate, I hope to bring to light the details of the planning process in a specific case and thus call attention to factors that have been overlooked or only briefly treated by others. In particular, I have been concerned with the ways in which changes in the status of women and in the day-to-day management of an upper-gentry estate translated into changes in both domestic planning and architectural style.

To date, little scholarly attention has been focused on the issue of gender as it relates to architectural history. By reinserting the experiences of women into the analysis of architectural style—a process which involves looking at family structure and power relationships—we can better understand the dynamics of stylistic change as a function, in part, of social life.[12] During the years which preceded its construction, and throughout the first phase of Wollaton's history as a country seat, the question of women's position in society was particularly pressing among the upper gentry and aristocracy. A number of significant factors—the presence of a female sovereign, new attitudes toward the making of wills and property ownership by women, new opportunities for social mobility among men of all classes, Puritan doctrines concerning the marriage bond and the quality of home life—conspired to produce what has been described as a widely felt anxiety about, and within, relationships between men and women.[13] In public, a heated debate about women's "true" role erupted in popular literature and in books of advice; in a recent study, Lisa Jardine has suggested, quite convincingly, that preoccupation with this issue underlay the ambivalent characterization of women in dramatic literature of the period.[14] In private life, the effects of this ideological debate varied according to the pressures of property ownership and the balance of authority. These not only increased as one moved higher up the scale of wealth and power, but obviously depended on individual situations and temperaments.[15]

This said, it should be added that there is at present little agreement among historians about the status of women in this period, either in general or as members of particular social groups.[16] The evidence presented here can, ultimately, add only a handful of cases to the pool of data, and while valuable, these can shed little light on the overall historical question. Yet by being integrally connected to the histories of well-known country houses, the women and men described in this study take on a special importance: they allow us to link together specific relationships involving women—as wives, mothers, friends, or participants in household groups—and individual buildings, producing a critical equation in the formation of architectural space. Like interactions between people of unequal social or economic power, relationships between men and women, whether they are from the same or different classes, are often charged with meaning which transcends the needs or personalities of the individuals and reflects the preoccupations of the culture at large. As such, these relationships become "political" in the broad sense of the term; they are used to play out the larger contradictions of the society as a whole.

The fact that architectural spaces reflect women's status and their place in household structure has for some time been recognized by environmental psychologists, social anthropologists, and geographers.[17] The relationship is clearly not only one of cause and effect, however. Once shaped, spaces and boundaries exert their own influences on the patterns of behavior enacted within them.[18] Thus the issue of gender and space clearly goes beyond the simple one-to-one relationship of women patrons and the buildings they pay for or their relationships to men who were patrons of architecture.

With or without direct control over architectural decisions, women clearly act as mediators and participants in the planning of built form. As property owners or transmitters of wealth through marriage, as housekeepers and bearers of children, women affect (and are affected by) the spaces in which they live. Further, both the shape of their houses and the quality of their experience can be seen as expressions of a set of relationships and cultural attitudes, in particular those which assign value to activities associated with children, household structure, and social life. That these attitudes varied over time is hardly surprising.

At Wollaton Hall, we can point to a number of architectural developments which directly affected the lives of women. Most obvious is the increase in the size and number of spaces (rooms, terraces, gardens) provided for socializing and polite entertainment. Second, the Elizabethan house was clearly more isolated than the old manor house had been: one was at the center of an active working farm on the fringe of a village, the other was shut away behind high walls and courtyards in the middle of a large park. Finally, the planning of the new house provided more diversification of private spaces and service areas—including private studies, muniment rooms, and storage rooms—than the earlier house had and separated these spaces from the large formal rooms which were the showpieces of the house. All of these features of the Elizabethan plan had significant implications, both positive and negative, for the lives of women and for their status in the household.

A second area of particular concern in this study is the relationship between architecture and the social-economic structures of Elizabethan society. The Tudor period was one which witnessed both increased opportunities for advancement and a heightened consciousness of class status.[19] These fostered the development of increasingly sophisticated codes through which to express difference: food, clothing, etiquette, education, and architecture, among other things, were all subjected to increased scrutiny, with the result that material objects and every aspect of human behavior were placed in complex hierarchical categories. Elizabethan sumptuary laws and etiquette books make such categories explicit; similar stylistic languages existed for the visual arts and literature.

During the period under consideration here, we can observe a widening gap between social classes, a division expressed in architectural terms by the separation of social and agricultural functions in the planning of large, self-contained country houses and by the creation of smaller and more private rooms in domestic structures of all types.[20] Further, in country-house design, we observe an increasing attention to the provision of small offices and private cabinets. Both are associated with increased emphasis on record-keeping, education, and professionalism. In estate management, these improvements in business technique and the provision of spaces specifically for the storage of documents made possible increased control of both property and tenants.

It is well known that the Elizabethan period is marked by rapid social and economic change. In the lives of the people who are the subjects of this study, these changes often expressed themselves as emotional ambivalence and uncertainty. Indeed, Wollaton Hall and its occupants frequently appear to be split between two different worlds. In appearance, the house itself draws on both the Gothic and classical traditions, uniting a trabeated surface of pilastered orders with a central tower distinguished by its castlelike bartizan turrets. The plan brings together traditional English sequences of rooms and Palladian axial symmetry, but these two very different planning strategies are never integrated—the mazelike spaces of the hall, screens passage, and service rooms on the ground floor are a world apart from the open and airy formal rooms above. Moreover, in the running of their household, the Elizabethan Willoughbys often seem torn between the old ways and the new: the husband maintained a large staff of officers and servants, insisting on traditional ceremony and on his rights over his wife's property and person; she, for her part, resisted him and claimed her right to an independent life at Court, in London, or wherever she chose to travel. Their troubles were clearly exacerbated by their personal problems and idiosyncracies, but their disputes seem to reflect a more widely felt tension over shifting social norms in contemporary society. Thus architecture and social relations appear to run a parallel course, with patterns in one area reflecting changes in the other.

Matters of taste in art and architecture are difficult to document at the best of times, and attitudes toward marriage and family life often go unrecorded. Letters, account books, and household orders enable us to sketch a picture of the daily activities in and around the country house; plans, drawings, and the surviving buildings themselves guide us in reconstructing the physical environment in which these things took place. Yet the historical evidence has many limitations: many seemingly straightforward narrative details about where people went, who they met, and what they did cannot be filled in at this point, and indeed they probably never will be. The private thoughts and feelings of individuals are even more elusive. Thus the fundamental questions of motivation and psychology at the intersection of social and architectural history cannot be answered directly but must be approached through incidental evidence and inference.

The method followed here is broadly interdisciplinary and broadly inclusive of various types of evidence; the goal is to reconstruct, recreate, and interpret the process through which the Elizabethan house and estate at Wollaton took shape. In dealing with questions of this kind, the method and discourse of art history has been greatly enriched by the concept of the "period eye," a phrase coined by Michael Baxandall to indicate the habits of mind and the "mass of information and assumptions" which the makers and observers of pictures bring to the process of looking at them.[21] These mental habits may be the result of specific skills (in Baxandall's example, for instance, the facility in reading proportional relationships, so important for the appreciation of fifteenth-century painting, was shown to relate directly to the practice of barrel gauging, a visual skill keenly developed among Florentine merchants) or of systems of signification, such as gesture, building materials, or clothes. Equally, the mental categories through which men and women order experience, that is, the way they structure a story, outline a speech or, indeed, divide up the spaces inside their houses and the area surrounding them, all contribute to their expectations and preferences in dealing with art and architecture—in short, to "taste" and artistic style. Thus, educational practices, business skills, devotional literature, handbooks of advice on marriage, or popular love stories all contain valuable clues to the interpretation of form. By influencing what we know, they determine what we see.[22] Often the relevance of such evidence to the history of architecture appears tentative at best, but it can bring us closer to understanding the most elusive and complex problems in the formation of architectural style.

The method of interpretive history used here owes a great deal to this concept of the "period eye" and to the notion in cognitive aesthetics which Ernst Gombrich has called "the beholder's share."[23] Here again we are concerned with culturally relative skills and assumptions (referred to by Gombrich as "mental set") but with a slightly different emphasis: the central construct of this theory is the psychological relationship between expectation and observation, "the waves of fulfillment, disappointment, right guesses, and wrong moves that make up our daily life."[24] For architectural history, this is a crucial notion. Past experience not only determines our ability to "read" a building in terms of its symbolic language (including, for example, the implications of the material of which it is made, its size, overall organization, and the presence or absence of the Orders or other surface detail) but also colors our judgment of it. As Gombrich put it: "A style, like a culture or a climate of opinion, sets up a horizon of expectation, a mental set, which registers deviations and modifications with exaggerated sensitivity. In noticing relationships the mind registers tendencies."[25] Gombrich used this principle to great advantage in describing the mannerist distortions of Giulio Romano's Palazzo del Te in the 1520s as an intentional disjunction in the terms of a system of formal relationships which unsettled the observer by frustrating or jarring his or her expectations.[26] Clearly this principle can be applied to the experience of other architectural or urban spaces: size, shape, sequences, juxtapositions, boundaries—all these are elements not only of form but of language, subject to cultural as well as individual differences.[27] A path of approach or a sequence of rooms is marked by signposts; the interpretation of them depends not only on a knowledge of the language in which they "speak," but also on a feeling for the range of choices and for the overall structure of the context in which they appear. In short, interpretation depends on expectation.

Many historians have recognized the value of the English country house as a building type and as an institution which provides evidence of social structures and cultural attitudes. These houses have been used to chart the progress of demographic shifts, to gauge opportunities for economic and social mobility, and as evidence of the ebb and flow of fashion in architecture and interior decoration.[28] As a group these studies define the map on which Wollaton Hall and the Willoughby family can now be located; they make it possible to reconstruct, in small part, the landscape of material conditions, relationships, attitudes, and expectations in which this splendid work of architecture took shape.

I

The Making of an Elizabethan Patron

As historians, our first view of Wollaton Hall should be through the eyes of a contemporary. Writing in 1600, just four years after Sir Francis Willoughby's death, the antiquary William Camden recorded his visit to Wollaton: "Where in this age Sir Francis Willoughby Kt., out of ostentation to show his riches, built at vast charges a very stately house, both for the splendid appearance and curious workmanship of it."[1] These scant comments draw attention to key questions and categories in our investigation of the patron's role. First, for Camden, as for many of his contemporaries, the house and its builder were closely identified. Thus he described Wollaton Hall in terms of Willoughby's personal ambitions, focusing on the issue of economic and social display. Size and substance were traditional architectural indices of power; the creation of a large and imposing new house, perched on a hilltop and surrounded by a substantial estate, served as a particularly unambiguous demonstration of wealth.[2] But in the Elizabethan world that Camden inhabited, social status and economic status were no longer equivalent; by calling Willoughby "knight," Camden added another designation to locate Willoughby's place in the minds of his readers, calling attention to both his wealth *and* his social status.[3]

Camden added another significant critical category to his short description by using the phrase "curious workmanship." Thus he not only emphasized the cost of the building but also called attention to artistic skill and craft, focusing on the specifically visual and material qualities of the building fabric. "Curious workmanship" was labor-intensive and cost money. In a society which was hypersensitive to personal status and "degree"—and in one which had brought the language of material display to a highly complex and sophisticated point—these categories added richness to the language of architectural symbolism, making it possible to present quite specific messages through built form.[4] Such changes in critical criteria reflect the transition from a military culture, in which the castle and fortified manor were the dominant types of domestic architecture, to one of relative political and economic stability where the range of variations in the size and style of country houses became greatly expanded.[5]

12

Francis Willoughby frequently moved between London and his estates in the country, promoting his political and business interests through meetings with his associates and maintaining his contacts through well-timed gifts and lavish entertainments. He was an important patron outside of the area of architecture: during the 1570s his household included a resident cleric, a physician, several musicians, and, at various times, traveling scholars and troupes of dramatic performers. He purchased paintings, expensive plate, and fashionable clothes.[6] Our analysis of his interest in architecture rests, in part, on what we can learn about his activities in other areas. A recognizable pattern of taste emerges, but so, too, does a pattern of ambitious investment both in business and the arts.

To assess the significance of Willoughby's accomplishments, we can look at the context of Elizabethan architectural patronage in general, pointing out other buildings, in both the monumental and vernacular traditions, which he might have known. These form the background against which he conceptualized his own new house. Further, Willoughby's desire to make his mark in the most knowledgeable architectural circles clearly determined his choice of Robert Smythson as his architect and building foreman. Nevertheless, the program depended on Willoughby's sense of what the building was going to be, who it was to serve, and how it would represent him in the world at large. This decision rested on considerations that were new to the Elizabethan era: the house not only had to serve as a center for estate management, it also had to accommodate the sophisticated entertainments and social life "in the country" of men and women familiar with London and the fashions of the Court. Thus, Wollaton drew on the precedent of the castle for its overall image but presented this in highly complex terms, with its plan subdivided into a sequence of grand and intimate spaces and its walls overlaid with costly and refined mannerist ornament. Emphasis on the niceties of architectural style and on increased spatial separation of the family from both the agricultural functions of the estate and the day-to-day operations of the household staff were recent developments in design. They are what make Wollaton Hall a country house rather than simply a house in the country. Willoughby's humanist education, patronage of the arts, and familiarity with architectural theory gave him distinctive personal tastes that found expression in his own version of this new building type.

Early Education and Youth

The Willoughbys were an ancient Nottinghamshire family whose steady rise in wealth and prestige from the fourteenth century onwards was made possible by expansion of their landholdings through marriage and well-timed purchases.[7] Trusted servants of the Crown for generations, they formed part of the network of provincial gentry so important to early Tudor administration. Their ties to the Court were long-standing: among the most distinguished members of the family (see table 1.1) was Francis Willoughby's great-grandfather, Sir Henry Willoughby, a Knight of the Body under both Henry VII and Henry VIII and Master of the Ordinance and Artillery under Thomas Grey, Marquis of Dorset, who served as justice of the peace and sheriff in the various counties where he held property. This man maintained an impressive court at Wollaton, and kept household accounts which reveal numerous expenditures for entertainment and lavish hospitality in the traditional grand style.[8]

Sir Henry Willoughby's sons were also notable figures of their time. Under Henry VIII, Sir John Willoughby enjoyed royal patronage and protection, receiving a letter of the signet from the king requesting his safe conduct during a pilgrimage to Compostella in 1518. In 1521 he traveled to Rome and was created a Knight of the Holy Sepulchre.[9] His brother Sir Hugh Willoughby, another of Francis Willoughby's great-uncles, was an explorer and navigator who died in 1553 while leading a voyage in search of the Northwest Passage.[10]

Through marriage and successful business ventures this generation of the Willoughby family acquired extensive landholdings in Nottinghamshire, Warwickshire, and Dorset; this property was eventually settled on Francis Willoughby's father, Sir Henry. Henry Willoughby's own marriage in the 1530s to Anne Grey, daughter of the Marquis of Dorset, strengthened his ties to an important noble house.[11] Willoughby's Warwickshire estates—at Middleton, Kingsbury, and Sutton Coldfield (see Map 1.1)—also brought him into close association with John Dudley, the Earl of Warwick, at whose side he died in defense of the Crown against Kett's Rebels in 1549.[12] Thus the Willoughbys were an important part of an extended network of gentry and noble families bound together by service, land ownership, and political patronage. They reaped the benefits of success and suffered the consequences of defeat together with their powerful allies at Court.

Moreover, during the 1530s and 1540s, Sir Henry Willoughby's estates generated substantial revenues: enclosure produced an increase in rents, and the development of coal mining on his land yielded a new source of capital.[13] With their political and economic power rising, the Willoughbys were thus set to join the ranks of Elizabethan upper gentry who came to power through the combined benefits of improved techniques of estate management and increasing royal patronage.[14]

Table 1.1. The Willoughbys of Wollaton

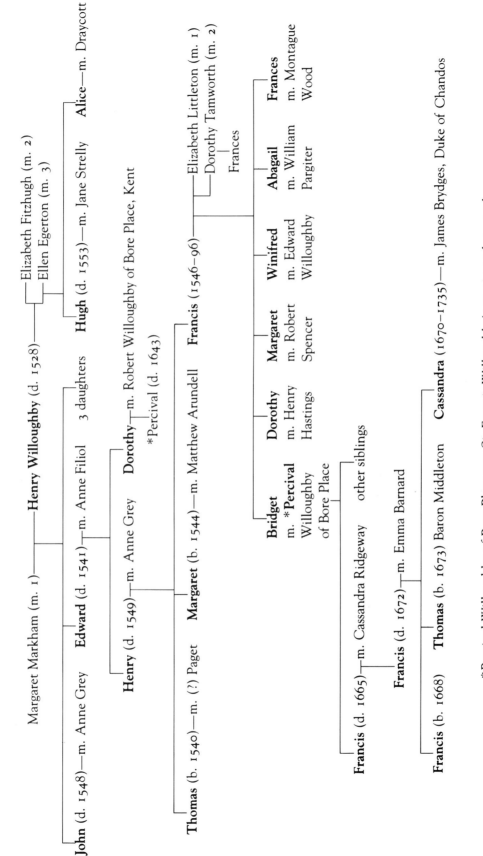

*Percival Willoughby of Bore Place was Sir Francis Willoughby's cousin and son-in-law

Map. 1.1. Southern
England and the
Midlands

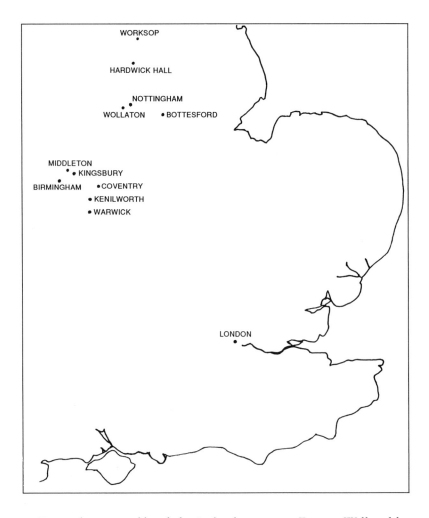

Yet at the time of his father's death in 1549, Francis Willoughby
had little expectation of controlling these impressive holdings. His
mother had died soon after his birth in 1546, and he was, moreover,
a younger son whose brother Thomas (born in 1540) was expected to
inherit the family fortune. Thus it was not Francis but Thomas who
became a ward of the Crown and began receiving a first-class education after their father's death; Francis and his elder sister Margaret
were provided for through the charity of their aunts and uncles.

Sir Henry Willoughby's will named his brother-in-law George
Medley and the chief officers of his estates—Gabriel Barwick, John
Hall, and Henry Marmion—as his executors.[15] These men were responsible for the administration of his property until his oldest son
came of age and for the maintenance of the two younger children
during their minority. Immediately after Sir Henry's death there was
a scramble to place bids in the Court of Wards for the purchase (and
control) of Thomas Willoughby's lucrative wardship.[16] These rights

were eventually awarded to Henry Grey, Marquis of Dorset and Duke of Suffolk, who was the children's uncle and Henry Medley's half-brother.[17]

Grey's purchase of the wardship was an important event for Thomas and for all of the children. It meant that they would remain in close contact with their mother's family and receive the benefits of participation in one of the most powerful and intellectually enlightened circles in England. Thus Thomas Willoughby was sent to Magdalene College, Cambridge, along with his cousins Henry and Thomas Medley, in 1550–51; between this time and his entry into Lincoln's Inn in 1558, he occasionally returned to Bradgate to visit the household of his uncle the Duke of Suffolk and frequently stayed at Tilty in Essex, the home of the Medley family.[18]

Francis and Margaret, the two younger children, were shifted between Bradgate, Tilty, and London. Now for the first time they came into contact with the world of the Court and began to learn the skills required for participation in it.[19] They found themselves on the fringes of a group which included the most powerful young people of their time—the Princess Mary, Lady Jane Grey and her sisters, the sons of the Duke of Northumberland—and it was their good fortune to receive an education similar to that of their more highly placed cousins.[20] A bequest in their father's will had provided a small sum for bringing them up "in vertue and learning," but the details were left to the judgment of their guardians. They were thus taught the skills which they would need as members of upper-gentry society.

From the moment they arrived in his care, every expense incurred in the younger Willoughbys' upbringing was dutifully recorded by their uncle, Henry Medley. His account book begins with the characteristically complete notation, "Memorandum that my nephvew Fraunces Wylloughbye and my nece Margarett Wylloughby, his sister, came to Tyltey, the xxith of Apryll, anno regni regis *Edwardi Sexti Quarto*, in the after none" and this is followed by a daily record of the children's whereabouts and expenditures over the course of the next eight years.[21] This unusual document not only enables us to learn about each child's day-to-day life in minute detail, but also provides us with valuable evidence for a comparison between them, revealing the very different ways in which young girls and boys were educated.[22]

Margaret, who was about six years old when she came into Medley's care, was soon presented with a Bible and other devotional literature in English.[23] Clearly she could read and write (and she presumably read other books in the household collection in addition to the ones she was given) but her education was limited to works in English.

This separated her immediately from the world of literature in Latin, a world of ideas which her brother and her distinguished female cousins were being trained to occupy. As contemporary theorists advised, she was taught to read moral and spiritual literature and learned such skills as would prepare her for a life as a wife and mother.[24] Thus she learned to cast, a simple method of calculation with counters useful in the management of domestic expenses, and she practiced needlework daily. This last activity had obvious practical advantages, reflecting the fact that women were placed in charge of fine linens and household stuffs, even in the largest and best-staffed households in England.[25] Margaret Willoughby was also taught the skills necessary to entertain herself and others in polite society. She learned to converse in French, took lessons on the virginals, and was given supplies for embroidery and fine handwork.

In these years, her brother Francis was educated for a very different role. As a younger son, he would serve as a gentleman of the Court or in the household of a powerful friend or family member. He might become a lawyer or a merchant.[26] Thus Francis embarked on a course of study which included both Greek and Latin grammar, and he learned to write and to translate simple sentences and aphorisms. At the age of five, he too was taught to play the virginals and he was given dancing lessons "several times."[27]

In 1553, the Willoughbys' happy world was abruptly shattered by the failed attempt to set their cousin Lady Jane Grey on the throne of England. They themselves were in little danger, but their uncle was lucky to escape the scaffold.[28] Neither the Duke of Suffolk nor a number of other members of their circle were so fortunate. With their deaths, the most illustrious members of the extended family were suddenly gone, and the survivors scrambled to realign themselves with those in power. The Willoughby children were moved from their uncle's house at Tilty to the Minories in London; a letter from their nurse to John Hall (one of the executors of their father's will) asked for money to see them through in the event that the house was seized.[29]

The children fared quite well under the circumstances. Thomas's wardship was bought for a thousand pounds by Medley and then sold again to Lord Paget, whose daughter Thomas later married.[30] Margaret became one of the Duchess of Suffolk's ladies-in-waiting and went with her to attend the new Queen, Mary Tudor. She was later placed in the service of the young Princess Elizabeth, traveling from Tilty to the palace at Hatfield with her clothes and possessions at Christmas 1555.[31]

Young Francis was sent to school. In 1555, he entered St. Anthony's school in London but stayed there for only two months before returning to Essex and entering the grammar school at Walden. During this period he lived with his uncle Sir Thomas Audley.[32] Francis's life at Walden is well-documented in the Medley accounts. As might be expected, he continued with his Latin studies, reading Terence, Cato, Cicero, and Vives.[33] These texts encouraged eloquent self-expression through imitation while presenting the student with elementary concepts of moral philosophy. A note in the accounts also records the purchase of a writing book and payments for lessons from a writing master. Clearly the young boys at Walden were following a plan consistent with humanist educational theory: greater emphasis was placed on rhetoric than on logic, and the students were drilled in grammar and translation.[34] The number of dictionaries listed in Medley's account bears this out. Francis was not only given a dictionary in English, but also Calepin's *Latin-Greek Lexicon,* the *De Copia* of Erasmus and Lorenzo Valla's *Elegantiae.* These were the most up-to-date texts of the period.

Among the most interesting aspects of Francis Willoughby's early education was the considerable attention paid to rhetorical style in written and spoken language. Francis's school books included both the *Floures for Latin speaking,* edited by Nicholas Udall, and Richard Sherry's *Figures of Grammar and Rhetorick.*[35] These mark his first exposure to the tools by which a mannered and aphoristic literary style could be perfected and his first real steps in learning the arts of rhetoric so important to aspiring members of his class.

This is worth noting here for several reasons. First, it appears that Francis Willoughby learned his lessons particularly well, developing a writing style in English characterized by a marked tendency to sententious phrase-making.[36] Second, the type of writing favored by him and taught by these texts shares with other art forms a tendency to artificiality and complexity; this "mannerist" approach to aesthetic experience reveals itself quite clearly not only in literature but also in the profuse and disparate elements of surface ornament at Wollaton Hall and elsewhere in contemporary Elizabethan art. While it would be unwise to push the comparison too far, it is nonetheless significant that the ability to recognize and appreciate many small details within a self-consciously complicated literary framework was paralleled in Willoughby's experience by comparable skills in looking at architecture and the visual arts generally. This was shared, to a greater or lesser extent, by other men and women who had been educated in the second half of the sixteenth century. Finally, the presence of these books among Willoughby's school texts reflects a growing shift in emphasis within English culture generally: now English language and traditions were awarded a new respect, giving rise to literature and art that was far less derivative of either Italian or other foreign precedents than it had been in previous decades.

Other aspects of Willoughby's early training also had a lasting effect on his later interests and tastes. Music was a lifelong passion. At Walden, Francis continued his lessons on the virginals, and he was taught to sing, to play the lute, and to write music; the early accounts also list payments for paper and for binding the manuscripts of his own songs.[37] In the 1570s, he employed a virginals player and a lutenist as permanent members of his household, and his account books from these years record numerous payments to traveling musicians. He was constantly on the lookout for first-rate musicians, writing to his sister at Court to ask for her help in finding players and singers.[38]

Toward the end of October 1558—a month before the accession of Elizabeth I—Francis went to Cambridge "to schole with Docketer Carre."[39] Here he continued his studies in Latin and Greek; precisely which college he attended is not made clear by the accounts. He was not destined to remain there long however, and in 1559, fate altered his course once again. On August 16th of that year, his brother Thomas fell sick and died "from overheating himself with hunting," catapulting young Francis out of the relative obscurity of the scholarly world of Cambridge and into the Court of Wards.[40] A memorandum in the executors' book for 1560 records charges for riding to London "to delyvr my cosen Francis to Sr Francis Knowele."[41] Other documents reveal that the wardship of the new heir was indeed granted to Knollys, with the provision of one hundred pounds to be paid out of rents toward his education.[42]

With this event, his life once again changed immeasurably. At the age of thirteen he had become an heir with expectations of a considerable fortune, and he was now the principal representative of his family in political and economic life. Thus he moved one step closer to the center of a world which he had previously known only from the fringes. He could now enter the charmed circle of the Court as a fully qualified participant—a well-educated, wealthy, and entirely marriageable young man.

Life at Court and in the Country

Francis Willoughby's entrance into the household of Sir Francis Knollys forced him to give up the scholarly course on which he had embarked. Knollys was Vice Chamberlain of the Royal Household when Francis first arrived, rising to the position of Treasurer of the

Queen's Chamber (1566), and later (1572) of the Royal House-hold.[43] He was expected to be in constant attendance on the Queen at Court and often traveled with her on her summer progresses through the countryside. Francis's sister Margaret was now a fixture at Court as well. In 1559 she married Sir Matthew Arundell, a young courtier with whom she could make a career of attendance in the royal household.[44] For Francis, then, the death of his brother was a mixed blessing. It gave him greater power and brought him some of the advantages that his older siblings had been privileged to enjoy, but it required him to enter a world which thwarted his independence and ambition, qualities which emerged in his later life and in his at-tempts to avoid the Court with its strict rules of conformity.

The first evidence of this resistance comes in the form of a license, preserved in the Middleton Collection at Nottingham and dated June 1564, transferring Francis Willoughby's wardship back to his father's executors for a sum of 1500 pounds.[45] According to the document, Francis Willoughby had refused to marry Elizabeth Knollys, the daugh-ter of his guardian, and was thus required by the conditions of his wardship to reimburse Knollys for the losses of property and revenues which would thus result. The paper is signed by Knollys, Willoughby, Matthew Arundell, Margaret Arundell, and by the executors of the estate. The reasons why Willoughby refused this marriage are not recorded, but the evidence suggests that he had already made up his mind to pursue his own course of action. An undated letter writ-ten by Francis to his uncle John Grey explained that he had been offered the hand of one Elizabeth Littleton, the daughter of his friend John Littleton of Frankley; Willoughby related the news that Lord Dudley—a man to whom he was bound, as we know, by ancient ties of marriage and service—had supported the proposed match. The letter concludes by stating the terms of the marriage offered by Littleton: he promised to pay 1500 pounds at the marriage, to bear the cost of his daughter's clothing, to pay any marriage charges, and to provide room and board for the couple at his house at Frankley (with six persons to attend them) for the next three years. For his part, Francis would only be required to promise his wife a jointure of one third of his estate, profits from his coal mines being excepted.[46] The offer struck young Francis as a very good one indeed.

Francis's decision to marry Elizabeth Littleton caused an uproar in the family. Letters flew back and forth between the sister and brother, making accusations and counteraccusations. Both Margaret and her husband questioned Littleton's honesty, and Margaret even asserted that her father's illegitimate brother George Willoughby (who was linked to the Littletons by marriage) had manipulated Francis into making the decision against his better judgment.[47] At the bottom of all this animosity—and it would continue unabated for the duration of the marriage—was perhaps a feeling on Margaret Willoughby's part that by marrying Elizabeth Littleton her brother was giving up the chance to make alliances at Court which would benefit them both. Yet as governor and constable of Dudley Castle, a former sheriff of Worcestershire, and the owner of estates not far from Willoughby's own in Warwickshire (Frankley was just ten miles to the southwest of Middleton), Littleton must have struck young Francis as a potential ally and business partner.[48] Willoughby viewed his marriage as an important step in the consolidation of his ties to the great Midlands families; like himself, Littleton was a follower of the Earl of Warwick and one of Sir Robert Dudley's "country gentlemen."[49] Moreover, he considered the terms of the marriage and particularly of the jointure (which was in later years to become such a sore point of contention between the couple) especially favorable.[50] Thus he went to great and costly lengths to secure the marriage which took place late in 1564.

We know nothing about Elizabeth Littleton's life before this time and, indeed, very little about her experiences after her marriage except in so far as she played a central role in the turbulent drama of her husband's household. From the start, the Willoughbys' life together was unhappy. Their problems began as a dispute over property between Willoughby and his father-in-law, but soon erupted into a full-scale battle which touched on every area of the couple's relationship, involving not only the members of their own households but also the Queen and royal officials.[51] Lady Willoughby was frequently ill, and her many pregnancies were accompanied by periods of extreme physical discomfort which contributed to her irascibility; her visits to her doctor in London and to the baths at Buxton were an added expense which her husband found insupportable. But the Willoughby's problems went beyond simple marital incompatibility: dividing his time between the Court and his country estates, Willoughby lived a life marked by false starts and frustrated ambitions. He entered into a series of speculative ventures and private alliances which were fraught with dishonesty and disagreement. Letters between family members were frequently filled with questions about his actions, betraying their authors' uneasiness about a man who was at once unsettled and unpredictable.

A letter from John Littleton written in August 1566 chided Willoughby for departing so suddenly from the Queen's entertainment at Kenilworth, thereby not only depriving Francis himself of a knighthood but depriving his wife of the opportunity to be a Lady; six men, including Littleton, were knighted by the Queen after Willoughby's hasty exit.[52] Willoughby's brother-in-law, Sir Matthew Arundell, also complained of his infrequent attendance at Court, writing in one letter that he would "not fail the Queen at Oxford, where he wishes Sir F. Willoughby would also be," adding, by way of encouragement, that "there is like to be great shows of learning, and a notable tragedy there is in hand." Arundell promised to "be his harbinger" if he would come.[53] As one of Leicester's supporters, Willoughby was often obliged to attend him, but the evidence overwhelmingly suggests that he avoided the royal presence whenever possible.

In 1575 the Queen was entertained at Kenilworth, in Warwickshire, for nineteen days. Willoughby was almost certainly present there, and rumor had it that his nearby house at Middleton would be the Queen's next stop.[54] A number of masques were presented for her pleasure during the lengthy festivities, and these were recorded by a retainer of Leicester's, Robert Laneham. The following description is typical:

> . . . her Highness all along this Tylt-yard rode unto the inner gate next the base coourt of the Castl, where the *Lady of the Lake* (famous in King Arthur'z book) with two nymphes waiting uppon her, arrayed all in sylkes, attending her Highness's coming: from the midst of the pool, whear upon a moovable island, bright blazing with torches, she floating to land, met her Majesty with a well-penned meter and matter after this sort: *viz.* first of the auncientee of the Castl, whoo had been ownerz of the same e'en till this day, most allweyz in the hands of the Earls of Leycester; how she had kept this Lake sins King Arthur'z dayz, and now undertanding of her Highness hither coming, thought it both office and duetie, in humble wize to discover her and her estate . . .

The pageant ended with "a delectable harmony of hautboiz, shalmz, cornets and oother looud muzic . . ."[55] On another day the story of the Lady of the Lake was presented with an explanation of how she had been imprisoned in a rock to avenge her spell on "Merlyne the prophet, whom for his inordinate lust she had enclosed in a rock."[56] Such was the typical fare at Court, complete with moving islands and a cast of characters dressed up in splendid costumes.

The now familiar revival of chivalry that dominated the culture of the Court was characterized by a love of the conceit, both literary and visual, and by a love of ceremony and ritual.[57] While he shunned the circle around the Queen, Francis Willoughby remained a participant in the culture she created. Although there is no evidence to suggest that he took part in the chivalrous pageants dedicated to the Virgin Queen (indeed, his household accounts record only a payment for "iiii hyltes for swerdes and daggers for my Mr to lern to playe at fench with"), his education and experience at Court made him familiar with the sorts of plays performed by her courtiers. Here such figures as the goddesses Diana and Venus might share the stage with a rustic, a knight and the Queen of Corinth, coming together in an encyclopedic pageant of personifications and emblematic figures. Indeed, such an assemblage would later form the basis of the sculptural program for Wollaton Hall.

Francis Willoughby's reception for the Queen at Middleton was set to take place on 21 July 1575, but no details of it are recorded by Laneham, who wrote only that "this day . . . I gave over my noting, and harkened after my horse."[58] Fortunately, two letters are included in the eighteenth-century *Account* of Cassandra Willoughby to show that the event did indeed take place. One was from George Willoughby and was summarized as follows: he wrote

> that he had advised with severall of the country gentlemen where and in what manner they intended to meet the Queen, and by what he can learn, their servants need only to have plain livery coats, but he think Sir Francis's number of servants should in no wise be less than fifty, as well because heretofore he had not shewed himself to the Queen, as also that his estate was very well known both to Her Majesty and the whole Counsel to be nothing inferior to the best. For himself . . . he thinks he cannot make [do with] less than three suits of apparell, for he is well assured that his attendance will be expected a week.[59]

This letter suggests that Willoughby was not only reluctant to appear at Court, but also anxious to hide his wealth and property from the Crown. A letter from Knollys carries the same message:

> Her Majesty is determined to tarry two days at your house, that is to say tomorrow night and Thursday all day, wherof I thought good to advertise you betimes. Wherefore I think it best for you not to defray Her Majesty, but rather that you should give her some good present of beefs and muttons, and to keep a good table yourself in some place, if you have any convenient room for it, two messe of meat. But do herein as you shall think best, but you had need to consider how your provision of drink, etc. may hold out. This Tuesday. the 20th day of July, 1575. Your loving Friend, F. Knolls.[60]

Cassandra Willoughby supposed that the reception took place at Wollaton, but it is obvious from the date and context that the house referred to here was Middleton. That Francis Willoughby was indeed visited and knighted by the Queen in 1575 is confirmed by the Herald's records; no mention is made of his own reaction to this event.[61]

It is clear that Sir Francis Willoughby was not by temperament a courtier but rather an independent land-owner whose own business activities and efforts to develop his estates absorbed his full interest and attention. In the words of contemporaries, he was a "projector" continually searching for "projects" that would use new technology or untapped natural resources to improve production and make more money.[62] While Tawney's portrait of the new Elizabethan landlord as a man of business who developed his estates "with the instincts of a shopkeeper and the methods of a land agent"—and he specifically mentioned Willoughby as an example of this type—appears overdrawn, it is nonetheless true that Willoughby's daily activities in the 1570s and 1580s were overwhelmingly directed toward estate development: coal mining, iron production, woad-growing, improved surveying techniques and rent collection.[63] Even his decision to build the new Wollaton Hall as a monumental showplace and as the administrative center of his Nottinghamshire estates fits this pattern. While he anticipated and expected the attention of the Court, his primary sphere of activity was in the country, where he built up a base of financial and political power on the land.

Coal mining was the heart of Willoughby's empire. In the 1490s, there were already five pits in operation at Wollaton, and these yielded profits of as much as £200 annually.[64] The coal accounts or "sinking books" for the years 1526–47 (the records are incomplete) suggest that production rose to about 6,000 to 10,000 tons per year in response to increased demand. Annual profits doubled from their late fifteenth-century levels.[65] The coal mines and colliers were clearly treated as a valuable asset of the Willoughbys' estates and were made a top priority of capital investment. In the will of Francis's father Sir Henry Willoughby, for example, he designated a sum of £1,000 for a new sough or drain in the Wollaton coal fields; this major engineering project, which involved the construction of a mile-long conduit, was completed in 1552.[66]

During the 1570s and 1580s, Francis Willoughby actively invested in coal and iron production in Nottinghamshire and elsewhere in the Midlands. In 1572, he joined with Nicholas Beaumont in operating the Beaumont-owned mines at Coleorton, Leicestershire. This partnership also owned and controlled the pits at Bedworth in Warwickshire and at Foleshill and Sowe near Coventry.[67] In the same year, Willoughby established a bloom hearth at Middleton and wrote to John Tyrer, his steward there, about the feasibility and cost of increasing iron production; Tyrer's letter details the costs of iron stone, fuel, and transportation, suggesting that competition from William Lord Paget (who operated a boom hearth at nearby Cannock Close) would be a significant deterrent.[68] As late as 1590, Willoughby was borrowing money at commercial London rates to set up and operate blast furnaces at Oakmoor (Staffordshire) and Codnor (Derbyshire) in an effort to generate additional capital.[69] His belief in the money-making power of such "projects" appears unshakeable.

At Wollaton, coal production was at peak activity in the late

1570s and throughout the period when the new hall was being built. Annual profits rose as high as £1,000 per year as a result of increased investment in labor, machinery, and transport.[70] For example, Willoughby was determined to make the Trent River more navigable in the Nottingham area and thus to improve distribution of Wollaton and Bilborough coal. In a letter of c. 1575, his sister wrote that she "wished he had not began his work upon the Treant [sic] (making it navigable) because it would be so chargeable."[71] Yet Willoughby ignored these warnings: he recognized that he could capitalize on rising demand for raw materials and consumer goods by gaining control of as many aspects of production and distribution as possible, thereby beating out the rival coal producers at Strelly and capturing the lucrative Nottinghamshire market.[72] Characteristically, this was just one of many areas in which he was actively investing in these years.

The story of Willoughby's investment in woad-growing and cloth production at Wollaton in the 1580s is a paradigm of his activity as a patron and an excellent example of the character of such entrepreneurial "projects" during the period.[73] Woad was a plant used in producing blue dye; English interest in the crop was apparently first prompted in the 1540s by a rapid increase in the price of foreign-grown woad supplied by the French and Portuguese.[74] Woad was thus under cultivation in a number of counties in the 1570s, but the idea of farming it as a cash crop was first brought to Willoughby's attention in 1585 by Robert Payne, an investor and "projector" whose zeal for new ventures matched Willoughby's own. Payne was the sort of man to whom Willoughby was continually attracted and in whom he invested both money and trust. In 1583, Payne had written two pamphlets on agriculture, including one on woad, and was thus a self-styled expert; he had big plans for employing female laborers at Wollaton (the men were occupied at the colliery) in a woad-growing scheme which promised not only profit but would also provide work for the poor. Willoughby gave Payne all the privileges of his support, providing him with money and a place in the household and making him a surveyor on the Wollaton estate.[75]

It is significant that, as with coal and iron, the major limitation on the profitability of woad production was access to the market. For Willoughby and Payne, it soon became clear that despite the best efforts of a number of Sir Francis's servants, who were impressed into service as woad salesmen in the Nottingham area, there was an increasing surplus of the agricultural product for which no market could be found. Thus Payne proposed to bring the process of dye-making and cloth production to Wollaton and Nottingham, and he went so far as to suggest that Thurland House, Sir Francis's Nottingham town house, could be converted to a sort of factory with a malt house "in the tennis court and the two floors overhead."[76] There is no evidence that these suggestions were ever acted upon, but it soon became evident that the project would not produce the hoped-for benefits, either economic or social. By 1588, Payne had left Wollaton in disgrace.

Willoughby's disappointment in the woad-growing experiment did not deter him for long. Throughout the 1580s, he was actively investing in a number of areas: his coal mines were at peak production, he had a stake in the iron industry, and he was actively acquiring lands, selling produce, and collecting rents. Like many Elizabethans, both gentlemen and yeomen, he used the increased capital generated by these activities to become a builder, investing perhaps the entire proceeds of his Wollaton coal mines (over £1,000 a year) in the construction of Wollaton Hall over a period of eight years.[77] His energy and enthusiasm for building, investing in and initiating new projects seems unbounded; he continually used his patronage and the resources of his household to support men with new ideas and money-making schemes. Thus when Payne approached Willoughby with the woad-growing scheme, he was virtually guaranteed a positive reception—indeed, it looked for a time as though both Payne and his project would succeed. Yet when the project eventually failed Payne was cast off as an enemy of Willoughby and his household. The accusations of dishonesty against Payne and his countercharges resulted in appearances before the Privy Council in a case which dragged on until 1592. This was a familiar scenario in Willoughby's life and on the Elizabethan scene generally. High hopes and enthusiasm were all too often followed by bitter recriminations and lawsuits when dreams were shattered.

Willoughby's activities on his country estates, his business schemes, his projects and the rising and falling fortunes of his many associates, servants, and followers were not only a way of life but a passion which absorbed him. While the world of the Court appealed to his intellectual tastes and to his social ambitions, and while this was a world in which he needed to maintain his good standing to ensure his political and economic influence, it was in the country that he found his greatest challenges. To these he devoted his considerable talents and energies full time.

Patronage of the Arts: Painting, Drama, and Music

Throughout the 1570s, Francis Willoughby maintained a large and powerful household at Wollaton in which the fashions of London and the Court were reflected in every aspect of daily life. Frequent notations in his household accounts record the purchase of books, fabrics, or other luxury goods in London, and it is clear that many of the activities in which he participated drew their vitality and inspiration far less from the culture of the surrounding countryside than from that of a network of powerful gentry and aristocratic landowners linked by shared interests and ambitions. At the center of this tightly knit system was the Court; households like Wollaton were satellites of it. Thus, while the evidence suggests a reluctance on Willoughby's part to come into contact with the Queen and her attendants (among them his sister and brother-in-law), he nonetheless remained closely tied to the world in which they operated, keeping abreast not only of changing fashions in the arts but also with political intrigues at the center of power. The distance which he maintained freed him to create a smaller court of his own at Wollaton, a place in which he, and not the Queen, was in control.

The portraits of himself and his wife (see plates 2 and 3), which Willoughby acquired in 1573, are typical of his purchases. The artist was George Gower, a painter of some reputation in London who would later become Serjeant Painter to the Queen.[78] The cost, thirty shillings for the two, was no greater than that of other luxuries he bought: he paid forty-six shillings and four pence for a silver sugar box, rewarded the musician Edward Edlin with forty shillings for playing, presented the same amount to "Mr. Waringe a scoller," and gave his own servant forty-six shillings and eight pence for books.[79]

These images of the husband and wife reflect their wealth: even Willoughby's comparatively sober jacket and ruff are obviously expensive, decorated with hundreds of small jewels sewn in clusters and hanging from slender threads at the neck, while Lady Elizabeth's dress and hat (so detailed that the painter charged them twenty shillings for her picture and only ten for his) are so heavily encrusted with ornaments that she seems quite lost amongst the feathers, bows, and lace. She wears a large jewel representing a triton surrounded by a bower; suspended from it are three large pearls, matching others festooned across her bodice. This ornament was probably imported from Italy and may have been purchased by the couple or one of their agents in London. Such luxuries were often proudly displayed in contemporary portraits of members of the Court circle.[80]

Further evidence of a network of patronage in which Willoughby participated can be found in the records of payments for musical and dramatic performances. Over the course of a three-year period, Willoughby was entertained by various troupes of actors who frequented the great houses and the Court: on New Year's Eve, 1572, "My Lord of Woster's players" entertained at Wollaton, returning two years later to appear on New Year's Day; in July 1574, the Earl of Essex's Men appeared twice and "Lord Monteigle's players" appeared once; the Earl of Sussex's Men performed for the household in September of the same year.[81] These groups toured the country presenting a wide repertory of romances and tragedies.[82] What they performed at Wollaton is not known, but works such as *Phedrastus*, *The Red Knight*, and *Phygion and Lucia*, which are known to have been among the dramatic presentations of these troupes in these years, were characteristic mixtures of traditional stories, chivalric romances, and classical themes.[83] Like the performances presented at festivals for the Queen, these private showings incorporated a wide range of literary and folkloric references into pageants for the entertainment of the household.

Numerous payments to itinerant groups of musicians (to the waits of Nottingham, for instance, or to "Mr. Stanhoppes weates") are also recorded in the accounts of the Willoughby household in the 1570s. Although the resident staff included Edward Edlin, a lute player, and a Mr. Astell, who played the virginals, performances by the waits marked ceremonial or special occasions; a "musicians chamber" is referred to in the accounts, but large musical performances were, like plays, often presented in the hall for the benefit of the entire household.[84]

The overall impression created by the Wollaton accounts and surviving letters from the 1570s is of a lively household bustling with activity. At any moment, servants or family members might be coming from London laden with goods, a band of musicians might be waiting for the master, or the mistress might be calling for fine linens to ornament the dining chamber. The household was run with strict attention to protocol and ceremony; a set of regulations written out by Francis Willoughby in 1572 (Appendix A) describes the service of meals in the hall and great chamber, the rules for receiving visitors, and the tasks of the usher, butler, and underbutler.[85] Watching over this small army of officers, servants, visitors, and laborers was Willoughby himself.

Willoughby's Library

In the late seventeenth century, Cassandra Willoughby wrote that her ancestor was "a man of great piety and learning" and described how there remained in the library at Wollaton "a great many very pious discourses writ by him, and several sermons which he made for his own chaplains to preach, and a collection of the most learned books of his time."[86] There was indeed a library of some fourteen hundred volumes at Wollaton during Cassandra's lifetime, and perhaps two hundred and fifty or three hundred of these dated from the sixteenth century. While it is possible to make a very approximate reconstruction of the contents of Sir Francis Willoughby's library, the surviving evidence is largely unsatisfactory. A shelf list drawn up at Wollaton in 1691 or 1692 can bring us only as close as the late seventeenth century; this list is damaged and in some sections records only authors' names and no titles. A Christie's sale catalog dating from 1925, when the library was sold at auction, lists 756 books, with 202 sixteenth-century imprints among them.[87] Many of these books bear the autograph of Thomas Willoughby, the heir who acquired the library in 1691 and had the list drawn up. None of the books in the library has been located, although the buyers (primarily book dealers) can be traced. Further, only two works listed in the catalog can be directly linked to Francis Willoughby: these are a copy of Erasmus, *Apophthegmes* (1542), which bore the autographs of both Francis and Elizabeth Willoughby, and a copy of Foxe's *Ecclesiasticall History* (1570) which was decorated with the initials "FW." A number of Willoughby's speeches before the Quarter Sessions included quotes from this volume.[88]

If we accept the conservative figure of roughly two hundred and fifty volumes as the total in Willoughby's library, we can begin to make some comparisons with other collections of books dating from the late sixteenth century. The largest private libraries in Elizabethan England belonged to scholars such as John Lord Lumley and Dr. John Dee, the mathematician and court astrologer. A 1609 catalogue of Lumley's library lists 2,800 printed books, while Dee's inventory of 1583 lists some 2,500 publications.[89] Yet these were clearly exceptional. Other scholars had much smaller collections of books. For example, Edward Hawforde, Master of Christ's College Cambridge, left only 106 books in 1582 while Ambrose Barker, also of Christ's College, left 130 books when he died in the same year.[90]

It is not surprising then that Willoughby's library was considered large by contemporaries, particularly as he was not a professional scholar. Books and bindings represent a major expense in the Wollaton accounts of the 1570s, appearing frequently as London purchases. One notation lists the payment of forty-six shillings and eight pence on a single bill, a huge expenditure in a period when many books cost less than a shilling.[91] It appears from the size and scope of the library that here, as elsewhere in his life, his approach was both ambitious and fundamentally utilitarian—he read to learn and his learning was motivated by an almost obsessive interest in the practical applications of new ideas in mathematics, mechanics, arithmetic, and, as a tool for use in government and local affairs, in rhetoric as well.

This preference for practice over theory is a theme which runs throughout the entire Wollaton library—it is as true of the seventeenth-century books as it is of the earlier volumes, suggesting that the intellectual tastes and habits we associate with Francis Willoughby can perhaps be seen as characteristic of his family and of the upper gentry generally. By comparison with the libraries of Lumley and Dee, the Willoughby collection is marked by the prevalence of books in English. No more than twenty-five percent of the sixteenth-century books are in Latin, while in Lumley's library only twelve percent were in *any* vernacular language—all of the others were in Latin, Greek, and Hebrew.[92] Further, both scholarly libraries contain numerous works of theology (Lumley's collection had come from Archbishop Cranmer) and natural philosophy, two categories which are scarcely represented among Willoughby's books.

At Wollaton, the largest category included books on mathematics, geography, natural science, and law (about eighty volumes). There was also a significant collection of books on medicine (about fifteen plus three bound with seventeenth-century texts), and a number on art and architecture (fifteen); approximately seventy popular works can be identified, along with twenty or thirty books on religious themes (including Bibles), a selection of Latin works of philosophy and literature, eight handbooks of advice, and four primers or dictionaries. While the numbers are necessarily approximate, it is nonetheless possible to characterize Willoughby's holdings as significantly different in character from either those of scholar-humanists like Lumley and Dee or from those of a solid Coventry citizen like "Captain Cox" whose inventory of 1575 lists mainly romances, plays, and ballads among his fifty-six volumes, including fourteen books of philosophy and one medical treatise.[93]

An overview of Willoughby's collection of medical books—including popular works which might more properly be included under the modern category of "health and fitness"—reveals the distinctively antitheoretical and hands-on quality of his interests. Willoughby acted as the patron for Dr. John Banister (see plate 6 in gallery) an anatomist and surgeon who lived at Wollaton in the 1570s and attended Lady Willoughby as her personal physician. In 1578, Banister dedicated his *Historie of Man* to Sir Francis. This work is listed in the shelf list as "Banisters Anatomie" but it is not included in the Christie's sale.[94] Works on anatomy and surgery are well represented in the library, but most are popular editions: Thomas Gemini's abridged translation of Vesalius (1559) and John Vigon, *The most ex-*

cellent works of Chiurgery (1550) are typical. The collection included a 1541 edition of Linacre's Galen in Latin and a copy of Hippocrates' *Works*, but most of the treatises were recent publications rather than scholarly editions. Copies of Sir Thomas Elyot's *Castel of Helth* (1547), John Barnard's *Tranquilitie of Mind* (1570), and Thomas Rogers's *The Anatomy of the Mind* (1576) all suggest that Willoughby was drawn to "self-help" books and actively sought the most up-to-date answers to his own health problems and those of his wife. The number of remedy books in the collection—Conrad Gesner's *New Jewell of Health* (1576), Petrus Gorraeus's *Formulae Remediorum* (1572) and Matthiolus's *De Medica Materia* (1569), for example—testify to Willoughby's interest in chemical and herbal medicine. Further, his excellent Latin, the result of years at school, brought him into contact with a wide range of medical works which would otherwise have remained closed to him.

The number of works on mathematics, mechanics, and experimental science reinforces the impression that Willoughby actively involved himself in the industrial projects on his estates. Jacques Besson's *L'art et science de trouver les eaux et fontaines cachées soubs terre* (Orléans, 1569) and Biringuccio's *La Pyrotechnie ou Art de Feu* (Paris, 1556) can both be related to coal and iron production. Blagrave's *Mathematical Jewel* (1585) describes the "making and most excellent use of a singular instrument so called." Euclid's *Elements* is also there, though not in the famous 1570 Billingsley edition with Dee's preface. A number of specialized texts, such as Ghaligai's *Practica d'arithmetica* (1552) survived from Willoughby's years at school and at the university.

When we turn to the collection of books on architecture, it is not surprising that we find a great deal of depth. For Willoughby, building was a "project" to which he could devote his talents and energies as an amateur and where he could join with a specialist to produce works of great novelty and technical virtuosity. Of the thirty-nine works listed by Lucy Gent in her index of treatises on art and architecture collected by Elizabethan and Jacobean patrons, Willoughby owned fourteen, plus two, Scamozzi and Bloum, not listed by Gent.[95] This number compares well with Dee's seventeen architectural volumes (five of which were editions of Vitruvius) and Lumley's four (including two editions of Vitruvius).

If we include all the sixteenth-century books on art and architecture recorded in either the shelf list or the sales catalog, we can reconstruct the following collection:

L. B. Alberti. *L'architettura.* No edition listed.
J. Bluom. *Quinque Columnarum.* Zurich, 1550.
P. De L'Orme, *Inventions pour bien bastir.* Paris, 1561.

————. *Architecture.* No edition listed.

J. A. Du Cerceau. *Livre d'architecture.* Paris, 1582.

————. "*Bastiments de France.*" No edition listed.

A. Dürer. *Geometricae.* Paris, 1532.

G. Lamazzo. *Trattato dell'arte de la pittura.* Milan, 1584.

A. Palladio. *I Quattro libri dell'architettura.* Venice, 1570.

V. Scamozzi. *Discorsi sopra l'antichità di Roma.* Venice, 1582.

S. Serlio. *Architecturae Liber Septimus.* Frankfurt, 1575.

————. No title given (shelf list "C21").

John Shute. *First and Chief Groundes of Architecture.* London, 1563.

Vignola. *Regole delli cinque ordini di architettura.* Venice, 1596.

Vitruvius. *De Architectura Libri Decem.* Venice, 1567. (Two copies, one bound with Shute.)

To this list should perhaps be added various works by Jan Vrede-man de Vries, which were the source for a number of the decorative motifs used at Wollaton. These works were widely circulated among London craftsmen and may have come directly from Smythson or from the master mason Christopher Lovell.

Architecture: The Genesis of an Idea

When Willoughby turned his attention to the problem of building a new hall at Wollaton, he seems to have followed the same approach that he used elsewhere in his life. He conceived of his own projects in bold terms, he went to London to find craftsmen of the highest quality, and, having educated himself about the subject through books and careful observation, he followed the fashions of London and the Court, seeking out the most qualified specialists to realize his ideas in built form.

Like Willoughby, most amateur builders owned substantial collections of architectural handbooks and pattern books in this period. Lord Burghley, for example, not only read widely in the field but also took an active part in the design of his own great houses of Burghley and Theobalds. During a period of intense building activity in the 1560s, he ordered a copy of Philibert de l'Orme's *Nouvelles instructions de bien bâtir* from France, a book which he had learned about from his friend Sir Thomas Smith, the builder of Hill Hall.[96] With his son Robert he collected two large portfolios of maps and architectural drawings which are still at Hatfield House. His expertise was recognized by other patrons who enthusiastically sought out his advice on their own projects. In 1579, for example, Sir Christopher Hatton wrote to Burghley regarding his own new house then under construction:

I fear me that as your Lordship shall find my house unbuilt and very far from good order, so through the newness you shall find it damp-ish and full of evil air . . . I humbly beseech you, my honourable Lord, for your opinion to the surveyor of such lacks and faults as shall appear to you in this rude building, for as the same is done hitherto in direct observation of your house and plot at Tyball's so I earnestly pray your Lordship that by your good corrections at this time it may prove as like to the same as it hath ever been meant to be.[97]

Burghley wrote back a long evaluation of the house which reveals just how conscious he was of the builder's intentions:

Sir, I may not pass out of this good house without thanks on your behalf to God, and on mine to you, nor without memory of her Majesty, to whom it appeareth this goodly, perfect though not per-fected work is consecrated . . . Approaching to the house, being led by a large, long straight fairway, I found a great magnificence in the front or front pieces of the house and so every part answerable to the other, to allure liking. I found no one thing of greater grace than your stately ascent from your hall to your great chamber; and your chambers answerable with largeness and lightsomeness, that truly a Momus could find no fault.[98]

Burghley's now well-known reply is particularly noteworthy in this context. To begin with, it is clear from his statement that these large houses were intended to be noticed and used by the Queen; they were built with her pleasure and approval in mind. Second, Burghley is explicit about the qualities he considered important: a long, cere-monious approach on axis, symmetry and order in the elevations and, inside, a "stately ascent" from the hall to the great chamber. The latter, of course, was of symbolic as well as aesthetic importance as it was both the route that visitors followed as they approached the mas-ter's presence, and the route taken by the servers as they brought his food from the kitchen, through the hall, up the stairs, and into the great chamber.

Outside the courtier circle, of which Burghley and Hatton were both a part, patrons of architecture appear to have been equally in-volved with design and construction. Even those who built primarily for their own pleasure rather than for the Queen's went to great lengths to acquire the most skilled craftsmen and up-to-date details for their projects. Thus, Sir Thomas Tresham, a devout Catholic not only out of favor but frequently in jeopardy for his religious beliefs, maintained an active correspondence during construction of his buildings in Northamptonshire.[99] In 1583, he was in touch with Hatton, thanking him for the use of his freestone quarry at Weldon. That he followed each step in the building process is revealed by a contract made in 1578 between himself and his mason, William Grombold, for "fyftye skutchins . . . with an arcketrave under and a cornishe over them, according to a plott alreadye drawen by the said William, showid unto the said Sir Thomas Tresham."[100] As with tombs, where contracts often include sketches of proposed designs, these building works were undertaken by patrons who knew what they were paying for.[101] Further, Tresham's library of books on architecture was the finest in England.[102] Like other patrons, he attended to the details of building, jealously guarding the services of his best craftsmen for his own projects. In the 1570s, he instructed his agent to quickly make a contract with the best masons for the upcoming season "ells happly they may be bespoken in Sir Jhon Stanupp's work this sommer, and know not I where to have so good workmen."[103]

Books were, of course, only a small part of the process by which architectural patrons formed their ideas. As Hatton's letter to Burghley clearly shows, other buildings set the standard against which one's own efforts were measured. For Francis Willoughby, the enormous houses of the professional courtiers and diplomats were, no doubt, of interest, particularly for the Italianate and Flemish details newly created by the patrons and the varied groups of craftsmen they hired.[104] Many of the details of these houses—the use of the orders, corner towers, and prominent gatehouses—were the hallmarks of fashionable architectural design. Yet Court fashion was only one thing with which Francis Willoughby was concerned in his building. The new house at Wollaton was to make a clear statement of family pride, wealth, and control over the countryside; thus Willoughby also looked to the tradition of English manor houses and castles, those buildings which Girouard has termed the "power houses," for inspiration.[105]

Medieval military architecture was a storehouse both of planning strategies and of significant details with strong symbolic messages. The revival of Gothic details in architecture was an important part of the revival of chivalry in Court culture.[106] But in looking around for models on which to base his own new house, Willoughby also understood the lasting effects of tradition: castles and manor houses were the center of power in the rural community, the places not only from which the great estates were run but also the focus of military life and hospitality. His own manor houses at Wollaton and Middleton were smaller structures, groups of low buildings ringing a series of courtyards.[107] Within English architectural tradition, the next step up in the building hierarchy from his own houses was a castle. Bartizans, crenellation, and other details immediately expressed military strength and power. These forms were also resonant with meaning in the chivalric revival of the Court.

Willoughby was familiar with the castle where his brother-in-law and sister, Matthew and Margaret Arundell, lived in Wiltshire. At Wardour (see fig. 4.30) the high thick walls, pointed lancet windows, and crenellated parapet gave the house a look of solidity and compactness. As a courtier, Arundell found it advantageous to maintain a house and household which gave him the image of landed wealth and power; Wardour, purchased by his father in 1551, made an extremely effective display.[108] In the 1570s, following the example of his friend and neighbor Sir John Thynne (the builder of Longleat), Arundell hired the architect Robert Smythson to undertake some renovations at Wardour, recutting windows and adding new doorframes on the exterior and in the inner court.[109] All this was no doubt watched by Willoughby with interest.

At Wardour, architect and patron alike studied the architectural language of power; it was a high house filled with light, its great hall illuminated by tall, traceried windows. As at nearby Longleat, the house stood on a substantial basement, its broad, homogeneous facade creating a formidable impression of size and strength.[110] This was the style which was fashionable among Elizabeth's courtiers. For example, at Kenilworth, the Warwickshire castle which the Earl of Leicester had converted into a sumptuous palace for courtly entertainment, the high tower and glistening windows were particularly noted by contemporaries. In 1575, for example, the diarist Robert Laneham set down his impressions of the building: "A daytime, on every side so glittering by glass; at nights, by continued brightness of candle, fire and torch light, transparent through the lightsome windows."[111] For Willoughby, who knew all of these buildings well, the lessons were obvious: they taught him the language of architectural display in the countryside. These he updated with references to the new learning—classicizing details and a sculptural program celebrating Roman gods and heroes—which made his house the envy of the Court.

There is even evidence to suggest that Willoughby himself may have formulated a preliminary design for the new house before he hired Smythson. A sketch plan in the Middleton Collection (see fig. 4.18), discovered by David Durant on the back of a sixteenth-century pedigree in Willoughby's hand, lays out the basic elements that would later appear in Smythson's project. The four-tower design is based on a plate in Du Cerceau's *Livre d'architecture* (1559), a book which Willoughby certainly knew.[112] Whether or not he consulted any architect at these early stages is unclear; the accounts of the 1570s contain only one mysterious reference to a "platt maker [who] came from London to measure groundes" in May 1573.[113]

At Wollaton Hall, the rounded corner towers eventually gave way to square pavilions, and the internal arrangement of rooms was very different from that shown in the sketch. Nevertheless, this drawing tantalizingly suggests the patron's role. Although the writing on the sketch itself is not Willoughby's, the two sides of the paper, one with a plan, the other with a family tree, bear witness to two issues which preoccupied him during the 1570s: his ancestral family status and his country house. Indeed, for him the two were one, and the strength of the metaphoric "house" of the Willoughbys found expression in the solidity of the real brick and mortar.[114]

Willoughby was a man obsessed with wealth and status; his life was a constant struggle to get to the top and to live as if he belonged there. As a powerful landowner in his shire, he was flattered, courted, and cajoled by many who sought his support; his position depended on his ability to entertain and bestow favors on his followers. Thus, while his patronage of the arts and of architecture reflected a genuine interest in these areas (his collection of books and devotion to music clearly show this) one senses that the largesse and grand style of the household were, in part, kept up for appearances. Willoughby jealously guarded his land and his money, living in an atmosphere charged with anxiety about his own position and that of those around him. Many paid the price for his free-floating mistrust—in particular his wife and children, who learned to forge alliances and avoid entrapment in a household filled with unscrupulous competitors for the master's favor. Writing in 1626, thirty years after Sir Francis's death, his son-in-law, Montague Wood, characterized him in a letter to Sir Percival Willoughby, who was then the owner of Wollaton Hall:

> I have often heard that ye olde Sr Fran when he came of yeares and had bene brede a greate scholler, his officers every one bringinge in ther severall accomptes both of mony and landes, he sawe that it was too much for him to manage him selfe, he wished he had bene lefte one hundrethe powndes by the yeare and his bookes and the rest to his friendes. Yett in that time of government he kepte as greate hospitalitye as any man in his shire. He bought as much lande as he sould, he spent as much in buildinge, yet in givinge to many confidence he was deceaved of more land than he soulde and more then would have payd his debts and his buildings.[115]

To those who bore the financial and emotional burdens of his sometimes ill-considered enthusiasm for people, projects and money-making schemes, Sir Francis would remain an enigma. He was both a great patron and a poor businessman who seemed to be continually in debt and forever surrounded by hangers-on. Yet in some respects he was a complete success: he was remembered for his hospitality and for his buildings, two things which were the mark of a great and powerful man.

2

The Manor House and Its Household

When Francis Willoughby came into his inheritance in 1568, he took possession of extensive landholdings in Warwickshire and Nottinghamshire; these estates were clustered around manor houses and farm buildings—Middleton Hall, Kingsbury Hall, Wollaton Hall—which served a wide range of administrative, residential, and agricultural functions. These houses were already old when Francis Willoughby came of age, and none had the architectural niceties which were becoming increasingly fashionable in London and at Court. In choosing to build a new house at Wollaton, Willoughby clearly expressed his need not only for a building that would look different from those he already had, but also for one in which a varied range of household activities would be accommodated, and indeed regulated, in a new way. Nevertheless, all of these houses and farm buildings continued to be used after Wollaton Hall was completed in 1588. For our purposes here, then, the medieval hall and service buildings at Wollaton are key elements for understanding the Elizabethan house; they not only provide us with the starting point from which Willoughby and his architect began, but also show us how and where essential activities continued to be performed once the new house was completed.

The First Wollaton Hall

By the time that Cassandra Willoughby came to live at Wollaton in the late seventeenth century, the "new" hall on the hill was the only structure still used as a family residence; the old hall in the village had been divided up and turned over to tenants while the service buildings continued to be used by the home farm. Thus she contrasted the two houses in her *Account:*

> The old hall was built near the church. What remains of that old building is turned into three or four farm houses, of which one is about a quarter of a mile from the rest, which was the dairy house to the old hall. The new house is placed upon a hill about half a mile from the old hall, from whence there is a very noble pros-

pect of the country round it . . . The house itself is a very noble pile of building, but it being less easie to describe it by writing than drawing, I design to place at the end of this book a draught and a plan of it, and shall therefore only mention here that Sir Francis Willoughby began the building, A.D. 1580, and finished it A.D. 1588.[1]

Disappointingly, the promised drawing and plan have never been found.[2] Moreover, nothing now remains of the old hall except a dovecote believed to have been built in the late sixteenth century; even before Cassandra's time some of the outlying structures had been pulled down and their stone reused.[3] Nevertheless, we are fortunate in having a number of surviving documents from which a reconstruction of the manor house complex can be suggested.[4]

The old hall at Wollaton was built in the late fifteenth century.[5] Estate accounts and inventories indicate that the manor was part of a group of farm buildings surrounded by a high wall; a gatehouse, which faced the town, controlled access to a large courtyard and to the sheds and other structures clustered around it.[6] These included dog kennels, a joiners' workshop, a blacksmith's shop, barns for the storage of corn and grain (barley, rye, wheat, etc.), a mill and mill house, a malthouse, brew house, bakehouse, coal yard and wool house, a cider mill, a pigeon house, swineyard, a shelter for geese and capons, and a dairy. A sluice fed a horse pool near the stables and may be the one shown in a view of Wollaton by Siberechts dating from the late seventeenth century (see plate 8). These buildings must have varied widely in appearance, size, and construction; some were of stone, but most were apparently of the local vernacular type in plaster and wood.[7]

Residential and service areas were interspersed throughout the complex, although the principal chambers appear to have been clustered near the great hall, parlors, and great chamber. An inventory of 1550 listed some ten rooms according to the names of the family members (three) and upper servants (seven) who occupied them; in 1585, fifteen such private chambers were noted.[8] These principal bedrooms were often furnished with one or two beds, a chest, a chair and, in some cases, a cupboard, but throughout the entire complex bedsteads and mats for sleeping were tucked away in rooms used for other activities as well. Beds were listed among the contents of the great chamber and were also found in one of the three parlors mentioned in the inventories.[9] A "Knights' Chamber" and "Sycke Folkes' Chamber" provided additional sleeping areas for particular groups.

No reference is made to the great hall in the 1550 inventory, but we know from a list of household regulations, drawn up by Francis Willoughby in 1572 for use at Wollaton, that it was the center of household activity there. The old manor probably followed the traditional arrangement in which the hall and its service areas—the kitchen, pantry, buttery, and so on—were separated by a screen and screens passage at one end of the room.[10] The great chamber and dining chamber, rooms in which the family ate and socialized apart from the ordinary household, were also adjacent to the hall, but at the opposite end from the service areas. These private spaces are described in both the 1572 regulations and in inventories as well: the great chamber was furnished with a bedstead, folding table, forms (that is, benches), and a cupboard (presumably for the display of plate), while the dining chamber contained two long tables, two trestle tables, two turned stools, a cupboard, a chest, and an old clock.

It is interesting to note that there was a chapel at the old hall, furnished with candlesticks, cruets, and a hanging of green and red saye, a woolen material; a separate category in the inventory of 1550 lists "chappell stuffe," including vestments, copes, and other religious garb of velvet, silk, and satin.[11] There was also a small armory filled with bows, arrows, and other items, while the principal armory contained large numbers of every sort of weapon including "fyve hand gonnes."[12] There was a room listed as a gallery, perhaps a short passageway between two larger spaces (a smaller room opened off of it), one of a seemingly infinite number of passages, closets, and storage areas tucked away throughout the complex.

The impression of old Wollaton conveyed by the documents is of a sprawling farmstead alive with activity. People and animals lived side by side; important visitors were received in the same courtyards through which farm laborers with their carts passed on their way from the fields to the barns. The proximity to the town and the variety of activities pursued there made the old manor a lively and varied environment. Yet it is clear why a young man like Francis Willoughby soon began planning to supplement this complex with another and far grander building separate from it: where the old hall was sprawling and various, fashion called for homogenity in appearance and a compact plan; where people of all classes and occupations met in the courtyard of the manor, current rules of etiquette called for a stricter separation of social rituals and work life; finally, as we shall see presently, where the old house at Wollaton tended to promote contact between members of the household, both men and women, and the outside world—in spite of its encircling wall and all of the rules laid down to restrict access to it—new concepts of privacy and propriety demanded a far more rigid boundary, a higher and less permeable wall, behind which the family, and in particular the lady of the house, would be protected. In this private realm, social life among the upper classes could go on undisturbed by the activities of those who served them.

The Household at Wollaton: 1572–80

Throughout the 1570s, while he was living at the old hall and preparing to build the new one, Sir Francis Willoughby maintained a household staff of between forty-five and fifty men (and a handful of women) who kept house, cooked, cleaned and sewed, paid the bills, and generally kept order throughout the complex of residential quarters and on the estate. There are four types of evidence that make it possible to reconstruct the composition and day-to-day activities of this group. The first is a set of household orders, written by Sir Francis in 1572, which were transcribed in part by Cassandra Willoughby in her *Account;* the original manuscript is now lost. The second is a detailed account book, in manuscript, listing expenditures at Wollaton from 1572 to 1575; this is supplemented by a list of men and women in the household and their quarterly wages in 1572. The fourth and in many respects the most important source of information about these years is the extensive correspondence exchanged by the Willoughbys and their associates; here again, the original documents no longer survive but substantial excerpts from them are preserved in the Cassandra Willoughby *Account.* [13]

The Willoughby orders of 1572 (Appendix A) describe the regulations for the service of meals in the hall and dining chamber at Wollaton. Because they are the only set of regulations to survive for an upper gentry household—all other known examples describe either noble or royal establishments—their contents, however fragmentary, are particularly interesting. What they show is that the protocol observed at Wollaton was a scaled-down version of that found in much larger households. A hierarchical order of command was strictly maintained, each servant was assigned to a specific area of the house, and particular attention was paid to etiquette for both the service of meals and the reception of guests. [14] Thus, we find that Francis Willoughby set down the duties of each servant in turn according to his role in the ritual, beginning with the usher and his groom and continuing through a list which included the usher of the great chamber, the butler, the underbutler, the pantler, cook, gentlemen waiters, yeomen waiters, slaughterman, carter, grooms, pages, and kitchen boys. Each of these men had specific tasks to carry out at certain times of the day. Each had his *place,* both literally and figuratively, in the household and knew to whom he should report.

The gentleman usher at Wollaton was Robert Fox.[15] His chief duties were to oversee the activity in the hall, both during meals and at other times, to ensure that protocol was observed there (calling in the clerk for help with this if necessary) and to see that dogs were kept out. He was to call on the butler (John Penne) and the pantler when beer or bread were needed. His badge of office was a "little fine rod" which he carried during the service of the meal as it made its way from the "dresser," through the hall, and beyond to the lord's table in the dining chamber; he was to display this staff as a sign of his authority. In wintertime he was "to appoint some one yeoman, at his discretion . . . to carry the torch before service in the nighttime."

As in a large aristocratic household, servants and visitors in the hall were seated and served according to the rank of their masters; the responsibility for setting this order also lay with the usher. If the number of visitors was quite large, he could require "the meanest sort of servants," such as the slaughterman, carter, and stable boys, to serve as waiters in the hall. Thus on special occasions even a relatively small group of servants could approximate the protocol of a nobleman's house by putting every available hand to work.

Willoughby's household orders also specified which of the servants had "the benefit of the play"—their share of profits from cards and dice—in each room: in the hall this was to go to the butler; elsewhere (Willoughby says "in most places") to the usher. This provision is consistent with the regulations for the largest households and reminds us of the importance of these games not only as leisure activities for the family and their guests but as a source of income and a privilege of service for household staff.[16]

At Wollaton the top positions were filled by a group of men whose names are listed at the head of the quarterly wage list for 1572: Henry Willoughby (paid £ 1/13/4), George Cam (paid £ 1/10/0), Thomas Shaw (paid £ 1) and Richard Wrigley (paid £ 1), who served as the steward, gentleman of the chamber, controller, and head gardener respectively. Throughout the account books for 1572–75 their names appear in connection with the making of payments, the ordering of supplies or provisions, and other administrative activities. Just below these are listed the names of William Marmion and William Blythe, two men who were also frequently entrusted with record-keeping and the payment of bills.

We learn more about Willoughby's servants from personal letters that mention a number of people who never appear in the Wollaton wage list. Many names are recorded in connection with daily activities in the household and on the various Willoughby estates. These include a number of men who acted as stewards, bailiffs and servingmen: Thomas Cludd, Henry Draycott, Geoffry Ithel, William

Catesby, John Squire, Henry Trussell, and Bartholomew Widdowson. Because the Willoughby letters are so frequently concerned with struggles for power and influence in the household, we are afforded a very close look at the day-to-day relationships among these men and with members of the family group.[17]

The picture that emerges from the letters and account books suggests a more chaotic world than that of the orderly hierarchical households found in the prescriptive literature, including Willoughby's own orders of 1572. As a group, Elizabethan and Jacobean household regulations support the notion that ritual and ceremony successfully mediated the tensions between individuals by reinforcing rank and status. Thus, most sets of orders establish a list of servants' titles that is organized by rank and physical place in the household. For example, the tasks of the gentleman usher are followed by those of the yeoman usher and groom of the hall; these are, in turn, followed by the yeoman of the pantry and the groom of the pantry, and so on. Each person had not only a set of tasks to fulfill but also a role to play in the ceremonial serving of food or reception of visitors.

What is missing from the orders because of their prescriptive nature is any indication of the extent to which jobs changed hands as a result of the patronage system and as a response to the ebb and flow of power in the household. This is what comes across so clearly in the letters: while ceremonial occasions were designed to present an image of order and control, behind the scenes relationships were rife with faction and intrigue. Perhaps the ambiguities of social and economic class that were endemic to Elizabethan society and which fostered demands for increased rigidity in the control of outward signs of status were taking their toll on the internal organization of large households as well. The unclear dividing line between the lower gentry and upper yeomanry blurred class distinctions fundamental to household organization and thus increased the tensions of the patronage system. Because Willoughby was particularly susceptible to the pressures of flattery and rumor amongst his officers and household servants, he used his patronage to reward and elevate or to punish individuals in his employ. This may have contributed to the instability of his household hierarchy and fostered the impression, as suggested by the personal letters at least, that positions were filled and vacated at the whims of the master.

What is particularly interesting is how many household members were tied to the Willoughby family through long-standing bonds of service, either because they were yeomen with traditional allegiances to the estate or younger sons of local gentry families.[18] Thus Marmion, Draycott, Catesby, Trussell, Ithel, and Widdowson are all names that appear in the household accounts kept by Francis Willoughby's ancestors at Wollaton from the 1520s to the 1540s; Marmion and Draycott are also listed in the Willoughby pedigree and in other records, revealing long-standing ties of marriage between the families.[19] William Marmion, Henry Trussell, and John Squire were all members of a Nottinghamshire gentry family and were themselves related to one another by marriage.[20] Another officer, Thomas Cludd, was the cousin of Sir Clement Fisher, a man who was Willoughby's closest companion throughout his adult life; like the Willoughby's, their family held lands in both Nottinghamshire and Warwickshire and was listed in the herald's records with the armorial bearings to which they were entitled.[21] Thus many household members had complex claims to rank and status that went beyond their individual talents or personal relationships to the family or other servants.

The family status of the gentlemen servants placed them in positions of trust and intimacy with the Willoughby family which would have been closed to servants in the modern sense. Although Cassandra Willoughby refers to them as "servants" throughout her *Account*, it is important to make the distinction between these officers and the lower ranks of men and women who cooked, cleaned, cared for children, and maintained the household from day to day. Theirs was a world apart. According to one Elizabethan list of regulations, written for "the household of an Earl" by the anonymous author "R. B.," the chief officers were to be "not only well borne and of good livinges, but also grave and experienced, not proude and haughty, neither too affable and easy . . ."[22] At Wollaton, the officers were in most cases cousins or distant relations of the Willoughby family, but their status in the household hierarchy was ambiguous. While certainly more powerful than the yeomen, grooms, and serving men, they were nevertheless not a part of the inner circle of the family proper. On the other hand, their day-to-day familiarity with their master's business affairs and their constant attendance on him placed them in a good position to gain his confidence and even to replace his own wife or children as his principal allies. Thus, at Wollaton, as in other wealthy households, the ambiguity of the officers' status expressed itself in constant angling for favors and privileges. They squabbled over the assignment of private rooms, jockeyed for positions as stewards and accountants in order to benefit from rentals or business ventures, and plotted to undermine their master's trust in other officers, servingmen, or family members.

By the latter part of Elizabeth's reign, fewer men of the lesser gentry and yeomanry were making a career of household service. "R. B." himself laments the decline of traditional customs: "In these daies," he writes, "noblemen . . . (for the most part) like better to be served with pages and groomes than in that estate which belongeth to their

44

degrees."[23] More and more often, it seemed, the services of well-born retainers were neither sought nor offered; large households were expensive to maintain and, as the example of the Willoughby family so eloquently testifies, difficult to manage; with greater economic opportunities available in business, trade, and even agriculture, more and more men came to feel that household service imposed too many burdens without granting sufficient rewards.[24]

Yet during the 1570s and 1580s, Sir Francis Willoughby's household was not reduced; only the private dissension among its members bore witness to the tensions that would eventually render it, and other grand establishments like it, unmanageable. From the outside, life at Wollaton in 1572 did not appear very different from that of 1522.[25] Patronage—political, economic, artistic—made the system work. Many men and women claimed allegiance to the household: the resident staff included musicians who were listed in the quarterly wage list as "the musitioners" and paid £ 5; an armorer was also in residence.[26] Thanks to Cassandra's transcription of the letters and to a chance comment made in one of them, we know that Willoughby also kept a woman named Mary as his "fool."[27]

Among the most distinguished members of the household at Wollaton in the 1570s was John Banister, a doctor who attended Lady Willoughby during her many illnesses. Both he and his wife were frequent visitors to the house (and may have been in residence for a time) and he received payments for treatments and medicines detailed in the account books.[28] Banister was also a writer and translator who was to become one of the leading surgeons of his time; in 1578, he dedicated his *Historie of Man, sucked from the sappe of the most approved Anathomistes* to Francis Willoughby, peppering his preface with references to classical literature and citing his patron's great devotion to study. Banister delivered the annual "visceral lecture" on anatomy to the Barber Surgeons in 1581 (see plate 6), accompanied the Earl of Leicester to the Netherlands in the mid-1580s, and later practiced both medicine and surgery in London. In the 1590s he was censured by the College of Physicians for practicing without their license, and he presented a letter to them from the Queen citing his skill and his years of service to the Earls of Leicester and Warwick.[29]

In light of the large and varied group with which Willoughby surrounded himself, it is perhaps surprising to find that the quarterly wage list for 1572 lists only nine women. Lady Willoughby's own name tops the list. This is followed by the names of her attendants and maids. Each had their prescribed tasks in the household. With the help of her lady-in-waiting, Elizabeth Mering (who was perhaps also a distant relation) and another gentlewoman, Marjory Garner,

Lady Willoughby was expected to oversee the care of the children; her other responsibilities were to produce and care for the fine needle-work used in the household, to entertain herself and any company who visited by playing on the virginals, to play cards or pass the time in conversation. Like the chief officers who ran the household and estate, her status was in many respects ambiguous. She was the wife of the master and the mother of his children, but her freedom was limited by his orders and she too had to resort to various machinations to gain his favor and economic support. Further, her contact with others was limited by her position as the mistress of the household. Yet while there were few people beyond her husband, her attendants, and any visitors deemed to be "of the better sort" with whom she was supposed to spend her time, no doubt her day-to-day movements throughout the living complex brought her into casual contact with a wide range of people.

The quarterly wage list also names two nurses for the children, and three other women (including Mary the fool) who lived at Wollaton. In the daily accounts we can find several others who served as wet nurses, as well as women who came to the house to deliver supplies, gifts, or messages. Among these were Mrs. Banister and Mrs. Undern—wives of the doctor and of the rector of the village church, respectively.[30]

The small number of women at Wollaton is typical of upper-gentry and aristocratic households in the period. Of the two hundred persons included in the orders written by "R.B.," for example, fewer than twelve were women.[31] These included the mistress of the house, her gentlewomen, and a small number of chambermaids and laundresses. Other regulations mention only the lady, her gentlewomen, and one or two nurses, prescribing very limited activities for them; only one gives equal authority in household matters to the husband and wife, and most don't mention women at all.[32] All of the cooking, cleaning, and serving in large households was done by men, just as they had been in traditional medieval castles. The status and power of the lord were communicated to the outside world and to those visitors who entered his house by the number of men he commanded and by the intricacy of the ceremonies observed by his officers and servants. In this display, women played only a minor role—but the situation was slowly changing.

The Daily Lives of Men and Women

Willoughby was a man of means in Nottinghamshire, and as such he kept a full staff of servants and dispensed hospitality to the poor and to every sort of visitor. Players, musicians, and performers stopped at the house to entertain, and each was rewarded for his efforts.[33] Wollaton was thus both a residence and a place of business: bailiffs, agents, and neighboring landowners came and went in a never-ending parade of visitors. The Willoughby orders suggest that every activity was carefully monitored, yet other sources indicate that the use of spaces both inside of buildings and outside in open courtyards and gardens was only imperfectly controlled by rank and etiquette.

The manor house and farmstead were used very differently by men and women. As the documents show, all of the tasks within the living complex (with the exception of maintaining the dairy, the laundry, and the nursery), and much of the work on the estate as a whole, were carried out by men. Access to the various rooms and service buildings was certainly open for the master and his chief officers, while men lower down in the household hierarchy enjoyed considerable freedom on the estate even if they were barred from entrance to the private rooms used by the family and chief officers. By comparison, the lives of women, and of gentlewomen in particular, appear to have been more circumscribed, both spatially and in terms of the activities in which they participated. Women are not mentioned at all in the Willoughby household orders, and the accounts of 1572–75 reveal a surprisingly narrow range of activities for Lady Willoughby and her attendants. Women's world was primarily private and sheltered—even for working women on the estate—while men's lives were more directly concerned with public and official activities. Thus, upper-class women's lives ordinarily included contact with very few people and they moved about in groups of two or three; throughout the lives of men, on the other hand, there were opportunities to interact with dozens of people through a clearly defined hierarchical network. In the words of one historian who described the lives of peasant women during this period, women "inhabited a separate culture parallel to but concealed behind the more powerful official male culture."[34] This can be said for women of the privileged classes as well.

These cultures intersected at significant times. Men and women in married couples could be entertained at dinners in the great chamber, at suppers or card games in the dining parlor, at banquets in the gardens or at musical performances. Further, on Christmas or on other holidays women and men were both in the audience for plays and entertainments in the great hall.[35] On a daily basis, however, women and men were ordinarily separated: at meal times, the master, his guests, and his officers shared a table in the great chamber or dining chamber while the mistress ate elsewhere; the surviving accounts suggest that the situation at Wollaton fit this model.

Yet serving women in many ways enjoyed greater freedom of movement than the mistress of the house. As noted earlier, women in the household were employed as laundresses, nurses, or chambermaids. Within the house, their activities were confined to the specific areas in which they served, and they had little cause or opportunity to move about the house or its grounds. On the estate as a whole, however, agricultural laborers included both young men and women who lived in the village or at nearby cottages.[36] Women ran the dairies and brewhouses and tended local farms. Thus, while the evidence suggests that women in the household were very few and their activities quite limited, we can assume that for those involved in the provision of foodstuffs and in the most fundamental physical maintenance of the household, the boundaries between the estate proper and the surrounding community were fairly permeable, particularly at the lower levels since the women of the Willoughby household carried out chores no different from those of their neighbors. By contrast, contact with others was severely limited for women at the top of the household hierarchy.

Household orders like those written out by Francis Willoughby carefully specify that the activities of strangers and, indeed, of all visitors, should be carefully monitored.[37] Willoughby noted that it was the responsibility of the butler and the underbutler to see that "no filching of bread or beer be suffer'd" and to make sure that "no breakfast, afternoon meats, nor hancks after supper be had or made." "R.B." cautioned that it was the duty of the chief officer "to goe unto the Porters Lodge, to see it be not the place for the receipte of the unthriftes of the house, nor the habour of drinking companions."[38] These comments reinforce the notion that the great house was not isolated from its surroundings but very much a part of them. It was in the lord's interest to see that the boundaries between inside and outside were carefully maintained in order to protect his property and prevent those not in the household from sharing his wealth; with many points of contact possible, this was a constant struggle.

As we shall discuss more fully below, the eventual removal of the country house from its agricultural context had significant implications for the lives of Elizabethan men and women. The changes were paradoxical: on the one hand, by enforcing a clear separation between public and private life, the increasing popularity of the freestanding country house further limited the sphere in which upper-class women could move, while on the other, it undoubtedly also provided them with larger and more beautiful spaces in which to live. These developments were accompanied by another important change as well. The increasingly rigid boundary between the domestic world and the world of the workplace eventually led first to the reduction and, in-

1. Wollaton Hall,
Nottinghamshire.
1588. City of
Nottingham.

2. George Gower,
*Sir Francis
Willoughby*. 1573.
Collection of Lord
Middleton.

3. George Gower,
*Lady Elizabeth
Willoughby.* 1573.
Collection of Lord
Middleton.

4. Anonymous, *Sir Percival Willoughby.* ca. 1610. Collection of Lord Middleton.

An° dñi 1607·   Ætatis svæ 4?

5. Anonymous, *Lady Bridget Willoughby.* ca. 1610. Collection of Lord Middleton.

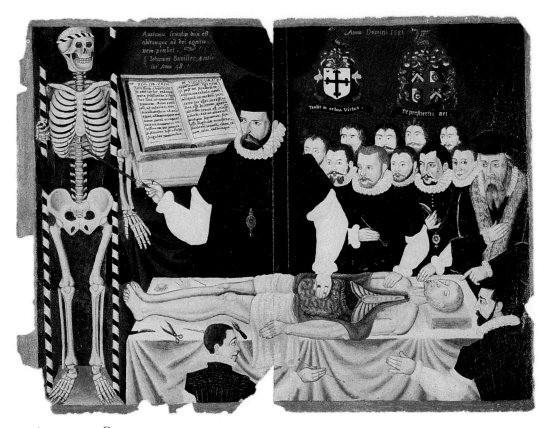

6. Anonymous, *Dr.
John Banister Deliver-
ing the Visceral
Lecture to the Barber
Surgeons in 1581.*
From Hunterian Ms.
364, by permission of
the Librarian of
Glasgow University
Library.

7. Jan Griffier (attributed to), *Wollaton Hall*. ca. 1695. Collection of Lord Middleton.

8. Jan Siberechts,
*Wollaton Hall From
the Village.* ca. 1697.
Collection of Lord
Middleton.

deed, to the elimination of the extended male household and then to a transfer of the seat of power from the home to the now more highly valued world of work. Thus, while the creation of the country house helped to place domestic work and family life directly under women's control, it also opened up the possibility for an identification of women with the home and for the virtual exclusion of women from public life.

In the household at Wollaton and elsewhere we find attitudes toward upper-class women's roles in transition. Women were no doubt an important part of the household, but their activities within it were limited by traditional rules of etiquette. While men learned increasingly sophisticated techniques of estate management and participated in the fast-moving public world of trade and commerce, upper-class women were expected to remain close to home where they were served (and surrounded) by men. Because the regulations for household management concern themselves with the rituals of household life, little is ever said about how the lady and her gentlewomen were to spend their days. A unique passage by an anonymous sixteenth-century author, however, describes their contact with the gentleman usher in a nobleman's house:

> He is to give notice to his ladies gentlewomen, that they attend in the great chamber for the better furnishing the same, viz. from nine of the clock until eleven, and then to attend their ladie to the chapel, or prayer; and from one of the clock after dinner until three in the afternoon, and then they may depart, if there be no gentlewomen strangers to be entertained, until five of the clock. [Also] . . . after supper so long as their lady is in presence and no longer.[39]

The Willoughby accounts also shed some light on what these women did in the great chamber all day. They list purchases of "books for the gentlewomen," supplies for needlework, and payments to them for their debts at cards. Lady Willoughby sometimes journeyed to the houses of neighboring friends at Colwick, Newstead, and Belvoir, where her losses were duly recorded by the accountant.[40] We know from contemporary descriptions of women's education that music and dancing were an important part of their training.[41] Gentlewomen were required to pass these skills on to their daughters, and thus female children would ordinarily spend much of their time with their mother and her companions. But in contrast both to the varied occupations of the master and his officers, and to the relative freedom of female servants, the lives of these women seem unusually dull and confined. Unlike those who freely moved about the manor house and surrounding estate, gentlewomen spent their days behind the doors of the great chamber, dining chamber, parlor, and nursery. Free access to the courtyards, service buildings, kitchens, and even to the great hall—still the symbolic if not the actual focus of household life—was denied them.

Writing in 1609, the ninth Earl of Northumberland set down his "Instructions" for his son Algernon Percy, focusing in particular on how he should treat his wife. Though obviously colored by his own misogyny (which was exacerbated by his marital troubles and his separation from his wife), Northumberland's description of household life is relevant here. The first two precepts he listed are striking: (1) "understand your estate better than your officers," and (2) "never suffer your wife to have power in your affairs."[42] This sort of generalized mistrust is not surprising; it is frequently found in documents relating to upper-class households in this period. What is significant here, however, are the reasons Northumberland gives for his exclusion of women from estate management. First, he says, their wits "are not naturally tempered as our be . . . for their ordinary ways of learning, consider but their educations, and it will appear almost impossible for them to be extraordinary, or nigh most men."[43] Second, since women are only educated in order "to keep them from idleness, the wind and the weathers," and not from "any intended desire to make them profit thereby . . ." they will never really understand business matters. According to Northumberland, women are only taught those things which will make them better ornaments in their husbands' households. If they learn Italian, for example, they learn only enough to read Ariosto; if they read books in English, they turn "to an Arcadia, or some love discourses, to make them able to entertain a stranger upon a hearth in a Privy Chamber." According to Northumberland, women's greed is what breeds factions in a household, and he warns that their skills in deception are many. Thus, he concludes, women should have no control over the estate or the servants, but should concentrate on bringing up children and caring for linens and household stuffs, appearing only at the necessary social occasions "when great personages shall visit, to sit at an end of a table, and carve handsomely."[44]

Yet while Lady Willoughby was expected to remain at home, her husband's activities frequently took him away. He divided his time between Wollaton, Middleton, and London, using his house in each place as a base in his travels. His days were filled with conferences and meetings concerning the business of his coal mines, his ironworks, woad-growing experiments, or the buying and selling of lands on his estates.[45] In addition to these activities, Willoughby served as a justice of the peace in both Warwickshire and Nottinghamshire during the 1570s and 1580s.[46] He became high sheriff of Nottinghamshire three times: in 1574, 1588, and 1593.[47] Other local knights and gentlemen, including Thomas Stanhope, Thomas Markham, and Gervase Clifton, also held these offices, as was expected of men of their class.[48] The names of these men frequently appear in the household accounts as visitors to Wollaton.

Given Willoughby's extensive involvement in business and politics, it is clear that record-keeping and the preservation of documents was of increasing importance at Wollaton. Throughout the second half of the sixteenth century, the habit of committing information to paper was becoming more and more widespread. Both men and women maintained extensive correspondence with friends and associates, and record-keeping of all kinds had become a mainstay of estate management. Thus we find rooms listed as "the Stuard's Chamber" or "my Master's study" in the accounts, and numerous purchases of paper and writing supplies are recorded.[49] Much of the record-keeping associated with the coal industry must have gone on at or near the "coal house" listed in the inventory of 1550.[50] Yet it is certain that with the shift toward increasingly sophisticated methods of estate management and with the push for greater profits from coal and iron came not only improved techniques of accounting but also a need for new spaces in which to carry out these activities. Storage of ledgers, account books, and contracts had become increasingly important. Spaces for these would be incorporated into the new house on the hill, but they were part of a business world that was increasingly specialized and increasingly separate from private life. Ultimately, one world would become the preserve of men, the other of women.

The new Wollaton Hall was built for a household where old-fashioned traditions were kept: hospitality, ritual, and knightly service were very much a part of day-to-day life. Even as Willoughby planned his new house, these were slipping into obscurity and being replaced by new attitudes toward service and social status on the one hand and toward the very nature of family life on the other. Yet Willoughby and Smythson planned the new hall to speak clearly to their own values and to those of their contemporaries. It would be a place in which the landowner could exercise all the privileges of his rank; all aspects of his life—public and private, personal and official, business and pleasure—could be carried out there. For Willoughby, as we shall see, this vision would prove elusive. In part this was just bad luck. Yet this was also a function of changes that went beyond his individual fortunes or those of his family. In many ways the last two decades of the sixteenth century marked not just the closing years of Elizabeth's reign but also the end of an era in art, in finance, in social life, and throughout English culture. The signs of change were to be found in Smythson's increasingly classicizing designs and in the complaints of conservatives who decried the passing of noble magnificence; they surfaced in Willoughby's own life and in his house, denying him the full pleasure of his greatest achievement.

3

A House Divided

Throughout the period in which Wollaton Hall was being planned and after it was built, the household of Sir Francis Willoughby was never free from discord, intrigue, and dishonesty; indeed, his children and their families continued to pay the price, quite literally, for the ruinous condition of his financial and personal relationships long after his death in 1596.[1] While the stated reasons for the difficulties between Sir Francis, his wife, and the members of their household varied from incident to incident, it is clear that the underlying cause was a frenzied cutthroat competition for his personal favor and, through him, for the rights to his property. Personal animosities between the various contenders led to charges of disobedience, infidelity, or maliciousness, but what lay beneath the surface of these allegations were two fundamental problems. First, from the time of his marriage in 1564 to the time of his death, Willoughby had no clearcut plan for the distribution of his property among his heirs and kinsmen; and second, to make matters worse, he was himself particularly vulnerable to the self-serving manipulations of others, alternately rewarding and punishing his wife and children as his confidence in them shifted from one day to the next. Thus he himself fanned the flames of discord raging in his household even as he protested this behavior in others.

The ongoing melodrama of the Willoughby household, which at times reads more like a modern soap opera than a real-life history, is important to us for two reasons. It enables us to form a picture of the day-to-day activities of the Willoughby family and household in the years just prior to the building of the new house and, thus, to enliven the architectural spaces under consideration here. Second, by looking at the Willoughbys' marital difficulties and at the conflicts among their servants and children in the context of other cases and of contemporary writings on marriage and family life, we can bring to light concerns that were not simply personal but widespread and, thus, identify problems shared by other Elizabethan households. These help us to reconstruct the program for the new hall by suggesting the directions in which the social order was changing, highlighting the inadequacies of both the existing household structure and of the

53

architecture which accommodated it. Willoughby's new house tells us a great deal about the way in which he wanted to live and how he viewed the organization of day-to-day household activity. The new Wollaton would provide him not only with a showplace and a center of operations from which to run his estates, but also with a more harmonious domestic environment that was easier to control than the one in which he had spent his early adulthood. Thus architecture was seen not only as a means to accommodate existing social relationships but as a tool to shape and define them.

Marital Difficulties

The Willoughbys' marital difficulties began even before their wedding—with the financial negotiations between Francis's family and that of his fiancée Elizabeth Littleton. Francis had met the young woman at her father's house, eagerly responding to the proposals by his kinsmen that he consider taking her for his wife. Writing to his uncle Lord John Grey, he took pains to underscore the appropriateness of the marriage for his family as a whole:

> After good deliberation it had pleased God to give him a liking to the young gentlewoman, who had a good education and was descended from a house of great antiquity, well frended and alyed, dwelling near his house of Middleton . . . Mr. Lyttleton offered to give with his daughter 1,500 £., to apparell her decently, to bear their charges at the time of their marriage, and to give them their table with six persons to attend them, for three years, and the keeping of six geldings.

For his part, Francis would be required to pay only "a very reasonable jointure and the settlement of but one third part of his estate on heirs male by her."[2] His uncle and guardian agreed that the match was a good one. Nevertheless, as noted in the previous chapter, Willoughby's proposal was met with immediate opposition from his sister Margaret, by then the wife of Sir Matthew Arundell and a fixture at Court. Her initial objection set the tone of tension and mistrust that was to divide the two sisters-in-law for the next thirty years. Margaret complained that she had not been consulted before any promises were made and she wondered why her brother had proceeded without her approval. Pointing a finger at their uncle, George Willoughby, whom she claimed had "some crafty designs of his own," Margaret wrote to her brother vehemently opposing his marriage.[3] Francis remained resolute, however, and even accused his sister of blocking the match out of her own desire to profit from his estate;

Margaret responded by accusing Sir John Littleton of being an "ill man" and a "great dissembler."

Financial problems arose as early as 1569. In a letter of that date, Sir John Littleton apologized to Francis for not making full payment of a debt (the marriage portion, perhaps) on time, saying he regretted that he could send only part of the money he owed.[4] When it became clear that Littleton was unable or unwilling to produce the money—and that, in fact, Francis was going to have to sue him to get it—Margaret wrote to remind her brother that she had warned him of his father-in-law's unreliability. She continually hounded him about Littleton's debts and the way he managed his own affairs. By this time the couple were no longer living at the Littleton home at Frankley (the three-year period agreed upon in the marriage contract was over) but stayed in various manor houses on Willoughby's estates in Nottinghamshire and Warwickshire. The time had come for them to set up their own household, but Margaret Arundell wrote to her brother that she doubted "whether his wife will like housekeeping, especially when she knows of the company he meant to have."[5]

As it turned out, the young wife did not like "housekeeping" at all, at least not if it meant living with her husband. While Francis chose to set up house at Middleton and Wollaton, Elizabeth often traveled to London or stayed on other estates, rejecting his frequent requests that she spend more time at home. She frequently claimed that her poor health required her to take the waters at Buxton—a fashionable retreat of the Court where the Earl of Shrewsbury and others maintained comfortable houses—or remain in London under her doctor's care; at other times she simply refused to comply with her husband's orders, thereby violating one of the traditional precepts of marriage.[6] In May 1575, Francis wrote to Dr. Smith, his wife's London physician, complaining that she was once again traveling to Buxton for the baths; he wrote that although he was willing to let her do it, she should "consider her duty rather than suffer herself to be guided by self will." He then wrote to Elizabeth herself at Buxton to make it clear that he wished that "with the recovery of her health she may also put on a tractable mind, and let her self-will give place to reason," saying that he desired her "to be as good a wife as she would make shew of being to the world, and let her example cause him to do the like."[7] Lady Elizabeth replied rather glibly that she was obliged to see her sister safely home and would thus not be returning immediately.

Each side claimed that the fault lay with the other. According to Francis and his sister Margaret, Elizabeth was self-willed, and unreasonable. She was accused of having an uncontrollable temper that caused her to fly into violent rages at the slightest provocation; in

1570, for instance, Margaret responded to her brother's complaints with the advice that the next time his wife was seized by one of her fits, Francis should "send for her father to come to her" and "they should both go with him home and board there with a convenient number of servants, till such time as she should have lost her wilfullness, and would apply herself to please him."[8] Francis frequently wrote to his father-in-law to complain of his wife's behavior, citing in particular her "frowardness" and her refusal to obey him.

The image of the shrewish and scolding woman was a familiar one in contemporary literature and books of advice.[9] A sharp tongue was a woman's most serious defect—as dangerous to her husband as her voracious sexual appetite—and thus a thing to be watched for and controlled. This view is summed up concisely in Thomas Bentley's *Monument of Matrons* (1582), a book of "Christian prayers and meditations to be used of all sorts and degrees of women . . .":

> Grant that my will, according to thy commandment, may be in subjection to mine husband, and obey him in all equitie. . . . Reform the manners of thine handmaid, and make me in my conversation modest, and honest; make me in visage shamefast, in words temperate; in wit, wise; in going, sober; in conversation, meke; in correction, pitifull; in life, circumspect; in companie keeping, warie; in promise, steadfast; in love, constant; take from me all crabbedness, curstness, stubborness, and shrewdness; and let me have an especiall care by virtue and friendlie words, to mitigate the anger of mine husband, if at anie time he be displeased, and let me absteine from all such things as I know will offend him.[10]

What Bentley obviously makes clear here is that women were expected both to curb their own tongues and to suffer the anger of their husbands in silence. That this was, of course, often not the case is made abundantly clear by the evidence from contemporary marriages and, indeed, from the very frequency of injunctions to silence and "shamefastness" found in the literature.[11]

Charges of shrewishness and frowardness went hand in hand. Thus, for example, the Earl of Shrewsbury claimed that his wife Elizabeth ("Bess of Hardwick") "scolded like one that came from the Bank"; he objected that she called him "knave, foole and beast, to his face and hathe mocked and mowed at him with words and gestures."[12] Writing to Shrewsbury in 1590, the Bishop of Coventry and Lichfield exhorted him to put aside his complaints of his wife, for "if shrewdness and sharpness may be just cause for separation I think that few men in England would keep their wives for long, for it is common jest yet true in some sense, that there is one shrew in all the world and every man hath her."[13] In his *Preparative to Marriage* of 1591, Henry Smith echoed this view: women were "stubborn, sullen, taunting, gainsaying, outfacing [and] with such a bitter humour that one would thinke they were molten out of the salt pillar into which Lots wife was transformed." He concluded, "We say not all are alike but this sect hath manie disciples." [14]

Often these charges of female insolence masked other conflicts within the household. The long-standing rift between the Earl and Countess of Shrewsbury, for example, did not originally stem from any particular fault in her personality or his but from their bitter disagreements about property and inheritance. At issue were the terms of certain documents transferring lands from the Earl to his wife and the question of who would receive the benefits of rents and other property; her sons claimed that they, with her, had been granted rights of ownership. [15] In the winter of 1585, Sir Francis Willoughby and Sir John Manners, acting as representatives of the Crown, heard complaints from representatives of each side in this dispute, dutifully recording the allegations of all witnesses. [16] Here charges of financial and personal misdoings were all mixed together. A similar pattern can be recognized in numerous other cases. For example, the marriage of the sixth Earl of Derby to Lord Burghley's granddaughter in 1595 began inauspiciously with his failure to pay his wife's portion and ended with the couple's separation amidst rumors of the wife's unfaithfulness—a charge that often seems interchangeable with stubbornness and frowardness since all were stereotypically female transgressions. [17] The marriage of Thomas Egerton, Lord Ellesmere, to the Dowager Countess Alice, widow of the fourth Earl, also declined into a series of quarrels over land and property; Egerton publicly complained of his wife's "biting tongue." [18]

At issue in all of these cases was the ambiguity of the land laws regarding transfer of property within families and amongst the heirs of married couples. [19] During the Elizabethan period, traditional common-law practices regarding the property rights of the eldest son, the wife, and the widow were increasingly subject to circumvention and reinterpretation by enterprising lawyers and their clients. The growing popularity of such devices as the "feoffment to use" (dating from 1535), the conveyance, and the will (dating from 1540) created a situation in which virtually any property could be transferred without limitation and thus every legal transaction was subject to dispute. Although the wife's consent was required for transfer of her jointure lands according to common law, there seems to have been considerable ambiguity about how strictly this was to be observed. In many cases the result was endless negotiation both about the specific properties that were to be so limited and the precise limitations upon them. Although it was generally agreed that the husband was liable for the wife's debts and wrongs and that she could not contract on her own behalf, there seems to have been considerable confusion in this period both about her relationship to her husband's estate and about his to hers. The chaotic legal situation was often compounded by the failure of the direct male line and the claims of female heirs to estate property. Bess of Hardwick was clearly able to hold onto her own property throughout a series of marriages (four, to be precise) and after her eventual separation from the Earl of Shrewsbury; other women, notably Elizabeth Willoughby and her daughters, were not so fortunate.[20]

In the Willoughby household, these concerns were at work in undermining the relationship between Sir Francis and his wife. A series of documents in the Middleton collection show that Lady Willoughby's jointure was renegotiated as many as four times during her marriage.[21] In 1575, George Willoughby wrote to Sir Francis that he should "banish his wife from him if after her many promises she would not at last yield to pass the fines"; another letter to his lawyer listed the property not in the jointure which would be included in the same fine, and also specified the terms by which these lands would pass to his heirs.[22] Ultimately, these bitter negotiations stemmed from property disputes between Sir Francis and John Littleton, but it was Lady Elizabeth who was in the front line of the battle. Sir Francis reported to his father-in-law that his wife had openly refused to obey him and that she had reproached him, threatening "that her friends would not see her destitute, [that] she would not bear so much as she had done, and that she would not with her good will tarry any longer with him, who . . . kept her but as a fool to jest and flout at."[23] Her jointure, her dignity, and her status in the household were all tied up together.

Throughout the 1570s, Lady Elizabeth's difficulties were aggravated by her problems during pregnancy and childbirth. She was obviously fulfilling her obligation to try to produce an heir: in about 1580 she complained to her husband that she had borne him twelve children in sixteen years.[24] Yet there is evidence that she was burdened by gynecological ailments throughout her life and thus refused her husband's sexual attention at various points in their relationship. At the height of these problems, Francis wrote to his sister that his wife had "burdened him in that by his dealing with her he had been the occasion of the loss of her children, which, tho' not true, he was contented to bear." Was this hard "dealing" simply mental cruelty, or was Willoughby physically violent or unwilling to give up his sexual privileges during her pregnancy?[25] The letter writers are silent on this point.

Despite the efforts of a number of doctors, Elizabeth Willoughby was ill for virtually all of her life. The pressure to bear children was enormous; no small amount of the difficulty between the husband and wife stemmed from their desire for an heir (six daughters but no son survived) and this was clearly perceived as her inability to provide one. A letter written from London in 1575 reveals the desperate situation in which she found herself:

> She writes that her phisitians think it very dangerous for her to travel. She would have got their leave to have gone to her cousin Thomas Willoughby's in Kent, but they would not consent to it. She writes that she thinks 'tis very unlikely that she should goe forth her time, if she be with child as she trusts in God she is, and yet some of her phisitians think the contrary. She desires they would give her something, either to help or dispatch her quickly, for she thinks death would be a thousand times more welcome to her than to live as she now does continually sick.[26]

The numerous recorded episodes involving Lady Elizabeth's erratic behavior and her uncontrollable rage must be viewed against this background of her financial insecurity and declining health. Her efforts to remedy her situation in both areas were met with frustration. Frequent trips to London to visit her doctor and the expenses of her separate maintenance on these occasions enraged her husband; worse, she didn't appear to be getting any better. Yet despite these difficulties, Lady Willoughby would perhaps have survived in the household had it not been for the calculated animosity of her husband's servants. It was their entrance into the constellation of forces opposed to her that eventually ensured her downfall.

Plots by Officers and Servants

Throughout his marriage, Sir Francis was attended by a large retinue in the traditional manner, and he maintained a staff of forty or fifty men.[27] His household—like others and, indeed, like the Court itself—was held together by a system of patronage based on allegiance and favors that could be granted or withdrawn at will. Competition, jealousy, and factionalism were endemic. Whatever animosity already existed between husband and wife was thus deepened through the efforts of servants who saw an advantage in their mutual distrust. Frequent attempts were made to arouse Sir Francis's suspicions that his wife kept company with his enemies, and it was even suggested that she sought out a friendship with a neighbor, Lady Stanhope, in order to pursue a love affair with Sir Thomas Stanhope, her husband. When investigated, these reports proved false, but more often than not Sir Francis accepted such rumors at face value.[28] He remained suspicious and mistrustful.

The evidence suggests that interference by servants and household officers was a familiar problem. A letter from the servant Marmion to Sir Francis, probably written in the early 1580s, described how he wished to leave the service of the Earl of Shrewsbury and his wife so that he could return to the Willoughby household, from which he had been dismissed some years before.[29] Marmion complained of being drawn into the couple's bitter arguments, saying that Shrewsbury had accused him of siding with Bess in their dispute over the costs of the Queen of Scots' maintenance during her confinement while under his supervision. Shrewsbury called for Marmion's dismissal, saying that if Bess would not remove him "he could never be brought to think that she loved him, neyther would he ever take her for his wyfe, but he would remove [him] and shutt her Ladyship up without suffring any sarvauntes about her than of his own placing."[30]

It is further revealed in Marmion's letter that the competition for the lord's favor was in fact a contest for substantial financial stakes: the rewards were not simply approval or protection but livings and annuities. Thus, Marmion requested that the lease of a small farm and a cottage be awarded to him since "Boothe being layde together will make a pretty living"; in return, he said, "I and all my pore frendes must think ourselves specyally bound to rest with all dutyful sarvice most faythfully at your worship's devocion."[31]

William Wentworth, head of a substantial gentry family in Yorkshire, addressed the matter in His *Advice to His Son* of 1604. He cautioned that servants should never be trusted, as "almost all trecheries have been wrought by servants, and the finale end of their service is gaine and advancement."[32] His son should beware flatterers and suspect their honesty, being careful to use the promise of rewards as a way to keep men attentive, for, he said, "After Annuities granted men are verie seldom found diligent and thankfull, for hope is at an end for possession of the thing desyred and mans nature is most corrupt that waye."[33] Wentworth also cautioned that wives should on no account be allowed to hear tenants' pleas or otherwise involve themselves in the running of their husbands' estates: "For flatteringe tenants will sone seduce a woman, who neither is lyke to have a true intelligence of the matter, nor so sound a judgement as the wiser sort of men have."[34]

In his *Advice to His Son* of 1609, the ninth Earl of Northumberland cautioned that the factions in his household should be monitored with the greatest attention. His wife and her supporters were most to be mistrusted:

> Gripe into your hands what poore soe ever you will of government, yett will there be certaine parsons about your wyfe, that you will never reduce; a gentleman usher, her tailor and her woman; for

they will ever talke, and ever be unreasonable; all which your officers will rather endeavor to pleas then yowr selfe . . . in a house
thus governed, factions will be ryfe, as well emongest your own servants as emongest your friends and hers; for her friends will ever be
the welcommest and best used, the traine of women friends being
ever the longest and most trooblesomme.[35]

Wentworth agreed: a wife's friends would take her part in property
disputes and corrupt the servants, undermining a man's authority in
his own house; the only way out was to monitor her every move.[36]

Sir Francis's efforts to control his wife met with little success. In
one incident, described in detail in Cassandra Willoughby's *Account*,
Sir Francis and his attendants held what appears to have been a semi-
official meeting with Lady Willoughby and her gentlewomen in the
gallery of their house at Kingsbury.

> Soon after he went himself to Kingsbury taking with him Sir Fowlk
> Grevell, Mr. Boughton, and Mr. Fisher. . . . After they had supper
> at Kingsbury Sir Francis Willughby sent to his Lady (who had be-
> fore refused to come to supper) to require her to speak with him;
> she sent word that she would speak with them in the gallery, where
> they all went. What Sir Francis said at first going into the gallery
> was not heard by the company, but his Lady answer'd in great col-
> ler "I will blaze your arms and make you better known." Sir Francis
> pressed her to be reconciled to his sister, which she refused. He
> then asked her if in all other things she would be ruled by him.
> Upon which she answered she would not be ruled by him. Upon
> which Sir Fowlk Grevell said "Why, madam, will you refuse to be
> ruled by your husband?" She answer'd she was the Queen's sworn
> servant and knew not but Sir Francis might command her some-
> thing against Her Majestie's proceedings; to which Sir Fowlk said
> that was an evil objection for a wife to lay to her husband. Mr.
> Boughton would have perswaded her for her children's sake and
> her own (for to discredit her husband was to discredit herself and
> posterity) that there might be a good agreement and love between
> herself and her husband. She answered that her heart was hard-
> ened against Sir Francis, and she could not love him as she had
> done. Sir Francis answered her that since his first marrying her to
> this day her actions had shewed the little love which now her
> speech made manifest . . . to which she answered in mockage that
> she thanked him, and if she had a cap she would have put it off
> to him.

Cassandra broke off her account of this conversation with a terse dis-
claimer: "Many more spitefull disrespectfull speeches she made which
are there copied [that is, in the letter from which she was excerpting]
but this I think is sufficient to show the nature of their uneasiness,
and too much to be noted down by a grand-daughter in the fourth

descent from this Lady." She concludes, "Mrs. Mearing, Lady Willughby's woman, was with her Lady in the gallery, and to Mr. Fisher
expressed her sorrow for what had passed."[37]

Violent public scenes erupted with increasing frequency. Once,
after her husband's departure from their house at Coventry, Lady
Willoughby attempted to discharge some of his servants, forbidding
them access to the house. They refused to obey her orders:

> Upon which she went down herself, being led by Mrs. Elizabeth
> Mearing and another of the maids, to have seen them turned out,
> but meeting with Cludde with his sword under his arm, Lady
> Willoughby cried out in a fright, "What! Will they murther me
> in my husband's absence?" And upon this, sending down some of
> her maids to raise the town, there came in Penn and Green with
> divers others with them, who not being able to appease or satisfie
> my Lady, she desired them all to guard her to the vicarage, which
> they did.[38]

This sort of public disturbance was unacceptable. In desperation,
Sir Francis placed his wife under a sort of house arrest of the type
reportedly threatened by Shrewsbury in his arguments with Bess.[39] He
ordered her to submit to the authority of two of his officers—Henry
Draycott and Thomas Cludd—and he restricted her movements to
specific rooms within his house. According to his orders, Lady Elizabeth no longer had any rights in the care of the children, who were
entrusted to the care of Joan, their nurse, and she was forbidden
either to "discharge or receive any servant" or to "strike or evil en-
treat any servant." She was barred from entering the room where
household stuffs were laid, she could make no purchases in the town
and had "no authority to command anything in the house except
necessary diet for herself." The children were to be in bed by eight
o'clock at night; at nine the fire in the great chamber—where Lady
Elizabeth and her ladies spent their days—was to be raked up and the
door locked.

Lady Willoughby objected to this treatment with all the violent
passion of which she was capable. The scene was recounted in detail.
She told her husband that

> whoever should take upon them to order her children in her pres-
> ence she would mischief . . . that Johan was his whore and that
> she would not be left amongst such villains [Draycott and Cludd]
> but would go into ye town . . . [that] she desired to goe to an inn
> and send for some of her friends to her, and upon his denying her
> that, she fell into a most violent passion, threatening to make away
> with herself, and being denied a knife would have struck her scis-
> sors into her belly if she had not been prevented. Then she said she

would never eat or drink more, but wth ye same knife she was next to eat wth would kill herself.[40]

Sir Francis ignored these threats, blaming her for her willfulness and unruly behavior.

Separation 1580–88

By December of 1579, John Littleton was writing to Sir Francis to arrange a separate allowance for his daughter.[41] In the coming months letters flew back and forth carrying rumors that Lady Willoughby was threatening to bring the case to the attention of the Queen; for his part, Sir Francis was ready with a list of his wife's faults. These included "her disorderly life, her watching late contrary to his liking, her keeping such company as he did mislike . . . her reviling him to his face," and "her running out of the house and raising the town." In 1582, he was obliged by the Queen to pay £ 200 a year for her separate maintenance.[42]

Over the next five or six years, Lady Willoughby wrote to her husband begging him to take her back. She pleaded for him to forgive her for her "unhansome speeches and disrespectful carriage" toward him, recalling the many false stories he had believed about her.[43] In a letter of 1585 in the Lansdowne Collection at the British Library, she promised that if he would once again receive her into his household, she would "study to conforme all my wordes as I may best content and please you, as also to performe all good duties that do become a loving and obedient wife towardes her husband."[44] She knew that this profession of remorse would please her husband, but she had no real intention of following through on her promises.

She wrote sarcastically that she trusted he would "hold [her] excused, if by the advise of [her] good and wise friendes, [she] shall refuse to enter into any hard condicions, or be drawne by any action into any chance of ye losse of that litle poor lyving [he] allowe[s] her." Moreover, if her husband wished her to return from London, she must be sure that the conditions would be favorable; had she not been told by a good friend "that I should take heed and beware how I come to yow againe, for yow had determyned and vowed that if ever yow took me agayne yow would kepe me shorter than ere I was kept, that yow lock and pynn me up in a chamber, and that I should not go so muche as into the garden to take the ayre, without yor leave and lycense."[45] She wrote that she hoped her husband would understand if she refused to return under these conditions.

In the same letter Lady Elizabeth caustically remarked that she suspected Sir Francis of trying to establish grounds for divorce by proving that she had had an illegitimate child. From our vantage point, this seems a particularly unjust charge on the part of the husband since there is evidence to suggest that it was Sir Francis, and not his wife, who was the parent of a son born out of wedlock in 1585.[46]

The accepted conventions of marriage were set out for Lady Willoughby in a letter written to her during this period by Lord Burghley's secretary, Sir Michael Hicks.[47] In response to her request for support, he replied that he could only offer her some friendly advice. She should commit her "unhappy case to God by [her] prayer and commend [her] honest cause to ye worlde by [her] pacyence." He reminded her that

> according to ye ordinance of God and the covenants of your marriage, yow [must] endevor to subdue and submytt yor will to ye plesure of yor hedd, in all honest and lawfull things seking rathr to wynne his good will wth covering his faultes, and bearing with his infirmyties, then to wreste hym to your owne, by reveling his shame and resisting his commandments . . . the wch although it may seme hard to fleshe and bloude, yett is it warranted by ye woorde of God, wch byndes all women of what birth or calling soever they be, to yelde due benevolence and obedyence to their husbands.

Here again was the familiar injunction to obedience and this was not, of course, what Lady Willoughby wanted to hear. But Hicks was right in a way: submission to her husband was her only recourse. Her only chance of producing a male heir was fading fast. The couple's young son had died in 1580, and since her separation from her husband the chances of her conceiving and carrying the baby to term were even slimmer.[48] Her allowance was inadequate and her position undignified. Her husband had won: it was she who begged him to take her back, swallowing her pride and ultimately accepting his terms. She had no real choice to do otherwise.[49]

In many ways, then, Lady Elizabeth Willoughby was a victim of circumstances. Her father betrayed her in the settlement of her marriage agreement, she was badgered by her husband's servants, and her poor health was a constant source of pain and anxiety. These conditions contributed to the uncontrolled and erratic behavior her husband found so objectionable. But her own problems were exacerbated by the ambiguities and tensions of the time in which she lived. As we have seen, the unsettled land law contributed to the heightened competition for her husband's favor. Two other factors can be added: first, the increasing opportunities for social and economic mobility which disrupted the hierarchy within the household and distorted relationships between its members; and second, the presence of a female sovereign on the throne of England. As the wealth of literature devoted to the "woman question" during Elizabeth's reign abundantly demonstrates, the example of the Queen, who was not only well-educated but outspoken and powerful, created considerable uneasiness in the minds of some of her subjects. This was accompanied by a heightened sensitivity toward "degree" and social status, which blurred traditional relationships by introducing new criteria of rank such as professional education and newly acquired wealth.[50] The effects were felt by both men and women. Exactly how these factors translated into personal relationships cannot be said with certainty, but examples like the Willoughbys and others referred to in this chapter suggest that a number of large households were disrupted by poor relationships between men and women within the upper segments of society. These disputes were often triangular rather than two-sided: the husband and wife were both ultimately pitted against the officers and upper servants, who manipulated their private relationships and undermined their public image. In many cases, the mistress's loss was the officers' gain; this was certainly true in the larger social context. The transfer of property and the maintenance of authority within the household were two areas in which uncertain legal conditions, economic mobility, and changing roles for men and women obviously came together; in this environment of shifting values and uncertain relationships, the effect was chaos.

For a woman like Lady Elizabeth Willoughby, the pressures within her husband's household became too great to withstand. She was not content to remain at home, silent and submissive as the moralists advised. Among her many reasons for this was certainly a desire for greater freedom than her husband would allow. Like other wealthy women of the time, she resisted her husband's traditional authority, and there was thus a grain of truth in his accusations of self-will. Indeed, without this motivation for independence, very few of the cases cited here would have come to our notice. Illness, fear of pregnancy, disputed inheritance, and the machinations of family or servants would perhaps have remained nothing more than isolated long-standing annoyances. But coupled with fundamental differences over the division of power and property in upper-class households, these problems blossomed into all-encompassing conflicts between husbands and wives. The atmosphere in her husband's house was clearly stifling to Lady Elizabeth, and she refused to remain there under conditions she was powerless to change. For this she was rejected by her husband and eventually by her father, the two men on whom she depended.[51]

Disputed Inheritance

In March 1582, not long after the marriage of his eldest daughter Bridget to Percival Willoughby, Sir Francis offered her some advice on
with her in-laws, had written to her father to tell him of her happy life. He replied that

> to continue it must be her own care, for 'tis not beauty nor fortune but good qualities and a virtuous disposition which makes a gentle-woman esteemed; therefore 'tis her good behaviour that must gain her own credit . . . she will learn by others in time (she may ghess who he means) to be wise and not repent too late. That now at first enterance she should frame herself a dutyful wife, and . . . take care to be in deed such a woman as she desired to be esteemed, and thus she might encrease and long enjoy her friends, in order to which two things were needful, serving God and knowing herself.

Both Sir Francis and his daughter had the image of her mother's intractibility constantly before them. Bridget replied that "her duty to her husband she will unfeignedly be carefull to perform, having the example of others seldom out of her mind, and cause to learn to be wise by other's harms."[52]

The marriage of Bridget to her cousin Percival Willoughby was arranged by Sir Francis following his separation from his wife and the death of their young son in 1580.[53] The terms of the marriage settlement were tied together with the revocation of Lady Elizabeth's jointure; her part of the estate would pass to this couple as the heirs of Sir Francis. Percival and his father, Sir Thomas Willoughby of Chiddingstone, in Kent, were to become Sir Francis's business partners (a decision which both would soon bitterly regret) and thus began to receive all his support and attention. The reaction of the household was predictable: the young couple soon became the focus of the servants' plots and thus began to suffer the consequences of Sir Francis's suspicion.

From the mid-1580s to the time of Sir Francis's death in 1596, Bridget and Percival Willoughby were embroiled in a series of disputes involving her father and his servants. All stemmed from their position as Willoughby's heirs. The first incident occurred as soon as Percival entered the household; it involved a Frenchman, Francis Conrados, whom the young man had hired on the Continent to teach him Italian. When the two arrived back at Wollaton, Percival unwisely pressed to have his teacher eat with him at his table in the great chamber; worse still, he asked that this man be assigned to a chamber already occupied by William Marmion, one of the more contentious servants.[54] When Percival became aware of the seriousness of the disruptions which this request was causing in the household, he reversed himself, but by that time it was too late. Joining with Percival's enemies, Conrados fabricated a story that Percival was plotting to murder his father-in-law and devised a means by which a note to this effect would fall into Sir Francis's hands. Thus the servants (Blyth, Marmion, and Cludd) rose in Willoughby's estimation and Percival abruptly fell. The malicious attention that Lady Elizabeth had suffered for years was now decisively focused on him.

The issue of inheritance seems to have been ever-present in the Willoughby household, a situation exacerbated by the presence of six daughters and no male heir to inherit Sir Francis's fortune. Property certainly played a central role in the marriages of his three eldest daughters; for the three younger ones it was less of an issue. Despite the fact that Sir Francis had written to a family friend that "lyking shall grow betwixt the parties, without ye which, I will never presse them," he nonetheless arranged his daughters' marriages to serve the financial interests of his family.[55] His second daughter Dorothy was married in 1587 to Henry Hastings, second son of the Earl of Huntington, a match viewed as financially advantageous to the Willoughbys; disputes over her marriage portion contributed to the breakdown of the relationship.[56] The possibility of a match between Margaret, the third daughter, and Gervase Markham was the subject of extensive negotiations between Sir Francis and his neighbor Sir Thomas Markham, but the boy's Catholicism impeded the match; she eventually married Robert Spencer of Wormleighton (created Baron Spencer in 1603), a far richer and more powerful man.[57]

The younger girls' lives were also profoundly affected by their parents' unhappiness. The fourth daughter, Winifred, fell in love with Percival Willoughby's younger brother, Edward, at a time when Percival had fallen out with both Sir Francis and his estranged wife. When she broached the subject of marriage, her mother responded by locking her up and beating her so severely that she wrote to her lover that she feared she would be lamed.[58] The two youngest children, Abagail and Frances, served in the household; both complained of ill treatment by their parents.[59]

The Program for the New Hall

These struggles reflect the need for change both in personal relationships and in household structure, pressures that produced major shifts in family structure and in social relations over the course of the next half-century. We cannot say with any certainty to what extent the planners of the new house consciously incorporated a new social and economic program into their design, but it is nevertheless possible to point to elements of the plan that seem intended to alleviate tension and to facilitate new ways of living.

While some problems in the Willoughby household were specific to the individuals involved and resulted from quirks in their own personalities, others, by contrast, seem to have been due to problems in the society as a whole. The most obvious of these was the competition between family members which resulted from the chaotic and confusing land law. In the Willoughby household and elsewhere, the ambiguity surrounding the procedure for the distribution of property gave rise to endless difficulties, as we have seen. This focused not only on the birth of a male heir and the marriages of the daughters but also on the immediate transfer of property by conveyances, mortgages, and leases. Before the advent of the strict settlement, tensions surrounding inheritance, property distribution, and status were significant undermining factors in marriage; where accumulated wealth was not at issue, the chances for success in marriage seem to have been greater. Further, the patronage system and the overwhelming presence of resident servants in large households clearly played a significant negative role, ensuring that the competition for the lord's favor would pervade every imaginable aspect of public and private life. As long as the business of estate management remained tied to domestic relationships, life in both areas suffered.

Moreover, throughout this period the position of upper-class women was clearly in transition. In noble and gentry families, pressure to produce an heir was considerable, and the terms both of marriage and of property ownership by women were clouded in ambiguity.[60] Further, there was apparently genuine confusion about the relative status of women and men in large households; new criteria rendered simple divisions of social hierarchy according to land ownership and blood ties more and more unclear. The highly visible example of the Queen surrounded by a court of educated men and women cannot have helped matters. For a couple like the Willoughbys, the extent of the husband's authority and his wife's duty to obey him remained undefined, causing them daily disputes and misunderstandings. Further, for them the ideal of the "companionate marriage," as Lawrence Stone has termed it, remained elusive, buried (if it existed at all) under layers of ambition directed toward economic and social advantage.[61]

These major areas of dysfunction in Elizabethan household life—and the need for changes which they signal—seem to underlie elements of the program for Wollaton Hall. Sir Francis Willoughby's household obviously retained remnants of the old military order and of the land-based feudal economy, but its members were clearly feeling the pressure of change. The increasing social and economic stature of Willoughby's officers, combined with their growing dependence on London and the Court, disrupted the balance of power in the household and reshaped the daily life of the manor house. Although Willoughby's identity in the country depended on family history and traditional service, these no longer sufficed in an increasingly professional and profit-conscious culture. He saw his new house as a place in which the values of the Court and the city were carried into the country: estate administration, record-keeping, and private study would take the place of agricultural activities (which continued in the manor house next to the town) while dinners, music, and other entertainments could be held in large and handsomely furnished rooms set aside for the purpose. The professionalization of estate management and of the business world encouraged the separation of public and private life; women, excluded from the public world by lack of education and by social pressure, would find their place in the now more isolated domestic realm of family and social life.

In this context, it is also interesting to speculate on whether Wollaton or houses like it were ever intended primarily as showplaces to impress the Sovereign, a claim which is often made about all the great houses of this period. Unlike courtiers such as Burghley or Hatton, however, men like Willoughby were not primarily concerned with the politics of the Court; on the contrary, their attention was focused on their own estates, on county politics, and on their status among the local gentry and nobility. As we have seen, Willoughby's relationship to the Court was ambivalent, and this is reflected in the design of Wollaton. On the one hand he was an independently powerful figure whose country house was his castle, but on the other, he remained a subject of a sovereign whose power, like his own, had increased with the improvement of administrative controls. This sovereign could choose to descend on him at any moment and claim his magnificence as her own. Thus Wollaton presents two faces to the world: it is a family home and the administrative headquarters of a powerful gentry landowner but at the same time a palace with apartments grand enough—and ready for—a visit by the Queen.

All this is, of course, an oversimplified and highly speculative description of causes and effects which were complex, a tangle of conscious and unconscious decisions. Yet, looking at the new house in comparison with the old, a number of changes stand out. First, the house is not only set apart from its agricultural context but looms high above it, an observation tower and a place from which the estate could be controlled. Second, on the interior, separate spaces were given over to the various classes of people and to their activities, isolating the service areas and offices from the principal rooms of the house.

Third, more extensive and varied spaces were devoted to entertainment and private leisure: these included the two great chambers, withdrawing rooms, gallery, roof-top banqueting rooms, terraces, and "Prospect Room"—all on the upper floors above the hall. These planning strategies represent a major shift from the spatially and socially enmeshed world of the manor house.

One final point sheds light on Willoughby's motivation as a builder and his hopes for his house. Writing to his wife's physician in the mid-1570s, he suggested that her health would be improved if she would "live in a wholesome air and eschue disorder in her diet and perturbations of her mind," adding that "she will not mislike the place where [I am] disposed to dwell, being unwilling [myself] to be in any air which [we] could find hurt by."[62] According to Cassandra's *Account,* Lady Willoughby often complained of the air in which she was living and frequently fancied that "the air she was in was unholsome . . . [desiring] to change it from one house to another."[63] The site of the new house at Wollaton was given special notice by Robert Burton in his *Anatomy of Melancholy* of 1622: "And he that built that faire house Wollerton in Nottinghamshire is much to be commended (though the tract be sandy and barren about it), for making choice of such a place."[64] Perhaps among all the many things that Sir Francis hoped to accomplish through his new building was an improvement in his wife's health and temperament. Thus it is significant that she returned to live with him at Wollaton in April 1588, ending their eight-year separation.[65]

Certainly, he had a complex and unfamiliar program in mind, one which required a bold and innovative solution. At Wollaton, Willoughby was to be the scholar-knight, the educated man at the head of a small army—now not of soldiers armed with weapons but of agents, stewards, and lawyers armed with papers and legal briefs. His house would be a palace in the country, where the Queen and Court could visit and the business of his estates could be transacted. Thus he called in Robert Smythson, a man whose connection to the Court and experience of current fashions gave him impeccable credentials.

4

Smythson, Wollaton, and the Elizabethan Building World

When Robert Smythson began working on the design of Wollaton Hall in the late 1570s, he was already an experienced craftsman at the height of his career.[1] At Longleat and Wardour he had worked side by side with some of the most knowledgeable master masons of his time, learning from them about new trends in architectural thinking and gaining valuable firsthand experience in handling the design problems then confronting the building professions. Patrons like Sir John Thynne at Longleat or Sir Francis Willoughby at Wollaton participated actively in the design process, trading pattern books and exchanging ideas amongst themselves and with their craftsmen, but it was ultimately in the workshops—among the masons, carvers, joiners, and carpenters themselves—that solutions were worked out, crystallizing in built form the suggestions, experiments, and personal tastes of all those involved.

On the building sites where Smythson worked, traditional practice was being reexamined and revised. The Elizabethan country house provided an ideal stimulus for exchange and experiment, bringing together skilled craftsmen and wealthy patrons committed to excellence and innovation. The large number of new private houses, the competition for display, and relatively recent improvements in education among both patrons and craftsmen combined to create a favorable climate in which a designer of Smythson's talent could grow. Smythson's early contact with men such as Humphrey Lovell, the Queen's master mason, and Allen Maynard, a French stone carver working at Longleat, opened his eyes to the complexities of the classicizing architectural style practiced by fashionable designers in Europe and now much in demand among English patrons.[2] From these men he acquired both a familiarity with the Orders and an understanding of the fundamental principles of symmetry and proportion that underlay the new style. It was, no doubt, his participation in this top-level world of architecture which recommended Smythson to Sir Francis Willoughby, a patron who was anxious to show off his learning and wealth by building in the most fashionable style of the day.

Yet Willoughby's commission also presented new problems in planning and design for which no satisfactory solutions or precedents existed. Willoughby was a reader of architectural pattern books and anxious to incorporate the latest fashions from Italy, France, and the Low Countries into his new building; he was also a wealthy land-owner whose conception of his new house included such traditional English features as traceried windows, turrets, a great hall, gallery, and great chamber. To bring this many-faceted image to life, he needed an architect of considerable experience and sophistication, an artist capable of synthesizing the formally discordant features of two different stylistic traditions. In Smythson, Willoughby found what he was looking for. Smythson's professional experiences not only provided him with the skills to satisfy the demands of his patron, but also motivated him to find his own responses to current trends as identified within the building trades themselves. These included new designs from the Continent, new forms of planning and ornament, and new program requirements. No doubt many ideas reached crafts-men like Smythson through the professional network long before ama-teurs were aware of them, while others appeared only in expensive pattern books read by wealthy patrons.[3] In practice, communication between the two groups reinforced their common goal: to discover a distinctive new English architectural style.

The significance of Smythson's efforts at Wollaton Hall and throughout his career as a designer of country houses stems from his ability to meet this challenge. Smythson's executed works and his portfolio of drawings at the Royal Institute of British Architects (RIBA) in London reveal a focused and sustained effort to develop an appropriate architectural form for each of the new monumental resi-dences of his patrons. Wollaton was his first independent venture. There he created a house specifically designed to sit high above the surrounding countryside, a high tower from which to observe the hunt and oversee the estate; it was neither a farm nor a castle, but combined elements of the two into a new building type through which wealth, power, and self-conscious erudition were all articula-ted. With no tradition to follow, Smythson's task at Wollaton was to devise the imagery and to provide the planning skills that would make his patron's goals realizable.[4]

England and "The Renaissance"

It is a commonplace among historians of art that Italian Renaissance architecture was not completely "understood" in England prior to Inigo Jones's Palladian works of the early seventeenth century.[5] But that view rests on a few significant and ultimately limiting premises: it favors the evidence of printed and published designs over drawings, which are less accessible to modern historians; it separates the individual "genius" from the workshop in which built form was conceptualized and ultimately realized; and it places a higher value on classical and classicizing art than on works outside this tradition. Jones's adherence to a conservative Palladian style, as codified by Andrea Palladio's *Quattro libri dell'architettura* of 1570, earned him the praise of neoclassical writers whose own eighteenth-century preoccupations not surprisingly determined their tastes and values. Jones came to represent for them the dawn of the English enlightenment, while Elizabethan architecture was seen as the darkness out of which he arose. Until quite recently, therefore, English architecture of the sixteenth century was relegated to the category of "primitive" background for later development, and it was thus studied very unsystematically.

Changes in Renaissance historiography have benefited Elizabethan architecture. Greater emphasis on economic and social context—patronage, social customs, market fluctuations—and their role in determining the history of style have made it possible to view Elizabethan buildings as significant in their own right and not just in relationship to Italian traditions. The study of workshop practice and training among artists and architects has also helped to refocus the historical picture, placing the isolated individual "genius" back among his coworkers and contemporaries.[6] Again, this has led to an improved understanding of English architecture, since the absence of famous names is no longer such a grave liability. The process of design has become as important as the final product and a significant key to its meaning. Thus broad stylistic affinities, habits of thought, and underlying (and perhaps invisible) influences now receive greater attention than in previous years. In the case of Palladio, where the implications for the study of English architecture are most significant, recent research has focused on the survival of local north Italian conventions, on the function of his buildings, and on the contributions of patrons, replacing the narrow image of the architect as independent innovator, academician, and scholar with a more complex and historically accurate analysis.[7] The recent publication of Palladio's drawings in the collection of the Royal Institute of British Architects arose out of this revisionist effort.[8] The drawings (figs. 4.1 and 4.2) reaffirm Palladio's role as a practicing architect engaged in a process of experimentation with classical sources and new building types. Like other members of his profession, he was constrained by the demands of tradition, finance, and practicality—the great value of the drawings is that they draw our attention to the process by which the elegant and refined images of the *Quattro libri* evolved. Ultimately, they show that Palladio absorbed a great deal both from his own observations and from the works of fellow architects, arriving at solu-

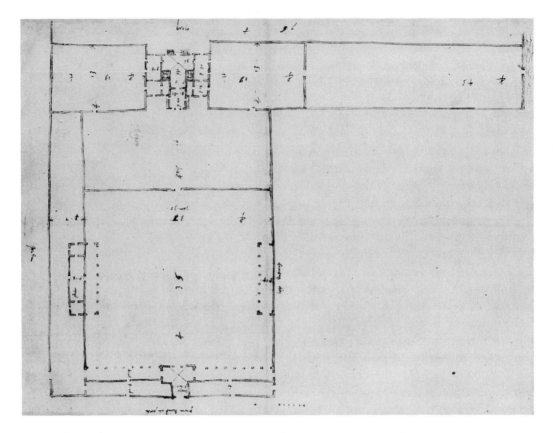

4.1. Andrea Palladio, *Site and Plan Project for Villa Pagliarino, Lanzè(?) and for Villa Poiana, Poiana Maggiore.* ca. 1544. (XVI/3)

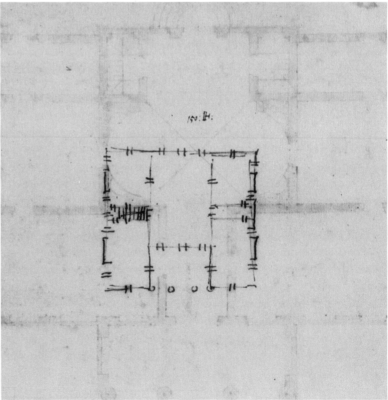

4.2. Andrea Palladio, *Sketch Plan for Villa Caldogno, Caldogno.* ca. 1548/ 1549. (XVI/20a *verso*) The British Architectural Library, RIBA, London.

tions to familiar problems which distinguished him as a designer of consummate skill and sophistication.

The brilliance and clarity of Palladio's illustrations for the *Quattro libri* (fig. 4.3) do set it apart from other sixteenth-century handbooks, but the work shared a common purpose with other portfolios of designs, both published and unpublished, which were produced throughout Europe in this period. It was meant to serve as a storehouse of models from which practicing architects could work. The importance of such collections to craftsmen is demonstrated by their frequent appearance in wills, explicitly cited along with tools and other workshop materials as the most prized legacy of masters to their followers.[9] The publication of the *Quattro libri* in 1570 made such a collection public, reflecting the increased participation of patrons and amateurs in building design. The audience was thus neither strictly professional nor solely Italian; the popularity of the book rested not only on its exceptional clarity and on the high quality of Palladio's work, but also on the widely felt need of patrons and architects *throughout Europe* for classicized designs of flexible format that could be adapted to local conditions and individual budgets.

Smythson's drawings and designs suggest that he knew Palladio's treatise, and there are obvious parallels between the sorts of strategies which Palladio devised for villa typology and those which Smythson

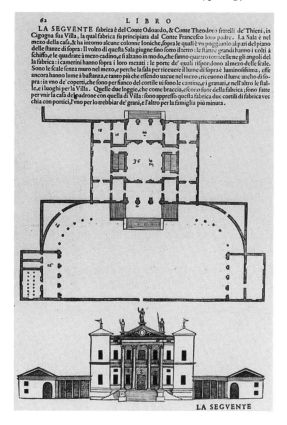

4.3. Andrea Palladio, *Villa Thiene*, from *I Quattro libri dell' architettura*, 1570. By permission of the Houghton Library, Harvard University.

proposed as variant designs for English country houses. Yet more important here than the question of direct influence from the *Quattro libri* is our recognition that both Smythson and Palladio shared common concerns with other European architects of the second half of the sixteenth century. It is Smythson's participation in a broadly defined European culture, and not the ability or failure of English architects to fully comprehend "The Renaissance," which gives his work its significance.

Transmitted through printed handbooks, workshop drawings, or by the architects themselves, a wide range of Continental motifs and building types began reaching England in the 1560s and immediately caught the attention of patrons and craftsmen. From this point on, England joined the European constellation, sharing a preoccupation with central planning and axial geometry and a fascination with the Orders and classicized surface ornament. All across Europe each region and, indeed, each architect interpreted these concerns in a distinctive local or personal style; it is this diversity of variations on a theme, rather than the supposed homogeneity of "the Renaissance style," which gives the architecture of late sixteenth century Europe its distinctive character. Following the lead of Serlio and Palladio in Italy and of Jacques Androuet Du Cerceau in France, Smythson applied a handful of classicizing *topoi* to the design problems he faced, and while these were interpreted in a distinctive English idiom, they nevertheless remained fundamentally similar to those which underlay the works of his Continental contemporaries.

Pattern Books, Portfolios, and Drawings

The motifs and conventions that Smythson's works shared with designs by French and Italian architects were the result of a two-level system of communication: first, between workshops and amongst the members of the building profession, and second, amongst patrons and amateurs themselves. While drawings and workshop portfolios were traditionally used to preserve and communicate designs (and remained the principal focus of craftsmen's working method), there can be no doubt that the invention of printing and the publication of printed portfolios greatly improved the exchange of information at both levels. Masons and stone carvers in England were suddenly deluged with handbooks from Italy, France, Germany, and the Low Countries, broadening a process of professional communication that had taken place sporadically and individually for years. Further, these handbooks of printed plans, elevations, and ornamental details opened the world of architecture to educated amateurs. Like the printed grammars and primers by Erasmus and Vives, from which young boys throughout Europe learned their first Latin lessons, the printed port-folios created a visual culture shared across national boundaries. This new commonality of interests and information facilitated communi-cation between patrons and craftsmen, deeply affecting the course of English architecture. For Smythson and Willoughby, it was a starting point from which to work.

The works of Sebastiano Serlio, published in separate books from 1537 on and in a single collected edition in 1575, featured systematic presentation of examples through clear illustrations and a simple text; they disseminated to a wide public the sort of images that would pre-viously have been available only through workshop drawings.[10] Serlio's rich repository of designs seized the imaginations of many readers who had never had the opportunity to see the monuments of Rome for themselves—amateurs and professionals who wanted to learn more about the practice of architecture at the source of ancient and contemporary classicism. Serlio's audience included the young Palladio, whose training in the Veneto during the 1530s left him as starved for new information as Smythson and Willoughby would later be in England.

Serlio borrowed from Roman builders and their Renaissance fol-lowers the rules of symmetry, order and proportion, but, like many of his contemporaries, he was primarily preoccupied with the problem of the centralized plan. In Book VII of his treatise, for instance, a series of illustrations shows designs composed of squares, rectangles, and circles that are presented as variant types for centrally planned, additive spaces (fig. 4.4). Here as elsewhere in his work the prolifera-tion of model solutions to a single problem betrays the author's desire to demonstrate his own versatility. Examples are often strung to-gether into a dramatic series of seemingly endless variations. Even a casual reader of Serlio's treatise would readily understand the crucial role played by the biaxial central plan in Renaissance Italy. Yet be-cause of his tendency toward repetition for its own sake, Serlio's work also implicitly emphasized the importance of individual elements and ornamental motifs, undermining a systematic approach to form and supporting a more partitive, decorative aesthetic.

This no doubt contributed to the immense popularity of the work in northern Europe, where the Gothic heritage remained strong.[11] Yet Serlio's wide influence in France, and later in England, was also due to the timely appearance of his treatise (and, briefly, of the archi-tect himself) in a world newly awakened to humanist culture. Indeed, Serlio's genius lay in his almost single-handed transformation of the medieval French castle into the classicized and yet still distinctively French chateau of the educated courtier (fig. 4.5). Capitalizing on a

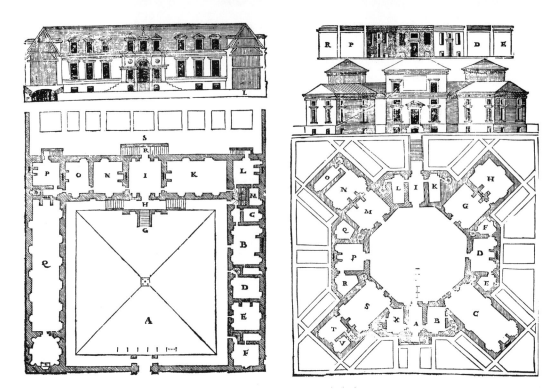

4.4. (left) Sebastiano Serlio, *Villa Design*, from *Tutte l'opere d'architettura.* Venice, 1619. VII, p. 29.

4.5. (right) Sebastiano Serlio, *Villa Design*, from *Tutte l'opere d'architettura.* Venice, 1619. VII, p. 57.

medieval tradition of central planning in military architecture, Serlio made this the basis for a modern house type, turning the traditional polygonal plan into an intellectual conceit and providing his readers with more patterns for elaborate ornamental details, grotesques, rusticated masonry, and colored marbles than any fashionable patron intent on modernizing his country estate could ever need.[12]

In Serlio's unpublished Book VI, *On Domestic Architecture,* we find a fusion of northern Italian villa design and elements drawn from the French castle tradition, resulting in a series of highly influential drawings.[13] Arriving in France in 1540, Serlio brought with him the knowledge of such important designs as the Villa Giustinian at Roncade (fig. 4.6); the plans presented in his treatise, composed in the 1540s, included variants in both French and Italian style intended to accommodate a new class of land-owning merchants, fashionable gentry, and noble families. Serlio's plans provided these patrons with great houses that both symbolized their power and served their needs as overseers of estates and participants in the activities of landed society.[14] Thus, the houses were compact and lacked open central courtyards; the site plans included perimeter walls (often with corner towers), open service courts in front and gardens in back of the house (fig. 4.7). Overall these projects are characterized by symmetry and tight organization, qualities which recommended them to the growing class of country house patrons (and architects) throughout Europe.

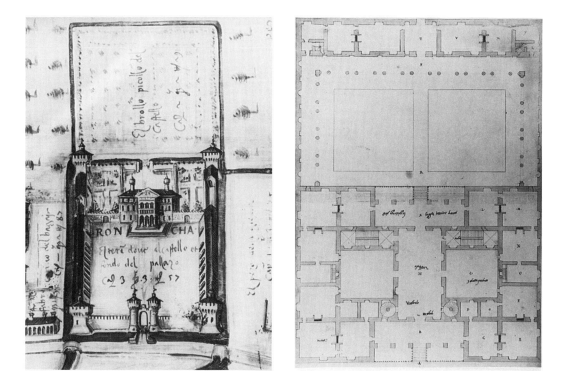

Among French architects, the influence of Serlio's work was profound. For Jacques Androuet Du Cerceau, the treatises served as models both for the mode of exposition and for the specific content of his own books. Other influential architects like Jean Bullant or Philibert de l'Orme worked in a style that was in many ways more true to classical precedents, but Du Cerceau, like Serlio, combined the traditions of north and south into a flexible and attractive version of mannerist style. This guaranteed the success of his work both at home and across the Channel in England.

Smythson seems also to have drawn a number of his ideas from the early handbooks of Du Cerceau, where emphasis was placed on the twin concerns of centralized planning and ornamental complexity. In Du Cerceau's *Livre d'architecture* of 1559, for instance, Smythson could find multiple examples of geometrical devices (fig. 4.8) fashionably arranged in groups of variant types. Further, Du Cerceau presented many examples of chateaux drawn in detail showing courtyards and service buildings, a feature which Smythson clearly found helpful in his own designs. Both architects faced the problem of designing individualized country houses for a homogeneous group of patrons, and both took this design problem to heart as a professional speciality. In many respects their problems were similar to those faced by Palladio in Vicenza or Serlio in France. As architects of late-sixteenth century Europe, all confronted the challenge posed by the

4.8. J. A. Du Cerceau, *Design for a Chateau*, from *Livre d'architecture*. Paris, 1559. Photo: reproduced by permission of the British Library.

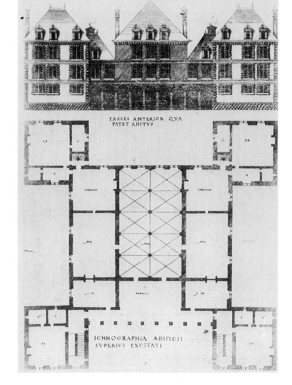

4.9. Robert Smythson, *Plan for a House in the Shape of a Greek Cross* (II/10). The British Architectural Library, RIBA, London.

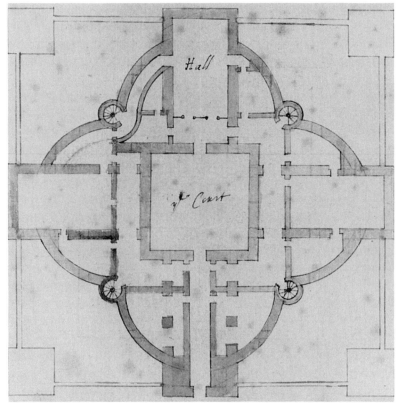

need for a new building type—called variously a villa, a chateau, or a country house—from which their educated patrons could control and survey their lands.

Robert Smythson's Drawings

The English building world of the 1570s drew inspiration from a wide-ranging architectural community: from portfolios of English workshop drawings passed on from one generation to the next; from printed handbooks of architecture produced in Italy and France; from drawings and printed portfolios of ornamental devices, many of which originated in Germany and the Low Countries; and from foreign craftsmen themselves.[15] Yet for an English master mason like Smythson, all this was quite separate from and secondary to the visible inheritance of built architecture itself, the environment with which he and his patrons were familiar. Conventional sequences of spaces and traditional compositions in elevation and massing exerted the strongest influence on English craftsmen, providing the conceptual framework to which they referred and compared new ideas. For Smythson, this contest of opposing forces was played out in his own portfolio of drawings.[16] Here the world of ideas and the world of real buildings could exist side by side.

Smythson's portfolio included a number of direct copies from printed handbooks and sketches of buildings he had visited throughout England as well as original designs. The overall impression one gets from this group is of a craftsman struggling to define his style through exploration and inquiry. As in the printed portfolios of Du Cerceau, there is a notable juxtaposition of Renaissance and classicizing motifs with local building types; there is also considerable attention paid to the various ways of handling axial and centralized planning. A sketch plan for "A House in the Shape of a Greek Cross" (fig. 4.9), for example, is among the most revealing original designs in the collection. Here Smythson placed the traditional suite of great hall, screen, and screens passage in one of the arms of the cross and a courtyard at the center, attempting to satisfy the demands of both the centralized plan and English tradition by creating a ceremonial approach to the hall, a room which was the symbolic focus of a great house. Here, however, the conventional route from entrance to hall, requiring at least one 90-degree turn through the hall screen, is abandoned in favor of the geometry of the plan. Further, the cross itself is circumscribed by a square boundary wall, integrating the overall site and the design of the gardens with the house block.[17] This concern for measurement and symmetry represents a new feature in English

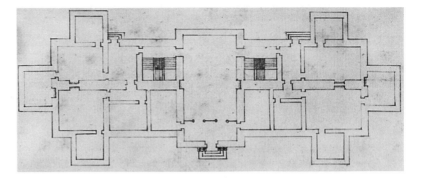

design. The sources for the "House in the Shape of a Greek Cross"
can be readily identified among the examples in Serlio's Book VII or
in Du Cerceau's *Livre d'architecture,* yet it is also distinctively English.
Through its juxtaposition of traditional elements and a new planning
type, it reveals the extent of Smythson's commitment to the integration of innovative design with that which was familiar to his
audience.

A number of Smythson's drawings and executed buildings bear
witness to his repeated attempts to resolve this problem. A plan
which Mark Girouard had identified as a study for Hardwick Hall (fig.
4.10), for example, includes both an emphasis on biaxial symmetry
and a centralized great hall. Here the hall is entered on axis, as at
Hardwick, and a flight of stairs is placed on either side of the dais end
as at Wollaton. Stepped back corners not only clearly reveal the
volumetric components of mass but also create rooms of square plan
that are open to the light on three sides. This last feature reappears
throughout Smythson's career, tentatively expressed in his earliest
experiments with window bays and rooftop banqueting houses at
Longleat and recurring later in the Prospect Room at Wollaton, in
the lantern houses of Worksop and Barlborough and, of course, at
Hardwick Hall itself.[18]

Other drawings point to Smythson's idiosyncratic use of the classical Orders in his work. A group of three designs for hall screens (fig.
4.11) reflects his efforts to relate arched openings and a trabeated system of bays to a conventional English type. English hall screens were
essentially immovable pieces of furniture used to separate the great
hall from the screens passage and service areas. In earlier houses, like
Penshurst or Hampton Court, screens were made of wood and decorated with traditional English carving; here Smythson transposed a
three-bay wall elevation such as might readily be found in Serlio or
some other architectural handbook into a typically English context.
Smythson's drawings for these relatively small-scale pieces are among
the most Italianate designs in his portfolio, but they were conceived
not as part of a homogeneous classical design, but as independent
motifs in a complex of various parts.

4.11. Robert Smythson, *Three Designs for Screens* (II/16). The British Architectural Library, RIBA, London.

4.12. Robert Smythson, *Entrance Front of a Large House* (II/11). The British Architectural Library, RIBA, London.

The "Design for an Entrance Front of a Large House" (fig. 4.12) shows a similar tendency to retain conventional forms while inserting classicizing details. The prototype for this sort of country house with two corner towers and a central loggia was the Roman portico villa, a form which survived throughout Europe. Revived and increasingly popular in sixteenth-century Italy, both this type and the centrally planned "villa-castello" were exported to the north by itinerant architects and through handbooks like those of Serlio and Palladio.[19] Smythson's portfolio reveals his familiarity with both, but here he significantly combines the Italianate three-bay loggia and balustrade with the typical northern forms, adding the tall mullioned and transomed windows of the English Perpendicular Gothic style. Thus the design testifies both to his awareness of current Continental fashions and, more important, to his continued retention of characteristic English traditions.

Smythson's drawings are clearly related to the triumphal arches, High Renaissance loggias, and choir screens illustrated in Serlio's treatise. But in translating his models from a Roman and Catholic context into an English Protestant one, Smythson not only reworked the designs to fit local tastes but also radically altered their meaning. England was a nation with its own local materials, building techniques, and conventions. In many cases, English craftsmen seemed to resist monumental classicism in favor of a style that emphasized surface detail, ornament, and color. Windows became elongated rectangles broken up by hundreds of shimmering leaded panes. Roof lines became jagged with balustrades, fingerlike chimneys, pointed gables, and complex carved ornament. All of these features contributed to the distinctive look that Smythson achieved: far from misunderstanding the Renaissance architectural system, Smythson turned it into something vital and meaningful for his own time. At Wollaton, he found the opportunity to bring the unique fusion of original and imported ideas in his portfolio to life in a real building. It was his first independent commission. Working closely with his dedicated but no doubt difficult patron, he set out to produce what both men hoped would be the most impressive building of their time.

Wollaton Hall: Planning and Design

Among the drawings in the Smythson Collection are a number that relate specifically to Wollaton: these include a plan (fig. 4.13), elevation (fig. 4.14), a design for a screen (fig. 4.15), and small ornamental details (fig. 4.16). These drawings, and the sources for Smythson's design, are discussed at length in Mark Girouard's monograph on

Smythson.[20] Smythson cast his net wide, pulling in motifs from the published pattern books of Jan Vredeman de Vries (fig. 4.17), Serlio, and Du Cerceau and freely borrowing from the storehouse of English examples well known to patrons and builders alike.[21]

Many borrowed motifs have been identified and described in earlier studies, yet what ultimately remains striking about Smythson's Wollaton design is its novelty. Various clues reinforce the impression of a strong desire on Smythson's part to absorb and improve upon the works of both English and Continental architects. Among Sir Francis Willoughby's papers in the Middleton Collection, for instance, is a drawing that shows the plan of a house with round corner towers and a large central salon flanked by symmetrically disposed staircases on either side (fig. 4.18). This is a variant design based on a plan published by Du Cerceau in his *Petites Habitations* (ca. 1560).[22] The author of the drawing is unknown, and yet it clearly points to the sort of building type at which Smythson—and Willoughby—were looking. Like the typical pattern-book examples discussed above, this is a centralized plan with a strong axial organization; the variant, unlike its source but like Smythson's Wollaton plan, uses bilaterally symmetrical stairways on either side of the central space to reinforce this axiality. Like Poggio Reale in Naples, published by Serlio in his Book III (fig. 4.19), or Serlio's own design for the chateau of Ancy-le-Franc, published by Du Cerceau, the plan derived from the *Petites Habitations* fused the conventional villa-castello with the typical centralized plan of the new style, yielding a type whose popularity was guaranteed by this combination of familiarity and fashion.[23]

There is no shortage of possible sources here; many buildings— built and unbuilt, published and unpublished—shared this affinity for centralized plans and corner towers. Among English examples, Castle Bolton in North Yorkshire (ca. 1380), Herstmonceaux (begun 1440) (fig. 4.20) and Mount Edgecumbe (built in the 1540s) might all serve as models for a medieval (or medievalizing) style of military architecture that had agreeable resonances of English chivalry and national tradition.[24]

Yet Wollaton marks a departure from tradition that separates it both from these examples and from others erected during the sixteenth century. Unlike contemporary houses such as Burghley, Kirby, or Theobalds—or Longleat itself for that matter—Wollaton not only lacks an internal courtyard but is surrounded by courts and gardens of roughly equal size and shape; this unification of the plan and integration of house and landscape was entirely new in England. In the plan, the site is enclosed by a square, which is itself divided into nine smaller sections; the central three divisions—the base court, house, and principal garden—create an elongated rectangular space accen-

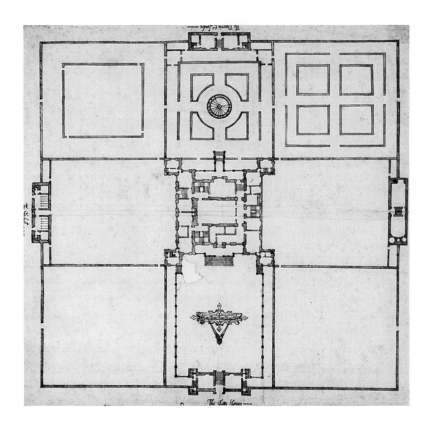

4.13. Robert Smythson, *Wollaton Hall: Plan* (I/25 [1]). The British Architectural Library, RIBA, London.

4.14. Robert Smythson, *Wollaton Hall: Elevation of a Corner Tower* (II/25). The British Architectural Library, RIBA, London.

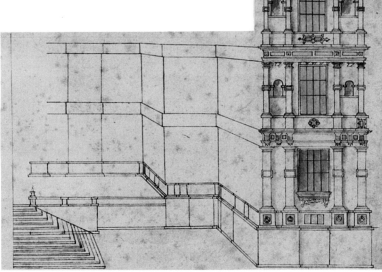

4.15. Robert Smythson, *Screen Design for Wollaton Hall* (I/25 [7]). The British Architectural Library, RIBA, London.

4.16. Robert Smythson, *Decorative Panels (after Vredeman de Vries)* (I/25 [2]). The British Architectural Library, RIBA, London.

4.17. Jan Vredeman
de Vries, *Gable De-*
signs, from
Architetura oder
Bautung, 1581. By
permission of the
Houghton Library,
Harvard Univesity.

4.18. Anonymous,
Sketch Plan for a
Country House (after
Du Cerceau). Univer-
sity of Nottingham,
Middleton Collec-
tion. By Courtesy of
Lord Middleton.

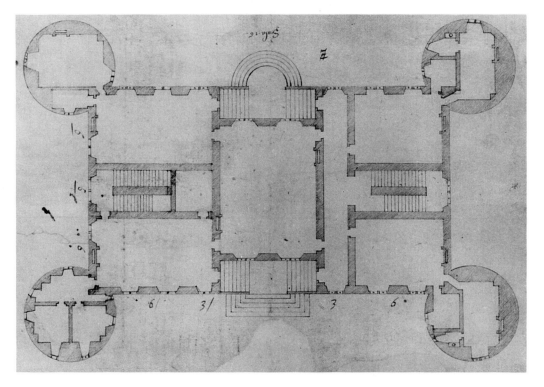

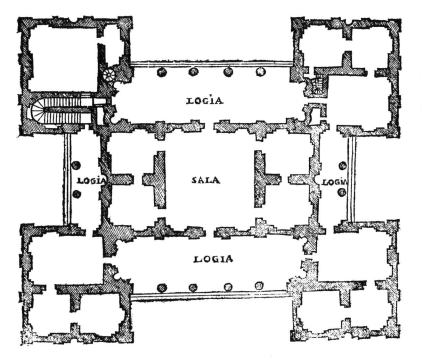

4.19. Sebastiano Serlio, *Plan of Poggio Reale*, from *Tutte l'opere d'architettura*, Book III, 122v. Venice, 1619.

4.20. Herstmonceaux Castle (1440). Photo reproduced by permission of the Royal Commission on the Historical Monuments of England.

tuated by the recession of the house between the projecting corner towers. The midpoints of each of the sides of the square are marked by a service building: at the front (north), a gatehouse; to the east, a stable; to the west, a bakehouse and brew house; to the south, beyond the garden, the dairy and laundry. The gardens were clearly meant to be fully visible from the house, which rose to a height of four stories at the very top; in the late seventeenth century, Cassandra Willoughby described the garden as "a little piece of ground in which was the plan of the house planted with box trees."[25] Thus spaces which appear in the plan (fig. 4.13) to be strange subsidiary courts at the southernmost end of the garden may in fact have been ornamental plantings intended as reflections of the corner towers of the house itself.

The view from the gatehouse was dramatic and novel. Willoughby had chosen his site at the top of a small but rather steep hill overlooking the town and old Wollaton Hall in the valley below. As at Wimbledon (fig. 4.21), which was built in the same years, the planning of the site at Wollaton exploits changes in level with courts and parapets, particularly in the approach from the north. The route to the house from the road would thus have taken the visitor through a carefully planned approach, leading first to the gatehouse, up a rather narrow flight of stairs, and into the base court. Directly opposite stood the house, imposing and tall. The spatial effect was calculated to impress the visitor with a view of changing levels, solid walls, and tunnel-like spaces. Moving through the base court to the house, the visitor was completely unprotected. This journey involved yet another change of levels, more steps and another terrace. The visitor thus crossed through a number of zones and passed numerous checkpoints before even reaching the house. Indeed, Smythson's plan gives the impression of a trap: having once entered the gatehouse, the route was direct and inescapable.

Inside the house, the dominant sense of axis and symmetry faded away, replaced by the twists and turns of short, narrow passageways. The approach was meant to impress the visitor; inside, the layout of the rooms was intended to confuse. Having passed the porter's lodge and followed a short corridor, the visitor and his or her attendants turned to enter the screen's passage. From this point there were two choices. Most visitors turned to the left, walked through the screen itself, and entered the high, open space of the hall. Lighted by huge windows, which dwarfed everything in the room, the hall served both as a passageway and a stopping place for those whose rank or business confined them to the more public areas of the ground floor.[26] For those continuing up to the great chamber or the gallery above, its length had to be crossed. At the dais end, the ascent to the upper

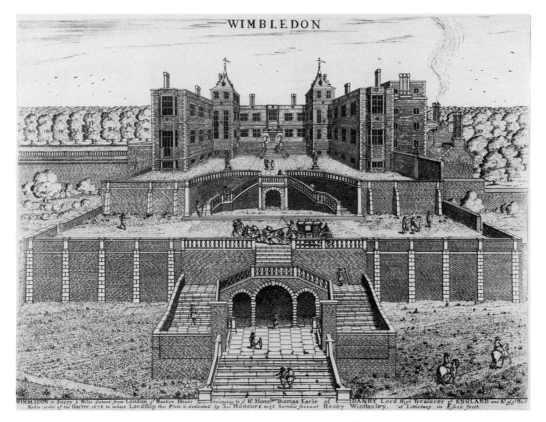

WIMBLEDON in Surry 6 Miles distant from London & Manhon House belonging to & R¹ Hono.ᵇˡᵉ Thomas Earle of DANBY Lord High Treasurer of ENGLAND and K⁸ of y² Most Noble order of the Garter 1678 to whose Lordship this Plate is dedicated by his Honours most humble servant Henry Winstanley. at Littlebury in Essex fecit.

floor would be made via the staircases on either side of the room. Each staircase had its own special function: one led to the suite of rooms on the north side, the other to that on the south; it was the latter that were probably the grander quarters, fitted out with the best furnishings for special occasions.

Looking at the plan of Wollaton Hall (figs. 4.22, 4.23, and 4.24), we can begin to recognize the calculated juxtaposition of conventional planning and innovative sequences of rooms in Smythson's design. As noted above, the ceremonial route past the porter's lodge, through the screens, and into the hall, requiring three 90-degree turns, had developed out of the traditional arrangement of the medieval hall and its subsidiary spaces. This distinctive layout symbolized the rituals of the male-dominated household and was thus an architectural form of deep resonance and meaning. As mentioned earlier, Smythson experimented with an axial approach to the hall in the "House in the Shape of a Greek Cross" (fig. 4.9) and in other drawings, actually constructing such a design at Hardwick in the 1590s (fig. 4.25). For Willoughby, a man whose image of his house included references to the past and maintenance of tradition, such axial movement would clearly have been unacceptable. What was required on the ground floor was the complete spatial sequence through a circuitous route; this is what we see at Wollaton.

4.21. Henry Winstanley, *Wimbledon House,* built in 1588. By Courtesy of the Trustees of the British Museum.

91

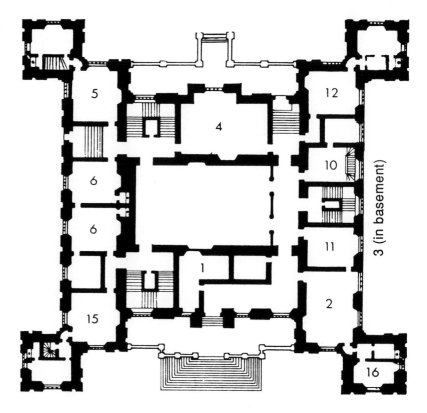

4.22. Wollaton Hall:
Ground Floor Plan
(after Smythson;
North at bottom).

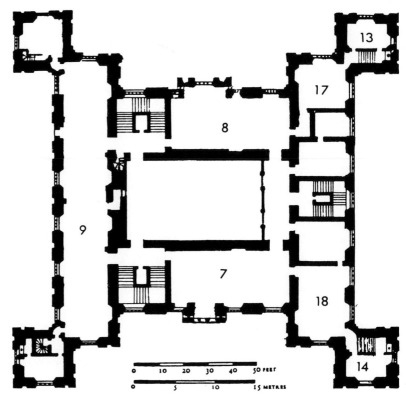

4.23. Wollaton Hall:
Second Floor Plan.
(Reconstruction.)

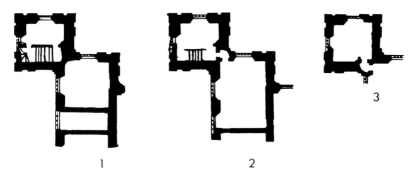

4.24. Wollaton Hall: Plans of the Mezzanine Levels in the Southeast Tower (Reconstruction): (1) Above the Ground Floor (2) Above the Second Floor (3) The Tower Room

Conversely, on tne upper floor it was the size and number of semi-public rooms which counted. Thus the suites on the north and south sides at Wollaton were laid out in virtually identical patterns: there were two great chambers, two sets of withdrawing rooms, and two identical approaches to the gallery that ran the entire length of the east side of the house. Here, for the first time, the English country house was touched by an overarching classicism which provided an optimally conspicuous consumption of space. The program required two ceremonial suites, one for ordinary household affairs, the other reserved for state and official visitors. Smythson's response reveals his mastery of Renaissance planning. Other solutions clearly existed, but Smythson chose the fashionable conceit of mirror-image symmetry. This he exploited for maximum effect.

This idea came ultimately from Serlio, but it was given new life by Palladio. The similarities between Smythson's design and the plans in the *Quattro libri* lie below the level of direct replication, yet there is an obvious stylistic affinity between them. Wollaton is compact and lacks a central court, unlike previous English prototypes; instead, the entrance hall and *salone* sequence often found in Palladian villa designs is paralleled by the hall and parlor at Wollaton. Because Palladio's axial arrangement was not possible if the traditional English approach was to be preserved, Smythson simply rotated the Palladian axis ninety degrees, thus placing the staircases at Wollaton on either side of the dais end of the hall. This strategy retained Palladio's strict symmetry but, instead of focusing attention on the Palladian vertical axis, it emphasized the typically English horizontal axis through the hall.

Another feature of the plan that seems to be related to Palladian models is the distinct separation of subsidiary spaces, courts, and service buildings around the main body of the house. Palladio's villa designs frequently employ this device, isolating each distinct component yet connecting the whole geometrically. At Wollaton, this technique enabled Smythson to place four service buildings at the periphery of the site along the outer wall, leaving the house block relatively free to function as a living space for social and business purposes. As in Palladian models, service and agricultural activities were

93

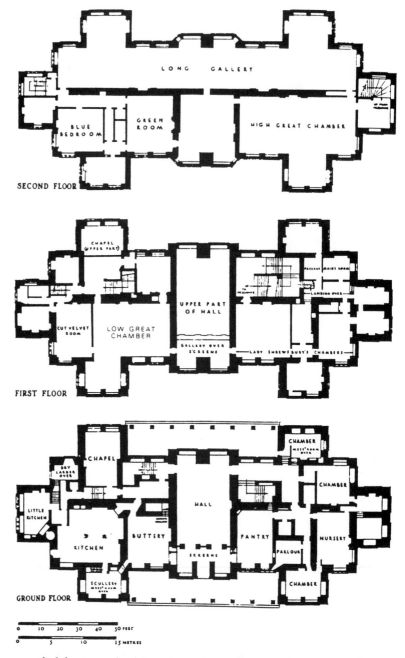

4.25. Hardwick Hall, Derbyshire. 1596. Plans of the Three Principal Floors.

SECOND FLOOR

LONG GALLERY

BLUE BEDROOM

GREEN ROOM

HIGH GREAT CHAMBER

FIRST FLOOR

CHAPEL (UPPER PART)

CUT VELVET ROOM

LOW GREAT CHAMBER

UPPER PART OF HALL

GALLERY OVER SCREENE

LADY SHREWSBURY'S CHAMBERS

GROUND FLOOR

CHAPEL

LITTLE KITCHEN

KITCHEN

BUTTERY

HALL

SCREENE

PANTRY

PARLOUR

NURSERY

CHAMBER

CHAMBER

CHAMBER

SCULLERY

0   10   20   30   40   50 FEET

0   5   10   15 METRES

provided for in outbuildings away from the main living space.[27]

Smythson also planned a full basement with kitchens and other serving rooms at Wollaton, following an idea described in a number of Palladio's designs, notably the Villa Godi at Lonedo.[28] This idea had been used elsewhere and may have been found in French examples, but it is consistent with the overall logic of the planning strategy devised by Smythson. This is true also of the mezzanines tucked between floors in the corners to provide more living and storage space without disturbing the clarity and organization of the principal rooms; they are suggested by Palladio, and whether Smythson learned this device from the *Quattro libri* or conceived of it independently, it is nonetheless consistent with the approach shared by the two architects.[29]

Smythson's essentially un-Palladian (in the sense of the term as applied to an architect like Inigo Jones) use of the *Quattro libri* is paralleled in a portfolio of designs by the architect John Thorpe now in Sir John Soane's Museum in London.[30] Among the drawings dating from the 1620s are a number that are related to the Wollaton and Hardwick plans because of their experimentation with geometry and mirror-image planning. In Thorpe's work, however, the connection to Palladio is overt: he often quotes directly from models in the *Quattro libri,* and in one very important drawing of ca. 1620 he copies Palladio's Villa Pisani plan and shows his own variant of it on the same sheet (fig. 4.26). Like Smythson's work, Thorpe's designs look anticlassical in elevation: with their flat walls, large windows, and ornamented surfaces, drawings like the "House of Sir John Danvers" (fig. 4.27) or, even more peculiar, the timber-framed Campden House (fig. 4.28a and b) may appear Palladian in plan, but they could hardly be more typically English in elevation. Thorpe was a generation younger than Smythson, yet their portfolios share a distinctive combination of Italian influence and English conservatism. The results are similar in each case; though Thorpe had no need to retain the typical hall/screens sequence as Smythson did at Wollaton, his original designs are no more classical than Smythson's. Unlike his contemporary, Inigo Jones, Thorpe steadfastly continued to absorb Italian models into his own English system of design rather than accept a new and foreign aesthetic.

Reflecting a similar impulse, Wollaton is a mixture of contrasts. Juxtaposed with Palladian planning we find diverse elements borrowed from English and Continental sources. The rectangular traceried windows (fig. 4.29) in the central space derive from Gothic ecclesiastical architecture, but similar windows were also traditionally found in medieval halls.[31] Most recently Smythson had seen them at Sir Matthew Arundell's Wardour Castle (fig. 4.30). As Mark Girouard has noted, there is also a strong possibility that Smythson knew Mount Edgecumbe in Cornwall, which included a central hall lighted by such high clerestory windows. Yet there are also resonant parallels among French and Scottish buildings of the mid sixteenth century as well—the bartizans of the massive central tower, for instance, appear also at Chenonceaux (fig. 4.31) and Azay-le-Rideau; recent research has shown that these were also frequently used in Parisian houses of the late sixteenth century.[32] Smythson could have

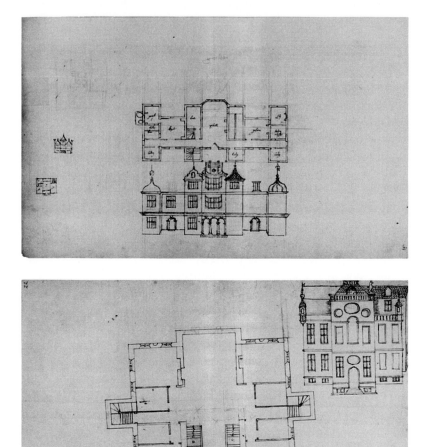

known these buildings through drawings, or he may have been introduced to them by Maynard at Longleat. Incorporated here, these details add yet another note to the range of visual and symbolic associations. The message was complex and, ultimately, rather discordant; it is urbane, sophisticated, stalwart, and menacing all at once.

The crowning glory at Wollaton was its Prospect Room, a huge glazed great chamber that seemed to float magically above the hall. Smythson's tower fused the imagery of the castle with a newer type— the hunting tower—and thus gave his patron a proud lookout from which to survey his lands.[33] A recent precedent existed at Nonsuch Palace, a royal retreat where medieval imagery and the observation of the hunt were equally important thematic and planning concerns. According to a late seventeenth-century survey, the palace, which was torn down in the eighteenth century, boasted both a battle-

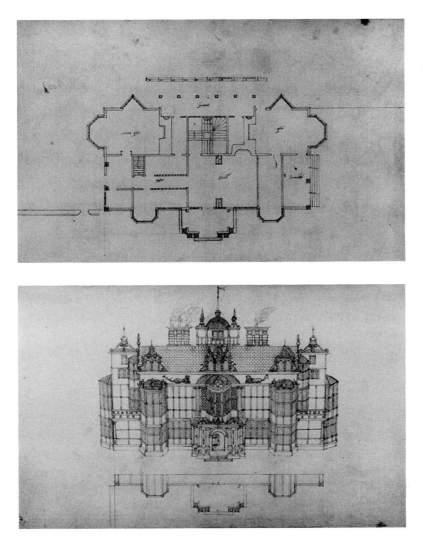

4.28 a. John Thorpe, *Plan of Campden House* (T96). By Courtesy of the Trustees of Sir John Soane's Museum.

4.28 b. John Thorpe, *Elevation of Campden House* (T95). By courtesy of the Trustees of Sir John Soane's Museum.

mented gatehouse of three stories and an impressive display of high turrets. The gatehouse was said to contain "a very large and spatyous roome very pleasant and delectable for the prospect," while the turrets were described as commanding "the prospect and view of both the parkes of Nonsuch and of most of the country round about"; these were said to be "the cheife ornament of the whole house of Nonsuch."[34] At both Chatsworth and Worksop, the country houses of the Earl and Countess of Shrewsbury, high turrets and upper-story rooms were featured elements, yet Wollaton was the only one in which a single tower dominated and gave the house its definitive character.

Here once again Smythson's ideas closely resemble those of architects on the Continent. In Serlio's unpublished Book VI, a range of variant plans for compact, tightly organized town houses and villas are presented; among them are two examples, one in the Italian style

4.29. Wollaton Hall:
North Front. Photo
reproduced by per-
mission of the Royal
Commission on the
Historical Monu-
ments of England.

4.30. Anonymous,
*View of Old Wardour
Castle, Wiltshire.*
Arundell Collection.
Photo reproduced by
permission of the
Conway Library,
Courtauld Institute
of Art.

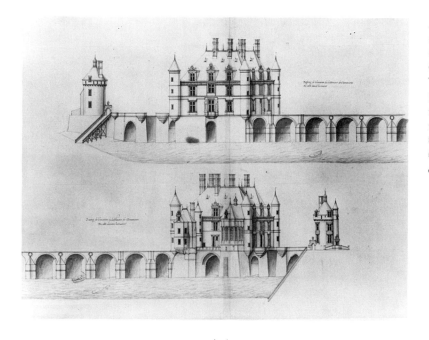

4.31. J. A. Du Cer-
ceau, *Chateau of
Chenonceaux*. By
Courtesy of the
Trustees of the Brit-
ish Museum. Photo
reproduced by per-
mission of the
Conway Library,
Courtauld Institute
of Art.

(fig. 4.32) and one in the French style (fig. 4.33), which include unusual towers closely related to Wollaton's rooftop room. In both the
French and Italian variants, Serlio placed a high lantern with a three-
bay arcade at the top of a blocky, two-story building, punctuating the
roofline around it with chimneys. In the Italian-style project these
have a rather fanciful shape reminiscent of north Italian examples
(such as those at Roncade) and also recall the bases of the Wollaton
bartizans (figs. 4.34 and 4.35). In the French example, corner towers
make the resemblance to Wollaton even stronger. Serlio's text describes these as dovecotes, but there is no reason for Smythson to
have known this or to have cared; such towers could be—and were—
used elsewhere as *belvederi*. Here as elsewhere the similarity between
the English and Continental designs may be coincidence, but it
clearly reveals a shared set of tastes and needs.

It is ultimately this high tower room that gives the house its character, for it was undoubtedly a room both marvelous to *look at* and to
look out from. It was above all designed to impress, a virtuoso perfor-
mance by the architect in the service of his patron. It was also an
amusing architectural conceit, and although it could be reached only
by winding corner staircases and had no fireplace for winter, it was
nonetheless an essential feature. From its windows the family and
their guests could survey the countryside and watch the hunt. Such
rooms made these country houses what they were: buildings from
which to enjoy and control the countryside, houses set down on the
estates of their owners and yet both physically and symbolically removed from them. In making the Prospect Room the final crescendo

4.32. Sebastiano Serlio, *House For a Citizen or Merchant,* Book VI, f. 7. Avery Architectural and Fine Arts Library, Columbia University.

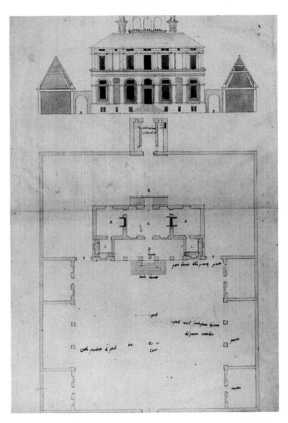

4.33. Sebastiano Serlio, *House For a Citizen or Merchant . . . in the French Manner,* Book VI, f. 8. Avery Architectural and Fine Arts Library, Columbia University.

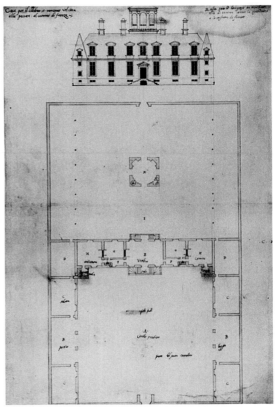

4.34. Wollaton Hall:
The Prospect Tower
from the West.

4.35. Wollaton Hall:
A Bartizan on the
Prospect Tower.

of his composition, Smythson revealed the essence of his design. Thus he created both a new building and a new building type which crystallized the tastes and aspirations of its patron, of its architect, and of its moment in time.

Building Wollaton Hall: Smythson's Role

Robert Smythson is buried at St. Leonard's Church in the village of Wollaton, where a simple monument describes him as "Architector and Survayor unto ye most worthy house of Wollaton with divers others of great account." The term "architect" was not in common usage when Smythson died in 1614, but for Smythson—and for his son John who erected the monument—the meaning was clear: he was a designer whose technical skills were guided by theory, an intellectual as well as a craftsman.[35] In England, the first published discussion of the term appeared in John Shute's *First and Chief Groundes of Architecture* of 1563.[36] Shute—who referred to himself in the treatise as "Paynter and Archytecte"—had been sent to Italy by a group of English patrons (among them the Duke of Northumberland) interested in learning more about the practice of architecture there.[37] His short visit seems to have done little more than give him a superficial familiarity with the terminology of Vitruvian theory, but this was enough to serve as the basis for a short treatise on architecture and an essay on the education of the architect. However muddled and pretentious, Shute's description succeeded in recording a constellation of Renaissance ideas that were gaining acceptance in London and Court circles.

English workshop training traditionally included both building technique and design, but Shute's new definition of the profession placed theory above craft.[38] His list of subjects to be included in the education of an architect included history, grammar, arithmetic, music, and philosophy. Although it was a matter of some fifty years before English practice even approximated the program Shute outlined, the ideas he described had resonance for craftsmen of Smythson's generation. Increasing literacy, widespread educational reform, and a greater emphasis on nontechnical training throughout the society had had their effects on the profession. Thus Smythson referred to himself as an architect with pride, indicating as he did so that for him buildings were not simply sound structure and careful measurement, but the embodiment of architectural ideas.

Smythson also referred to himself as "survayor" on the same monument; the two roles were distinct, though complementary. The Wollaton building accounts provide a rough sketch of what this job entailed. Smythson's name first appeared in the accounts late in 1584 and early in 1585 in connection with the payment of wages to masons at the quarry at Ancaster.[39] He was later recorded as having received funds from which he could make payments to others for "task work" (that is, for subcontracted jobs). Smythson's position as the head of a crew of stonecutters at the quarry and as one of the chief contractors on the site gave him considerable authority to direct the work of others. As his drawings indicate, he had responsibility for much of the measurement and layout of the design. Yet there were other masons at work on the building who also held positions of importance, including Christopher Lovell, son of the Queen's master mason Humphrey Lovell, Thomas Accres, and John and Christopher Rodes. Unlike the other workers, who were paid a daily wage, these men, like Smythson himself, were often paid in lump sums and oversaw the carving of large areas of stonework.[40] They headed a team of some fifteen to twenty-five masons whose numbers varied accordingly to the season and year.

The hierarchy of craftsmen on the site was constantly changing over the course of the eight or so years that work continued at Wollaton. The Rodes—father and son—were sometimes paid a daily wage and sometimes were not present at all; Christopher Lovell was also frequently absent, in London or at work on other projects. Smythson's name disappears in 1587, but he seems to have returned to the site toward the end of 1588. At this point, he worked closely with a mason named William Styles, who was paid a daily wage in the early years covered by the accounts but began receiving payments of lump sums for task work in 1586–87; in the final account book, Styles appears as the principal site-foreman, delegating work to others.[41]

Smythson's role was to oversee the whole project, mediating between the various construction specialists, the paymaster, and the patron. His duties were various. An itemized bill titled "Glasse mesured at the new haulle the xxth of november 1587" and signed by Robert Smythson shows that he ordered and paid for building materials.[42] This was the sort of specialized activity that took Smythson out of the world of craft and into the world of business. Other evidence also points to Smythson's relatively high status and diverse employment both on and off the site. A slip of paper, described in an unpublished thesis of 1957 but now lost, listed rents collected by Robert Smythson in 1588 and turned over by him to the steward of the Wollaton estate.[43] Another document, dated 1602, was drawn up by Henry Willoughby (a cousin of Sir Percival Willoughby's and a member of the household at Wollaton), and referred to "my very loving frende Roberte Smythson of Wollaton," giving him power of attorney in a business transaction.[44] Thus Smythson appears to have represented the family in various legal and financial enterprises, becoming part of the small army of agents who oversaw the management of the vast Willoughby properties. Smythson's education enabled him to enter this world, moving from technical and design concerns to the calculations and contracts generated in an increasingly document-conscious and litigious age.

Smythson clearly became a man of some means at Wollaton. He settled down in the village and continued to serve the Willoughby family until his death in 1614. Over the years he directed the completion of the building—albeit not to the full extent originally drawn out in his plan—and monitored the additions and changes to the house that followed Sir Francis's death in 1596. Maintaining his Wollaton residence as a base, he undertook building projects for other Midlands patrons; at Hardwick in the 1590s he built his most innovative house, taking advantage of his years of experience and the freedom afforded him by a wealthy and relatively unintrusive patron to experiment with new ideas. Later, he spent less and less time on such matters, having trained his son John as an architect to follow in his footsteps.[45]

The Craftsmen

The skilled workmen at Wollaton were recruited from two sources: one group accompanied Smythson from Longleat and Wardour, the other was made up of men based in the Midlands. Among the former were Christopher Lovell and John Hill (or Hills), both of whom had been at Longleat and thus knew the sort of overall image Smythson hoped to achieve in his new building. At Wollaton, Lovell was a foreman paid for task work and Hill was a master mason paid twelve pence a day, but both were high in the chain of command. Hill's name appears at the top of the ledger pages, signaling his authority over the other workers.[46] In the latter group were John and Christopher Rodes (often referred to as Rodes junior and senior), two masons frequently paid in lump sums for the carving of specialized stonework, such as pilasters, entablatures, and balusters (fig. 4.36).[47] Their experience at Wollaton obviously served them well, and they became the principal contractors for carved stone at Hardwick (fig. 4.37). It is likely that they had previously worked for the Countess or Earl of Shrewsbury at Chatsworth or Worksop. This was certainly the case with Thomas Accres, a mason at Wollaton, who had carved at Chatsworth and later completed a number of chimney-pieces for Hardwick Hall.[48]

4.36. Wollaton Hall:
The Southeast
Tower.

4.37. Hardwick
Hall. Photo re-
produced by
permission of the
Royal Commission
on the Historical
Monuments of
England.

Craftsmen tended to move from site to site in groups, thus contributing to the formation of a workshop style. But part of the impetus for this came from the patrons, who observed these men's activities very carefully, noting good work and asking their friends for referrals. The Countess of Shrewsbury visited both Wollaton and Holdenby in the late 1580s as she was beginning to think about the new Hardwick Hall; many years earlier she and her then-husband Sir William Cavendish wrote to John Thynne asking for the name of a good plasterer.[49] Burghley, Hatton, Thynne, and Willoughby all exchanged letters with others describing their projects and asking their friends to search out fine craftsmen. This avenue of communication between the patrons contributed to the homogeneity of fashionable tastes, reinforcing and complementing the exchange of ideas amongst the members of the workshops.

This was true throughout the building trades. The three chief plasterers at Wollaton—Jaxson, Raphael, and Ragg—were responsible for all the ornamental ceilings (called "frett" in the accounts) and perhaps for modeled overmantels as well.[50] Two of them appear on building sites elsewhere: at Hardwick, Ragg worked under the master plasterer Abraham Smith (one of Bess's most prized craftsmen), while Jaxson (who received a wage of twelve pence a day, the highest rate paid for plaster work) can perhaps be identified with the John Jackson who became master of the newly chartered Plasterers Company in London in 1597.[51] The name is a common one and the connection is therefore extremely tenuous, but the rank of the other craftsmen at Wollaton suggests that he was an artist of the highest reputation, the sort who was capable of London employment. None of the plasterwork now remains, but we can get an idea about its appearance from surviving contemporary work such as the ornamental ceiling illustrated by Henry Shaw in his *Details of Elizabethan Architecture* (fig. 4.38).

The same is true of the wooden carving and wainscot, both of which have long since disappeared. The joiners at Wollaton were a highly specialized group: their number included a foreman, Thomas Greenaway, who received fourteen pence a day, and ten other men who received twelve pence a day.[52] Greenaway is mentioned more than once in connection with the "seeling" of rooms at Wollaton. It is unclear who was responsible for the ingenious method of laying the foundation floor of the Prospect Room, with its wide span, according to a scheme of pegging together short lengths of timber in an overlapping pattern to form a matrix of considerable strength. This underflooring (which is similar to the one described and illustrated in Serlio's *First Book*) was revealed when the renovations of the Prospect Room began in the early 1980s. Advanced construction tech-

4.38. Plasterwork Ceiling from Henry Shaw, *Details of Elizabethan Architecture*. London, 1839.

niques could also have been the contribution of the equally skilled and knowledgeable team of carpenters headed by Richard Crispin, a man whose previous credits included Longleat. Among this group was also a local carpenter named Cornelius Spurre, who is recorded in an account book of 1591–92 as having made new doors for the hall. He appears to have remained in the Nottingham area following the completion of the new house at Wollaton.[53]

While stone and wood occupied the attention of most of the skilled labor at Wollaton, it would be wrong to overlook the extensive use of brick in the construction of the building. Throughout the accounts, payments are recorded for loads of brick which were delivered to the site and laid up by rough masons and "layers" who were listed by name. At the height of building activity, there were six layers on site who were paid between eight and ten pence per day; their number dwindled to one (listed as "Jack") in 1588. These men were responsible for building simple walls of brick or stone. Brick was used in the cellars, wells (including the one known today as "The Admiral's Bath" cut deep into the rock below the house), and conduits. Although the infill of the thick lower walls of the house appears to have been made of local sandstone, there is evidence to suggest that the inner walls on the upper stories were made of brick. Not only was this material cheaper and lighter than stone, it could also be used in concealed relieving arches above the long stone lintels of the window bays. The examples of other Smythson buildings (Doddington Hall, Burton Agnes) suggest that he was interested in experimenting with brick construction as a technical means to achieve success with his increasingly tall and skeletal structures. The use of arches and buttresses in the walls behind the dressed ashlar blocks at Hardwick, noted by Girouard, offer further evidence of this experimentation.

The most highly paid worker on the site was not a mason but the head painter, John Matthews. He received a wage of sixteen pence a day and occasionally received money "in prest" for subcontracted labor. From 1586–88, he was at work at Wollaton, painting window bars and casements, decorating two little chambers on the east side of the house, and undertaking other odd jobs, which included "blacking verses on the table on the garden side."[54]

Matthews was a local Nottingham craftsman of some reputation. His activities in the area were various: he worked for the Countess of Rutland at Belvoir and Bottesford in 1591–92 painting the tombs of the earls put up by the London-based sculptor Garret Johnson and restoring wall decorations.[55] In the early 1580s, and again in 1591, he was questioned by the local authorities for his part in the making of wax effigies, which were said to have been used in black magic rituals.[56] Like other craftsmen of his time, he found work wherever possible and practiced his trade when he was hired to do so, regardless of whether the job was large or small. His patrons thus included such great men as Willoughby and the Countess of Rutland and others with more modest goals—in the case of the wax effigies, for instance, he was paid by a local doctor with a deep-seated grudge against his mother-in-law.

Of the sixty or so men whose names appear in the records, very few seem to have been local artisans.[57] Many must have worked at sites elsewhere in England and their names may thus appear in building accounts and associated documents not yet published. There is still a great deal of work to be done in this area and much that remains unknown, but the wealth of documentary evidence in the few cases that have been studied in depth suggests that more names that can be linked to specific building projects will come to light.

The Sculpture

Wollaton Hall is best known for its exterior sculpture, the profusion of complex ornamental cartouches, grotesques, portrait busts, and applied orders with which its surface is encrusted. No documentary evidence concerning this important work survives. Yet enough is now known about Smythson's earlier buildings and about the style of contemporary carving to permit us to suggest some dates and attributions here. Thus far, the most fruitful research has been in the area of funerary sculpture, for here surviving contracts link specific works with named individuals. From these it has become clear that during this period there were two different categories of fine stone-carving workshops: those of the provincial masons, whose carving tended to be rather crude and unsystematic, and those based in London, where Dutch and Flemish immigrants produced sculpture of generally higher quality.[58] At Wollaton, a third group emerges: English masons capable of working in the style associated with London, the "Southwark school," and the Court.

All of the names that appear in the Wollaton accounts are English. Nevertheless, there are reasons to suggest that much of the specialized carving was done by London-based sculptors paid by Smythson or Lovell from sums recorded only as "task work." Work at the quarry was never itemized, and the relatively easy matter of transporting carved stone by cart meant that payments for this would not require special notice in the building accounts. With their London connections and wide circle of highly skilled associates, Smythson or Lovell could easily have arranged to have this carving done.[59] Although both men were capable of producing satisfactory designs themselves, they may have gone to London to find carvers of the highest skill. According to the scheme proposed here, then, the work of these London carvers would include the strapwork frames, portrait busts, and many of the grotesques which ornament the exterior elevations. The applied orders and cresting on the corner pavilions, on the other hand, were undoubtedly carved by skilled English masons (the Rodes, Accres, Hill, or William Styles—a mason who appears late in the accounts), who cut some figural details as well.

Strapwork frames, like those which surround the oculi on the two upper levels of the corner pavilions at Wollaton (fig. 4.36) are typical of London-made stonework. In the well-known tombs of the third and fourth Earls of Rutland at Bottesford (fig. 4.39), for instance, designed and set up by the Dutch sculptor Garret Johnson and his son in 1591, these complex linear motifs appear in the achievements and escutcheons.[60] Much contemporary tomb decoration by London-based firms reflects the strapwork mania that gripped Court society, but Wollaton is the only example of an extensive application of these motifs to architecture. As we have already seen, however, Smythson also devoted himself to the study of these designs, and his drawings for the Wollaton project included a variety of ornamental motifs

4.39. Garret Johnson, *Tomb of the 4th Earl of Rutland.* Bottesford, Leicestershire. 1591. Photo reproduced by permission of Fred H. Crossley and Maurice H. Ridgeway and the Conway Library, Courtauld Institute of Art.

4.40. J. A. Du Cerceau, *Design for a Chimney-Piece,* from *Livre d'architecture.* Paris, 1561. Photo reproduced by permission of the British Library.

4.41 a and b. Hieronymous Cock, *Cartouche Designs,* from *Compertimentorum,* 1566. Photos reproduced by permission of the British Library.

based on examples published by Jan Vredeman de Vries (figs. 4.16 and 4.17). His design for the screen (fig. 4.15), for example, incorporated these motifs into a lively decorative scheme related to the exterior surface of the building. French and Flemish influences are mixed here; ornamental designs published by Du Cerceau (fig. 4.40), Hieronymous Cock (fig. 4.41 a and b), Martin de Vos, and Nicholas de Bruyn were widely available in printed handbooks, and at Wollaton they were used extensively.

Thus it is not style so much as quality of carving and complexity of design that separates the work of the Smythson team from that of London-based carvers. For example, the strapwork pediments on the corner towers (fig. 4.42), clearly depicted in Smythson's elevation design (fig. 4.14), are drawn from a detail published by de Vries (fig. 4.43), as are the Doric order and entablature (figs. 4.44 and 4.45). The frames of the oculi on the ground floor (fig. 4.46) are associated with other ornamental designs by the same author (fig. 4.47). Yet the frames on the second and third stories (figs. 4.48 and 4.49), while obviously in the same general stylistic tradition, relate more closely to the work of Du Cerceau and Cock; they are more complex in design, three-dimensional, and weighty, and the carving of them required a facility in handling cut stone that the lower reliefs did not. The carving at Wollaton is sufficiently varied to suggest the presence not only of a number of hands (something to be expected on a work of this size and complexity) but of at least two different workshops of specialized carvers.

The most distinctive work on the building is the figural sculpture—the portrait busts and grotesques. Nothing of comparable quality or style appears at Longleat or Wardour. Indeed, much of the carving there is marked by the distinctive influence of Allen Maynard and reflects French precedents.[61] A plaque, coat-of-arms, and bust at Wardour (figs. 4.50 and 4.51) bear a close resemblance both to Maynard's work at Longleat and to sculpture at Wolfton House, Dorset, also attributed to him.[62] Sculpture in this style does not appear at Wollaton. By contrast, the rusticated door frame at the entrance to Wardour (fig. 4.52) and another in the inner court (fig. 4.53) are quite similar in style and execution to work at Wollaton, particularly the Doric order used both on the exterior and in the hall screen. These comparisons suggest that the same members of the Smythson team (Lovell or Hill?) were responsible for some architectural elements and for the details closely connected to them (like the lion's head represented in an important Smythson drawing taken from de Vries (fig. 4.54) at Wardour and Wollaton, but that most of the specialized carving and figural sculpture at both sites was undertaken by others.

4.42. Wollaton Hall: Strapwork Gable.

4.43. Jan Vredeman de Vries, *Gable Designs*, from *Architectura oder Bautung*. Antwerp, 1581. By permission of the Houghton Library, Harvard University.

4.44. Wollaton Hall:
The South Entrance
(detail).

4.45. Jan Vredeman
de Vries, *Doric
Order*, from *Variae
Architecturae Formae*.
Antwerp, 1563. By
permission of the
Houghton Library,
Harvard University.

4.46. Diana, Wollaton Hall.

4.47. Jan Vredeman de Vries, *Designs for Ornament*, from *Differents portraicts de menuiserie*. Paris, 1565. By permission of the Houghton Library, Harvard University.

4.48. Wollaton Hall: Bust of a Roman Emperor in a Strapwork Frame. Second Floor.

4.49. Wollaton Hall: Strapwork Frame on a Corner Tower.

4.50. Old Wardour Castle: Inscription Plaque Over the Entrance.

4.51. Old Wardour Castle: Detail of Sculpture Over the Entrance.

4.52. (above left) Old Wardour Castle: Principal Entrance.

4.53. (above right) Old Wardour Castle: Door Frame by Smythson in the Inner Court.

4.54. Robert Smythson, *Ornamental Panel* (after Jan Vredeman de Vries, *Variae Architecturae Formae*). Antwerp, 1563. (I/25 [4]). The British Architectural Library, RIBA, London.

A comparison of the grotesques suggests the range of skill. The relief figures at Wardour (figs. 4.55 and 4.56), while lively and interesting, show none of the vitality or inventiveness of the Wollaton carvings (figs. 4.57 and 4.58). The former tend to be rather shallow and undifferentiated in comparison to the latter. Details like hair and facial features are handled with assurance in many of the Wollaton masks. Other figural elements, such as the sculpted heads in the frieze on the second level (fig. 4.59) or the lion's head over the north door (figs. 4.60 and 4.61), are in yet another style, but overall the sculpture at Wollaton is of a higher quality than that in former Smythson works, reflecting the addition of new talent to the building crew.

The reasons for attributing the best sculpture at Wollaton to London-based carvers require further discusson. The absence of comparable sculpture at Wardour (and the presence there of fine carving in a distinctly different style) clearly suggests that other craftsmen were called in for the specialized stonework at Wollaton. Why not an English workshop? The evidence in the accounts would certainly suggest this, but the problem remains that no English sculpture of similar appearance is known to have been produced at this date. As we have seen, nothing known to have been made by the Smythson team compares to it, and the evidence from contemporary English tomb sculp-

4.55. (left) Old Wardour Castle: Detail of a Door Frame in the Inner Court.

4.56. (right) Old Wardour Castle: Detail of a Door Frame in the Inner Court.

4.57. (above left) Wollaton Hall: Detail of Ornament on a Corner Tower.

4.58. (above right) Wollaton Hall: Detail of Ornament on a Corner Tower.

4.59. Wollaton Hall: Detail of Ornamental Sculpture on the Facade.

4.60. Wollaton Hall:
North Facade. Photo
by Bill Hunter.

4.61. Wollaton Hall:
Detail of Ornament
over the North Door.

ture argues strongly against any attribution to another English shop. For example, the figural work of two English carvers, Richard and Gabriel Royley, represented by the tomb of Thomas Fermor at Somerton, Oxfordshire (1580) (figs. 4.62 and 4.63), is awkward and ill-proportioned, and the faces are flat and unexpressive.[63] These men were from Burton-on-Trent, the center of English carving, and their work has been widely identified throughout the Midlands on the basis of documentary and stylistic evidence. In 1587 the two men were hired to erect a tomb for a friend and neighbor of Willoughby's, Sir Gervase Clifton, but the cost and quality of the carving were far lower than that of work at Wollaton Hall.[64] Although the Royleys appear in the Wollaton accounts (1582), they were paid less than the foremen and had no responsibility for detailed carving. At Wollaton, the standard was clearly set by London and the Court. While Accres, a first-rate marble carver, or Lovell, himself a London-based mason, could possibly fulfill these requirements, the weight of the evidence leans toward the most experienced carvers working in the Court style. These were, of course, in London itself.

A number of London-based firms were capable of producing high-quality sculpture, among them the workshops headed by Garret Johnson and Richard Stevens.[65] The effigies and "weepers" at Bottesford (1591), for example, are skillfully carved (though reduced by tradition to what can only be called a lifeless formula), and the ornamental dragons' heads in the cresting reveal an animated forcefulness that associates them with Wollaton. Nicholas Johnson's Thomas Sutton tomb at the Charterhouse in London (fig. 4.64), while of later date (1615), is also relevant here, as it falls within the span of years to which some of the Wollaton sculpture can be assigned.[66] Both the principal figures and the personifications along the cornice reveal the high quality of the best English carving (some in this case by Nicholas Stone) that dates from this period. Finally, a much earlier monument, that of John Lord Russell (1585?) (fig. 4.65), perhaps by the Stevens workshop, shows distinctive naturalistic qualities, particularly in the Victories in the spandrels.[67] These examples make a strong case for associating the best figural at Wollaton with London, but whether the sculptors were Huguenots or Englishmen remains unclear.

The portrait busts present an even more difficult problem as they vary widely in both style and date. In her *Account,* Cassandra Willoughby wrote that 'the master workmen which built the house were sent for out of Italy, as also most of the stone figures which adorn the house."[68] There is very little possibility that this is true, as it is supported neither by visual evidence nor by any reference to Italian workmen in the building accounts. As we shall see presently, how-

4.62. Richard and Gabriel Royley, *Tomb of Thomas Fermor and Wife.* Somerton, Oxon. 1580. Photo reproduced by permission of Fred H. Crossley and Maurice H. Ridgway and the Conway Library, Courtauld Institute of Art.

4.63. Detail of the Fermor Tomb (fig. 4.62).

4.64. Nicholas Johnson, Isaac James and Nicholas Stone, *Tomb of Thomas Sutton*. The Charterhouse, London. 1615. Photo reproduced by permission of the Royal Commission or the Historical Monuments of England.

4.65. Richard Stevens (?), *Tomb of John Lord Russell*. Westminster Abbey. ca. 1588.

ever, there may be a grain of truth here which—fueled by Cassandra's early eighteenth-century prejudices in favor of neoclassicism—grew into the assertion that all the carved stonework was made in Italy.

The earliest busts seem to be those on the ground floor labeled with the names of the figures: Virgil, Aristotle, Plato, and Cato (figs. 4.66–69).[69] To this group can be added the figure of Minerva (fig. 4.70). All are characterized by strong modeling, deeply incised hair, strong brows, and dark pupils carved into their eyes. That they are contemporary with the original building is suggested by their similarity to the grotesques carved on the exterior walls; a lion's head (fig. 4.71) over a door on the garden side of the house, for example, is remarkably close to the figure of Virgil. None of these busts is represented in the mid-seventeenth-century view by Hollar (fig. 4.72), which shows sculpture in the second-floor roundels only, but the accuracy of details in this sort of image is questionable.

The busts on the second and third floors, representing Roman emperors and sibyls, are no doubt later but appear to date from the first half of the seventeenth century. Among them is a portrait of Charles I (fig. 4.73) derived from a design of Hubert Lesueur and made between 1631 and 1642, the year of the king's death.[70] It is unlikely that any of this sculpture would postdate 1642, the year in which a fire at Wollaton caused extensive damage that was never fully repaired. In 1643 Sir Percival Willoughby died and the house was left vacant (except for occasional family visits) until 1687.[71] Only minor repairs were undertaken during this period. Within the first half of the century, a comparatively early date is suggested by the close relationship between the figures of the sibyls and a series of prints by Crispin van de Passe the Elder dated 1601. The resemblance is clearest in the cases of the Samian Sibyl (figs. 4.74 and 4.75) and the Egyptian Sibyl (figs. 4.76 and 4.77). These are among the best works at Wollaton, recalling the lifelike figure treatment of Nicholas Stone. Although Stone often used the device of roundel and portrait bust in his work (as did Epiphanius Evesham, a member of the Stevens workshop closely associated with Stone's teacher Isaac James), there is no evidence to suggest that he himself or any members of his shop worked at Wollaton.[72] The overall style, however, suggests that these busts were all made in the 1620s.

Finally, there is a group of figures on the ground floor that appear to date from the late seventeenth or early eighteenth centuries. These include Flora, Mercury, Diana, Hercules, a Roman Soldier, and—in the same style—a bust traditionally regarded as a portrait of the first Lord Middleton (figs. 4.78–81). All are softly modeled, massive, and rounded; they share a neoclassical fullness of form, which suggests that they may well have been made by Italian craftsmen.

4.66. (above left)
Bust of Virgil,
Wollaton Hall.
Photo by Bill
Hunter.

4.67. (above right)
Bust of Aristotle,
Wollaton Hall.

4.68. Bust of Plato,
Wollaton Hall.

4.69. (above left)
Bust of Cato,
Wollaton Hall.

4.70. (above right)
Minerva, Wollaton
Hall. Photo by Bill
Hunter.

4.71. Lion's Head.
Wollaton Hall:
South Front.

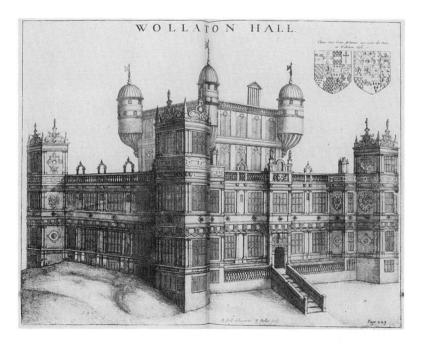

4.72. (above left) Wenceslaus Hollar, *Wollaton Hall*, from Thoroton, *Nottinghamshire*, 1677.

4.73. (lower left) Portrait of Charles I (after Lesueur). ca. 1631–42.

4.74. (lower center) The Samian Sibyl.

4.75. (above center) Crispin van de Passe, *Samian Sibyl.* 1601.

4.76. (lower right) The Egyptian Sibyl.

4.77. (above right) Crispin van de Passe, *Egyptian Sibyl.* 1601.

SIBYLLA SAMIA QVAE ET HEROPHILE PROPRIO NOMINE DICITVR

SIBYLLA AEGYPTIA QVAE ET AGRIPPAA QVIBVSDAM DICTA

Ecce dies, moras quæ tollet læta tenebras,
Nos tenet, soluens nodosa ictumina fatum
Gentis sudabit, referent et carmina plebis.
Hunc poterunt clarum viuorum cernere Regem
Humano quem virgo sua intitulata reuexit
Annuit hoc Coelum, rutilantia sydera monstrant 5

Summus erit sub carne satus, charissimus atque
Virginis et veræ complebit viscera sane tum
Verbum, consilio sine noxa, spiritus almi
Despectus multis tamen ille, salutis amore
Arguet et nostra commissa piacula culpa:
Cuius honos constans et gloria certa manebit. 11

4.78. (left) Flora,
Wollaton Hall.

4.79. (right) Mer-
cury, Wollaton Hall.

These works date from the period of renovation under Cassandra and
her brother that began with her arrival at Wollaton in 1687.[73] Contemporary fashion called for the work of continental craftsmen; in
later years, as Duchess of Chandos, Cassandra and her husband
would employ foreign painters and carvers in their great house at
Canons.[74]

Inside the house, some Elizabethan carving survives. Here it becomes apparent that the same hand that shaped the form of the
Orders and the strapwork pediments on the exterior was responsible
for the design of the screen (figs. 4.82 and 4.83). This is of course
also supported by the surviving Smythson drawings. Although the
extremely crude figure drawing found in Smythson's sketch is improved upon in the work as executed, the spandrel figures nevertheless remain characteristically cramped and awkward. The bearded
heads in the keystones are somewhat better, but as we have seen, this
too is entirely consistent with the work of the Smythson team.

The chimney-piece in the hall (fig. 4.84) may have been carved by
Thomas Accres, the skilled mason responsible for many of the more
elaborate works in marble at Hardwick.[75] But the piece raises questions far broader in scope than its relatively unimpressive appearance
would suggest. It is based on a design in Serlio's Book III (fig. 4.85)
and includes a plaster medallion of considerable interest. The sim-

plicity and flatness of the carving suggests the hand of the Smythson team, but the medallion is taken from a London-made design.[76] We know this from a presentation drawing (fig. 4.86) for the Henry Willoughby monument (1591) at St. Leonard's Church in Wollaton village; a variation on the motif was used (and survives) there. The same motif appears on several tombs in Westminster Abbey of the 1580s and 1590s that were clearly London-made, perhaps by the Stevens workshop. The same firm very probably designed the Willoughby monument and may have supplied the chimney-piece as well.

It is well known that tomb-makers took commissions for other types of fine carving, including chimney-pieces, garden sculpture, and, as I suggest here, carved portrait busts and ornamental figures.[77] The presence of the medallion here suggests that they supplied such work for Wollaton. In addition, Cassandra's *Account* describes how she found fragments of elaborately carved chimney-pieces on the upper floor at Wollaton when she first arrived in 1687. These had been destroyed by fire in 1641.[78] She specifically mentions an elaborately modeled coat-of-arms that remained among the fragments. Although the evidence is slight, it is enough to point to the presence of London-based carvers at Wollaton and to establish the basis for suggesting that a number of works there were fashioned in their shops.

These puzzles serve to remind us of just how many anonymous

4.80. (left) Hercules, Wollaton Hall.

4.81. (right) Bust of a Roman soldier, Wollaton Hall.

4.82. Wollaton Hall: The Screen. Photo reproduced by kind permission of *Country Life*.

4.83. Wollaton Hall: The Screen (detail). Photo by Bill Hunter.

4.84. (above left) Wollaton Hall: The Chimney-piece in the Hall. Photo by Bill Hunter.

4.85. (left) Sebastiano Serlio, *Doric Chimney-piece*, from *Tutte l'opere d'architettura*, Book III.

4.86. (above right) Richard Stevens (?), *Design for a Wall Monument to Sir Henry Willoughby et al.* 1591. University of Nottingham, Middleton Collection. By courtesy of Lord Middleton.

hands, how many unrecorded ideas and dreams, have come together in the creation of the house as we know it. Smythson's own conception, as revealed by his drawings, was an important point of departure, but once on the page his designs began an inevitable process of evolution. Many causes had to be heard, many needs answered; Smythson and his workmen were only part of a larger group of contributors. It was they who created the design at a specific and limited moment in the building's history, but here as elsewhere the craftsmen worked around the limits and obstructions imposed by economic constraints, their own experience and skill, and the tastes of their patrons. Wollaton, like any other building, represented a compromise of conflicting desires. All were subject to change. Poised between the old ways and the new, the house absorbed the tensions which produced it, integrating tradition and innovation in a design of rare drama and novelty.

5

Life at the New Hall:
1587–1610

A Troubled Start

During the first decade after its completion, the new Hall on the hill was used infrequently. Willoughby's other houses—the old Hall, the Chantry in the village, Thurland House in Nottingham, and Lincoln's Inn Grange in London—were all fully occupied throughout the period.[1] Like Smythson's later house for Bess of Hardwick, the new building at Wollaton was brought into use slowly, and it remained a showy satellite of the existing manor house throughout much of its early history. Thus, the account books for 1587–88 testify to Willoughby's frequent provision of hospitality and entertainment of local gentry—the names of Stanhope, Clifton, Markham, Manners, Sacheverell, and Strelly all appear frequently—but only two or three of these gatherings took place at the new Hall.[2] By far the most lavish celebration was a dinner for 120 people held at the new Hall on 11 November 1587 when the guests of honor were the Earl and Countess of Rutland.[3] Nevertheless, the documents suggest that Sir Francis's household was not fully in residence at the new Hall at the time of this event, or, indeed, at any time before Sir Francis's death in 1596. Day-to-day household activities went on elsewhere.

In April 1588, Lady Elizabeth returned to Wollaton, ending an absence of eight years, and the couple began to "keep house" together at the Chantry.[4] The reasons for this important change are unclear. In 1587, at the time of his daughter Dorothy's wedding, Sir Francis wrote to the Earl of Huntington to excuse himself for not providing the wedding feast and entertainment at his house "because by reason of his wives absence and the furniture of his house being much decayed, he had not designed to keep house this year . . ."[5] This suggests that the reconciliation was brought about, at least in part, because of Sir Francis's genuine need for his wife's help in the running of his various households: his youngest daughters would themselves soon come of age, and he looked forward to an increasingly busy social life in the new Hall. A letter from the bailiff Henry Trussell to Lady Elizabeth dated February 1588 conveyed his hope "to see such a reformation in Wollaton House as shall make Sr Francis sufficiently sensible of ye loss he has sustained in [your] absence," adding "that he shall be glad to see Wollaton reassume its former credit."[6]

Sir Francis's reconciliation with his wife at the moment that the new Hall was coming into use is significant. The new house was designed to facilitate social contact between men and women: its spacious parlor, great chambers, and gallery were ideally suited for the dinners, entertainments, and banquets favored in polite society. While such gatherings were infrequent in the Willoughby household in the years prior to the completion of the new Hall—first because of the disagreements between Sir Francis and his wife and later because of their formal separation—it appears that Sir Francis hoped to be able to entertain in this way at the new house after his wife's return. Further, although the existing household structure was set up to carry out all of the tasks of day-to-day living, there was a genuine need for someone to oversee the care of furnishings and fine linens, particularly in a large and fashionably outfitted new home; that person was traditionally the mistress of the house. Thus, while he was able to get along without his wife up to this point, Sir Francis may now have found that he genuinely needed her: the new house, its furnishings, and the comfortable way of life that he and his friends expected to find there all demanded it.

If, as these documents suggest, Sir Francis allowed his wife to return home to Wollaton so that she could take an active part in the running of the household, then he was—once again—to be sorely disappointed. Soon she was moving about the countryside with her accustomed unpredictability, writing first from London to warn her husband "of a plot of knavery amongst his own men," then writing again to complain about the house in which she was staying (it was too cold and the furniture was "so mean that she was fain to have all her own found"), and finally repairing to Buxton in April 1589 where she became so ill that her husband was forced to borrow a horse-litter from the Countess of Shrewsbury to bring her home again.[7]

Disputes over the transfer of property were ongoing. From day to day, Sir Francis changed his mind about the settlement of his estate, promising to write a will on one day and backing down the next.[8] As his principal heirs, his son-in-law Percival and daughter Bridget were at the eye of the storm, buffeted about not only by Lady Elizabeth but also by the other daughters and their husbands as the struggle for Sir Francis's favor continued. Thus the new Hall, intended as a monument to family tradition and longevity, remained the focus of a battle for control within it. In 1588, news reached Percival Willoughby that his brother-in-law Robert Spencer was currying favor with Lady Elizabeth and that he had "told her that Sir Francis Willoughby was a most wise man for not disposing of his land in his own lifetime, and for his part if Sir Francis should dye, he would keep possession of one of the turrets of the new house."[9] Many others, it seemed, had the same idea. This was only the beginning of a contest—and ultimately a court battle—which would disrupt family life for the next twenty years.[10]

In 1594 Lady Elizabeth died and the balance of power was again thrown into chaos. Sir Francis announced his intention to remarry, withdrawing both his affection and his promises of inheritance, and rejecting his daughter and son-in-law in favor of his bride and her family. Having sent one of his officers, William Russell, to London to find him a wife a month before, in August 1595 Sir Francis married Dorothy Tamworth, a widow, who, according to other sources, "had been called in question for her honesty and [had been] separated from her husband."[11] A new series of attacks on his daughter and her husband began immediately. Willoughby claimed that he wanted the manor at Middleton for his own use and sent a troupe of men to have them turned out of the house; later he accused his daughter of trying to steal some jeweled gowns of her mother's, which he claimed belonged to him. He charged both with "disobedience," writing that "her husband was grown so froward that nothing would content him but what agreed with his own humour." He reproached Bridget for failing to show his friend and kinsman Sir Clement Fisher the respect that he deserved.[12] These criticisms echo his earlier charges against his wife; now their daughter was out of favor, replaced by yet another heir apparent.

Throughout these troubled years, Sir Francis's suspicions about his family were deepened through the malicious efforts of his servants and friends, among them Sir Clement Fisher, Thomas Markham, and Thomas Cludd. Much is revealed by a letter written to Fisher by Bridget Willoughby soon after her mother's death:

> I have received at this instant letters from my father wherein I have his displeasure for not pleasing of your worship; I am sorry he knows you no better, but I hold your tongue for no slander that is so busie in all matters, and spareth not ladys and gentlewomen of greater account than myself. Thou hast used thy pleasure in bad speeches of the Countess of Shrewsbery, of Mr. Thomas Spencer's wife, and others. Thou hast practiced dissentions betwixt my husband and me from the beginning. Thou has set my father and him at jares, because thou mightest the better fish and inrich thyself, as you hast done, with their spoyles.
>
> Thou wouldest (being in thy house) have married me to thy cousin Clud, a poor cozening knave of my father's, that came lowsy to him, and therefore in thy heart couldest never since abide me, tho' hitherto I have concealed it.
>
> I was once before thy pleasure and perswasions little better than

hurled out of this house, being great bellied, when thou didst hope both by that means might have perished.

And now again I and mine for not worshiping of thee must upon small warning goe wander, as thou thinkest, a great conquest of such a worshipfull justice as thyself, that employest all thy wits and means to doe mischief. It is well known to all the country that my father of himself never offer'd such measures to the worst servant or tenant that he had.

At thy being at Middleton thou toldest me that thou camest to cross my father's marriage, and to take that stumbling block out of my way, and yet now no man so ready to cog and desemble with them as thyself. And notwithstanding all this and much worse then this thy ordinary protestation is by the faith of an honest man. Malicious knave thou art that canst not spare poor gentle-women and infants with thy tongue and practices; gentleman thou know'st thyself to be none, and tho' at this instant I have no better means of revenge then a little ink and paper, let thy soul and carkes be assured to hear and tast of these injuries in other sort and terms then from and by the hands of a woman.

And seeing by thy practices and theirs, to whom by oath thou art confederate with, I am like to lose my father's favour (which was all the world to me), while I am able to speak thy treacherous knaverys shall not rest altogether concealed, and complain to my father if thou dare again.[13]

Between the machinations of the officers, the presence of a new wife, and Sir Francis's own tendency to mistrust, the family and household were thrown into turmoil and the new house at Wollaton rarely occupied. Further, Sir Francis's estates were increasingly bur-dened by debt. Since the early 1580s he had been borrowing money to finance his building projects, his investments, and other financial commitments (coal mines and ironworks in Warwickshire, woad-growing projects at Wollaton, and a large number of annuities granted out of his lands), and while the profits from the coal pits at Wollaton totaled £1,000 a year, these could not match the increasing demands on his resources. Last ditch efforts to raise cash through enclosures, the sale of woods and new mortgages only dragged him down further. Worse still, Willoughby soon decided to convey his remaining lands to his new wife, leaving his daughter and son-in-law to bear the bur-den of his debts.[14]

In November of 1596 Sir Francis fell ill; his family suspected that he had been poisoned.[15] Percival Willoughby wrote to his wife from London to tell her of her father's sad condition: "He writ that her father's case was lamentable, that he had been ill a fortnight, and shut up from all his friends, that the whore and her minion had stripped him both of goods and land, and left him nothing where he lay but what hung upon his back, and that now he sits haling for life and breath." [16]

A few days later he died. He was buried in the church of St. Giles Cripplegate without ceremony; no mourning cloaks or gowns were given out by his widow and his children were not present. [17] News of these events soon reached the family and with it the news that the new wife was pregnant. Percival, upon whom the leadership of the family had fallen along with its debts, was forced to obtain a troop of the Queen's guards "to watch and search everybody that came to the house" where she was lying in, lest she should secretly try to exchange a girl child for a boy and thus improve her claims on the estate. [18] To the family's great relief, the child was a daughter, but the struggle for her wardship was fierce: it was one more strand in the web of Sir Francis's tangled affairs that his family was left to unravel. In the end, Sir Percival Willoughby and his wife were lucky to inherit Wollaton, Middleton, and a number of smaller manors in Warwickshire; the others got nothing.

The Use of Rooms at Wollaton Hall

These events overshadow the history of the house in the last years of the sixteenth century, driving a wedge between the purposes for which the house was intended by its builder and the use to which it was actually put during his lifetime. The evidence for a reconstruction is uneven: extensive nineteenth-century renovations have obscured the original arrangement of rooms, but various drawings by Smythson and John Thorpe (ca. 1610) (figs. 5.1 and 5.2), as well as a number of inventories made in connection with the transfer of the property after Sir Francis's death, provide an indication both of how these rooms were used and of how they were furnished. [19]

In the inventories of goods and furnishings at Wollaton made between 1596 and 1609, the principal rooms were referred to by various labels, making it difficult to follow the sequence followed by the writer. [20] Further, there were no rules governing which rooms were listed and which ones were left out. The hall (fig. 5.9) for instance, was almost never mentioned, but this is hardly surprising as most of the inventories recorded only bedding and linens rather than other furniture—such things were rarely stored in the hall. Among the frequently mentioned rooms indicated by number on the plans of the principal floors (figs. 4.22, 4.23, and 4.24) are the porter's lodge (1), wardrobe (2?), kitchen (3), parlor or dining parlor (4), chapel or "chapel chamber" (5), two painted chambers (6), north great chamber (7), south great chamber (8), and gallery (9). From notations on

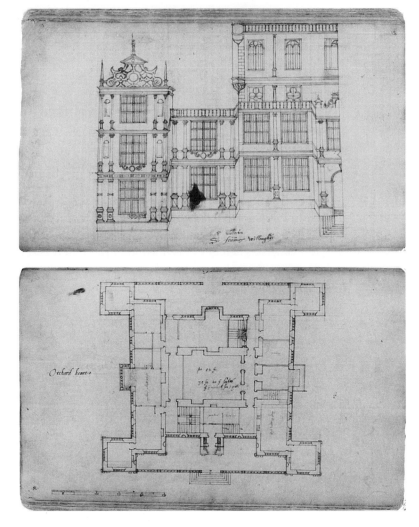

Thorpe's drawing, we also know the location of the pantry (10) and
buttery (11). The placement of both at the screens end of the hall is
consistent with traditional planning. Thorpe also noted that the gallery was on the east side of the upper floor. His plan, which may have
been drawn from memory, contains two errors, however: it shows the
location of the kitchens in the northwest corner (they are in the
basement) and it reverses the location of the staircase on the south
side of the house.[21]

The four corner rooms on both principal living floors were used as
bedchambers. An inventory taken in 1596 and signed by Robert
Smythson indicates that the "best chamber" was on the second floor
on the southwest side; this was distinguished from "My Mr's chamber" (15) on the ground floor to the northeast.[22] Most of the largest
bedchambers and the inner chambers next to them were listed by location labels ("northwest corner chamber" or "chamber next the

wardrobe") rather than by occupant's name. As these were probably intended for use as state or guest bedchambers they would not have been assigned to individuals. Smaller rooms, however, are sometimes designated by the name of a person, usually a member of the household rather than a family member.[23]

Part of the confusion in assigning rooms to particular people results from the instability of the household during the years in which these inventories were taken. After Sir Francis's death in 1596, the house was left vacant for some time before his son-in-law and daughter took up residence. Thus, between 1596 and 1599 the household was in a state of flux, and many of Sir Francis's personal servants were gone or replaced by men and women employed by Sir Percival. The turmoil in the Willoughby family in the period preceding Sir Francis's death necessitated a complete changeover of staff when the balance of power shifted. The assignment of rooms was thus in an unsettled state. Another cause of confusion in the documents was the removal of all of the household furnishings by Sir Francis's second wife.[24] As Sir Francis's widow, she was entitled to the entire contents of the house and a significant portion of his landholdings, as stipulated in his will, despite the short period of their marriage.[25] According to a deposition of 1597, the widow, who married Lord Wharton soon after her husband's death, carried off some ten thousand pounds worth of "goodes, platt, jewells and readie money"—most of this surely came from Wollaton Hall.[26] The sparse furnishings listed in the earliest inventories thus do not accurately represent the original contents of the house.

By 1609, the house was permanently occupied by Sir Percival Willoughby's household, and it had been restored to something of its former glory; an inventory made in that year lists furniture and hangings comparable to those found in other well-kept country houses. Although more strapped financially than his father-in-law, Sir Percival seems to have furnished his house in a grand manner.[27] Household ceremony and taste may have changed in the twenty years since the completion of the house, but it is unlikely that the decoration of the principal rooms had altered substantially over that short period.

The 1609 inventory indicates that, after the hall, the principal room on the ground floor was the parlor on the south or garden side. Here there was a long table with two forms, a small table, two cupboards for displaying plate and storing linens, two chairs (one leather and one embroidered), two joined stools, seven "Turkey" stools (some with carpeted seats), a map, three green table carpets, a pewter cistern, tools for the fire, a fire screen, and gameboards for backgammon and chess. The parlor was used for informal dining (in some early inventories it is called the "dining parlor"), but it was also clearly a place where family and friends could gather for conversation, cards, or games.

The room on the southwest side of the ground floor listed as the "Duke's Chamber" (12) was furnished with a bed hung with green and white silk and included other expensive items. Its name in the inventory perhaps commemorated the visit of the future King Charles I in 1604; the names of the "Prince's Chamber" (14) and "Queen's Chamber" (13) on the upper floor probably date from a visit by the royal party in 1603.[28] Each principal chamber had an inner chamber next to it with a mattress for a servant to sleep on. The "West chamber next the gates" (16) on the north side contained a field bed, a cupboard, a stool, and cushions. This, too, had an inner chamber. "My Mr Bed Chamber" (15) was in the northeast corner. It contained a field bed with curtains, but the inner chamber next to it was furnished with a "standing bed" of the substantial type with posts and a broad base. The hangings for this bed were embroidered with Sir Percival Willoughby's coat of arms.[29] This room was probably the one which Sir Francis intended to use during his lifetime, as indicated by a payment in 1586 for wainscotting in "my Mrs [Master's] chamber by the North tower."[30] A chamber listed as "Mris Sturles" (that is, Storley, a daughter of Sir Percival and Lady Bridget Willoughby) can perhaps be identified as the former "chapel chamber" in the southeast tower. The wardrobe, a separate room on this floor (2?), was used for storing blankets, hangings, and assorted weapons and tools; it was replaced by the armory in the nineteenth-century plan. Among the most interesting items listed in it are five instruments with cases, a white lute of bone, and a drum and drumsticks.[31] These may well be survivors of the musical entertainments of Sir Francis's day.

Upstairs were the state lodgings, the Prince's chamber, and the Queen's chamber, and these were fitted out in the best fashion. In the Prince's chamber, in the north corner of the house, the bedhangings were made of red and yellow silk with a tester of red damask, and there was a blue velvet chair, two matching stools, and a large blue velvet cushion. The curtains in this room were also blue. In the Queen's chamber, in the south corner, the bedhangings were made of yellow silk, and the tester was of red velvet. A blue velvet chair, this one embroidered, and a cupboard were among the other furnishings.

On this floor the two principal suites were arranged symmetrically, the first example of this type of planning in England. On each side of the house was a flight of stairs leading to a great chamber, withdrawing chamber, and bedchamber. Each of the two best bedchambers (that is, the Queen's and the Prince's) had a smaller chamber above it for servants and included a small closet with a privy.[32] The withdrawing chambers (17 and 18) were furnished with beds, stools, and, in the one on the north side, a cupboard. These rooms were used as private sitting and dining rooms for visitors or by the family, in conjunction with the great chamber, which lay beyond.[33] At Hardwick, there were two withdrawing rooms as at Wollaton, but they were on different floors: one was next to the high great chamber, the principal room of state, the other was near the low great chamber and connected with Lady Shrewsbury's own bedchamber; it was thus aptly labeled "Lady Shrewsbury's Withdrawing Chamber" in the inventories of the house.[34]

At Wollaton, as in other Elizabethan houses, the most important rooms on the upper floors were the two great chambers on the north and south sides, and the gallery, which ran nearly the entire length of the east side of the house. The more lavishly furnished of the two great chambers was on the south side, overlooking the garden. It contained two draw-leaf tables, two large cupboards, benches, cushions, embroidered chairs, and stools.[35] The furnishings of the opposite room were similar, but there were fewer pieces and they were more simple. Both rooms were used for dining and entertainment on formal occasions or when important visitors were present, although large-scale dinners might also be held in the hall. Here maps were hung on the walls and, as at Hardwick, the rooms were dominated by monumental fireplaces. Each of the great chambers was separated from the gallery by a wide staircase and a landing; one could thus make a ceremonial entrance to either room by proceeding through the hall and up the stairs.

At either end of the gallery was a small room containing only a table, and in the mezzanine above each of these (see 4.24[2]) was a chamber with another bed in it.[36] The gallery itself was sparsely furnished: the 1609 inventory lists only a stone table, a round table on a pedestal, a red leather chair, twenty-two "maxes" (or "maxres" = maces?), and a coat of arms "in glasse." This was perhaps painted on the windows. Because our inventory lists neither pictures nor wall hangings of any kind, it is impossible to say if there were pictures here, but we know that it was customary to hang portraits and tapestries along the walls of these rooms. As visitors or members of the household walked up and down the length of the gallery, they could admire the view out of the windows on one side and look at an impressive array of family and official portraits on the other.[37] At Ingatestone, Essex, for example, the gallery of Sir William Petre (1600) was hung with pictures of Henry V, Henry VIII, Cleopatra, Diana, a "Man Turk" and a "Woman Turk," a portrait of Petre himself, and "nine painted shields with poseyes [mottos] on them."[38] Here the walls were wainscotted and the floor was covered with rush matting, as was the custom both for galleries and for most other rooms, even

5.3. Hardwick Hall: The Gallery. Photo reproduced by permission of the Royal Commission on the Historical Monuments of England.

the most grand.[39] At Hardwick, for example, the floor of the gallery was laid with rushes and the walls were hung with over forty pictures; there were also tapestries illustrating the story of Gideon, each nineteen feet long.[40] The vast expanse of uninterrupted space there (fig. 5.3) gives some idea of the effect of the gallery at Wollaton before the seventeenth-century fire and the remodeling by Wyatville in the early nineteenth century. This room was a typically grand feature of the Elizabethan house.[41]

The so-called Prospect Room (figs. 5.4 and 5.5) was in fact yet another great chamber, one which was particularly attractive in summer when guests could wander in and out from the roof terraces and enjoy the view. Unlike the lower great chambers, it had no ceremonial approach but was accessible only by a winding, narrow stair. Thus its function was really very different from that of the high great chamber at Hardwick Hall which was in every way a more grand and ceremonial space than the low great chamber on the floor below. At Wollaton, the Prospect Room was part great chamber, part hunting tower and part banqueting house: it was outside the ordinary path of circulation through the house, a private, almost secret place which could be used for dancing, music or cards and from which the hunt and the vast prospect of Willoughby's estate could be enjoyed. Like the great chamber and the gallery below, it was a place in which to entertain and to impress, but unlike them had a more informal and purely social function.

5.4. The Prospect Room (in the course of renovation). Photo reproduced by permission of the Natural History Museum, Wollaton Hall. Photo by Michael P. Cooper.

5.5. The Windows in the Prospect Room (in the course of renovation). Photo reproduced by permission of the Natural History Museum, Wollaton Hall. Photo by Michael P. Cooper.

5.6. Robert Smythson, *Design for a Closet or Office.* (II/13). The British Architectural Library, RIBA, London.

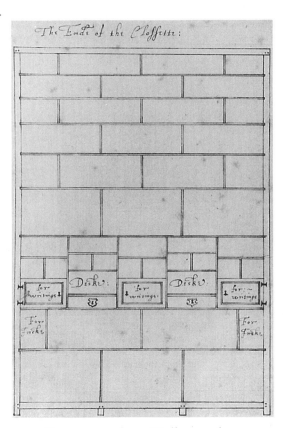

Although there was no library as such at Wollaton, there must have been some sort of room to replace the one at old Wollaton Hall listed in the early inventories as "My Mr. Study."[42] Willoughby's collection of manuscripts and books was substantial, as we have seen. Thus it is tempting to connect a drawing in the Smythson collection (fig. 5.6) for a study with fold-out desks, numerous drawers, and pigeonholes for manuscripts with the Wollaton project. Girouard has dated this design to ca. 1600, at which time Smythson was still working for the Willoughbys and also engaged in the building of Hardwick; if the date is correct, it is too late to relate to Sir Francis's project, but in the early 1590s work was still being done on the interior of Wollaton.[43] The dimensions of the design and the shape of the window certainly suggest a connection to the house.

The many private rooms at Wollaton were among the most innovative features of the house. Unlike the old manor house, the new Hall easily accommodated a number of smaller spaces in the basement and corner towers. These small rooms served as privies, private studies, or places for storing both personal effects and official documents (figs. 4.22 and 4.23). Reflecting a new emphasis both on personal privacy and on the written word, whether in printed form or in manuscript, closets and chambers were tucked away in the four corners of the house on the principal floors and formed the inner recesses of the suites. They were used both by members of the household and by distinguished guests.

Other small rooms were hidden in the mezzanines between the floors of the corner towers and in the basement (fig. 4.24[1–3]). These were used as storage rooms, service areas, and as private chambers for servants. The basement was entered either by a side door on the east side of the house or via the stairs off the screens passage; the mezzanine rooms were reached by internal stairs. This ensured that activities related to service and estate management could be efficiently carried out in the new house, and further, it separated these activities (and service circulation generally) from the ceremonial or private family functions that might be going on elsewhere in the house.

If our reconstruction is correct, then Sir Francis intended to make his own suite at Wollaton the hub of business and social activity in the house. Located in the northeast corner, his rooms were not only at the head of the hall but immediately next to a staircase leading to the great chamber on the upper floor. Further, his withdrawing room communicated with one of the two painted chambers, small rooms perhaps used as libraries or studies (in the nineteenth century these spaces were opened up to form one large library on the east side of the house). Finally, from the innermost chamber in his suite, Sir Francis could easily reach the rooms of his officers in the mezzanines and basement above and below him. Thus he had a central command post from which to oversee activities throughout the house.

Whether the other grand suite on the ground floor, a cluster of rooms in the southwest tower, was intended to be used by Lady Willoughby remains unclear. The documents are silent on this point; no mention is made of a chamber claimed by either Lady Elizabeth or by Lady Dorothy (Sir Francis's second wife), or indeed by Lady Bridget, mistress of the house from the late 1590s on. This mystery is, unfortunately, characteristic of the circumstances surrounding the planning of the house and its use during the early years. While all of the signs point to a program in which Sir Francis's wife would play a major role in the life of the household—strongly suggesting that a personal suite would be planned for her use—this was, in fact, never to become a reality in her lifetime. The inventories thus fail to mention her and the evidence on this important point remains elusive.

Gardens and Roof Terraces

The planning of gardens and open spaces around the house is consistent with the effort to impose order that we have observed elsewhere.

The creation of a precinct of walled courts and gardens around the main building and above it on the rooftop replaced the irregular courtyard of the old manor with an area that could be easily monitored from the house. The gardens shown in Smythson's project parallel the configuration of spaces on the interior, forming a series of small compartments and long *allées* around a circular fountain (fig. 4.13). This pattern of hedges and low walls was intended to be seen from the roof terrace and Prospect Room above.

Wollaton was among the first country houses in England to incorporate the house and garden into a consistent design. As at Wimbledon (fig. 4.21), a design of contemporary date, the approach to the main block is treated as a scenographic challenge: the route through the courtyard is made via terraces and gradually changing levels. Thus the conception of design is perspectival as well as two-dimensionally ordered. Roy Strong has cited Wollaton as an early example of French influence (cf., the Chateau of Anet) in England.[44] Here, as elsewhere in Smythson's designs, we observe the attention to proportion, symmetry, and consistency of geometry that reflects the influence of Palladio and of Continental planning generally.

On the south side of the house, the garden was laid out on a flat lawn defined by hedges or low walls. An orchard beyond this could be reached via a flight of steps. Kitchen gardens were cultivated on the west side where service buildings separated the estate from the park beyond. This irregular cluster of sheds, shown in some topographical views of the seventeenth century, took the place of the elegantly sited service buildings on Smythson's plan. There is no evidence that any of these buildings was constructed as Smythson originally intended. Moreover, it is likely that most agricultural activity continued at the home farm in the village and that these service buildings only served as storage for garden tools, foodstuffs, and perhaps also as stables. Their hodgepodge arrangement was a far cry from the idealized Palladian planning of Smythson's original conception. This was, of course, also frequently the case with many of Palladio's own designs for villas that remained half-finished or in which logistical considerations forced reluctant builders to depart from the perfect symmetry of the original projects.

The roof terrace provided an open space for walking, looking out, or—more formally—for banqueting. Like the gallery and the garden, the roof was used for exercise, particularly by women. In the diary of Lady Anne Clifford, written about 1616, for example, she notes that each morning she would "walk upon the leads" of her house before going to prayer.[45] At Wollaton, the terrace gave access to a series of rooftop rooms: the tower rooms in each of the four corners could be reached via exterior doors (fig. 5.7), and staircases off the Prospect Room lead up to another terrace at the very top of the house. Here were two tiny banqueting houses—miniature rooms set high above the estate (fig. 5.8). From these one could enjoy the view of the gardens and the surrounding countryside at one's leisure, embraced by the house and thus fully receptive to the pleasures of the company and the view.

The high Prospect Room served the same purpose. As it had no fireplace, its glorious height and openness made it the ultimate display of its builder's wealth and status. Here was a room with no other purpose than to be enjoyed. It was large enough to accommodate a sizable banquet or dance but accessible only by two narrow, winding staircases. This was the ultimate Elizabethan conceit: like the private study in a tower called "Paradise," which Leland described in the 1530s, the Prospect Room floated high above the ground, a room full of light that could be entered only by a darkened passage, a room of glass in the tower of a walled castle. It was this extravagant display of wit and wealth which caused the house to be christened "Willoughby's Glory" in the late sixteenth century.[46]

Finally, if we place the rooms at Wollaton into categories according to their uses by various members of the household, a number of critical distinctions arise. First, in comparison to old Wollaton and other medieval manors, the new house was both more compact and more clearly divided into layered "zones" distinguished by function and the status of their occupants. The basement housed the kitchens and offices and was also used for the storage of supplies and provisions. It could be reached by doors on the east side of the house or by internal stairs on the west used by servants. The ground floor was primarily the zone of public household life. It was dominated by the porters lodge, the screens passage, and the hall, all familiar spaces of the traditional medieval household. These rooms were primarily occupied by men and carried in their form and arrangement a very clear message about the status, strength, and order of the household. On this floor were also the wardrobe, the parlor, and four bedchamber suites, including the master's own chamber and his study. This area could be used for entertainment, for ceremony, for the private lodgings of Willoughby and his officers, and for transactions of estate business. With these activities, the ground floor functioned like the core of the old medieval house. The corner towers served as its lodgings, providing space for numerous small bedrooms and storage chambers.

By contrast, the upper floors were given over almost entirely to spaces that accommodated activities shared by both men and women. Here were the two great chambers, the gallery, and the best bed-

5.7. Wollaton Hall: Entrance to a Tower Room from the Roof Terrace.

5.8. Wollaton Hall: Looking across the Roof of the Prospect Tower.

chamber suites. Here, too, were the Prospect Room, tower rooms, and turrets, spaces given over to entertainment and enjoyment. Although the great chamber was traditionally the most important room of the house and the place where the lord took his meals, it was also quite private when compared with the heavily populated hall. Friends (including women) or dignitaries might be entertained there, but in contrast to the parlor downstairs it was formal and stately. At Wollaton, the magnificence implied by the presence of the two great chambers went beyond the simple doubling of space: two great chambers signified a departure from strict economy—now there was so much space that rooms could remain unused most of the time. With the long gallery on the east side, entered ceremoniously by staircases and generous landings at either end, the second floor became a place of entertainment and lavish display.

The plan of the house thus reflects the division between the old and the new. On the ground floor, tradition and masculinity prevailed. Above, a new order—both in design and in the use of rooms—was beginning to emerge. The upstairs space was less accessible and more separate from the rest of the house; it thus became more private. At the same time it became more formal and grand, but what was new here was that its rooms were shared by men and women. Further, the size and elaboration of the gallery, great chambers, and reception rooms soon equalled—and even exceeded—those of the hall and its approaches. This was, of course, a major break with tradition.

At Wollaton there is a new emphasis on privacy for the family and its closest associates in the upper zones of the house. Here again we see increased contact between men and women—or at least an increase in the size of the spaces in which this was possible. Yet even with these changes, the hall, with all its complex connotations of traditional values, was not abandoned altogether. This would come later, in other houses.

The existence of a traditional hall and screens passage side by side with a symmetrically planned upper floor at Wollaton marks it as a house conceived and built at a point of transition in social and architectural history. We know from the Willoughby Orders of 1572 that the hall was indeed the focus of household life at the old manor, and we can see that importance reflected in the survival of its traditional form in the new house (fig. 5.9), but Wollaton was among the last of the great houses built or used in this way. At Hardwick in the 1590s, and in most later houses, the hall was stripped of its characteristic approach and, more significantly, planned so that it would be entered on axis—that is, via a door at the midpoint of its short side. At Hard-

5.9. Wollaton Hall:
The Hall, from John
Britton, *Architectural
Antiquities of Great
Britain.* 1809.
Vol. II.

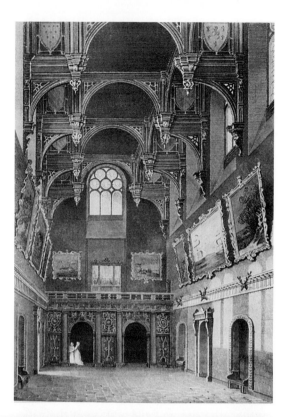

5.10. Hardwick
Hall: The Screen in
the Hall. Photo re-
produced by
permission of the
Royal Commission
on the Historical
Monuments of
England.

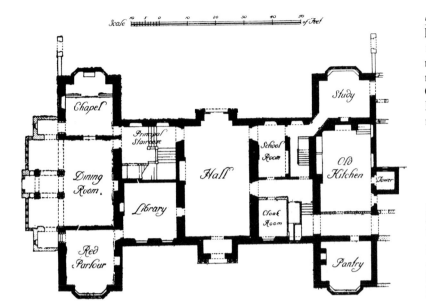

Scale of Feet

Chapel

Study

Principal Staircase

Dining Room.

Hall

School Room

Old Kitchen

Library

Tower

Cloak Room

Red Parlour

Pantry

5.11. Charlton House, Greenwich. 1607. Plan. Photo reproduced by permission of the Royal Commission on the Historical Monuments of England.

5.12. John Smythson, *Plan of Worksop Manor* (III/17). The British Architectural Library, RIBA, London.

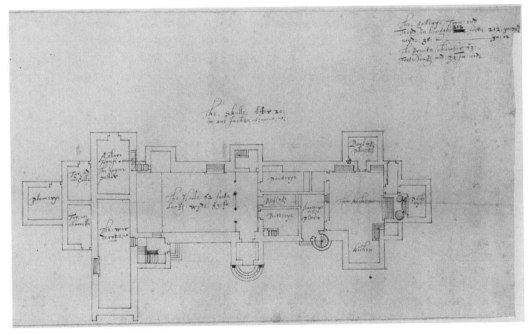

wick (figs. 4.25 and 5.10), it is clear that the character of the space is severely altered by these changes: now the screen is merely a symbolic barrier, and the hall takes on the quality of a longitudinal passage rather than a focal point in itself. At Charlton House, Greenwich (fig. 5.11), built for Adam Newton, the tutor of Prince Henry, in 1607, the hall was again planned on axis with the front entrance; the screen was abandoned altogether.[47] A similar experiment was attempted at Hatfield House, built for the Earl of Salisbury in 1607–12.

These changes came about as a result of two equally powerful forces: a shift in program which deemphasized the importance of the hall, and an increasing preference among artists and patrons for classicizing symmetry. The three houses which dominate Smythson's later career mark the transition: traditional halls were included at Worksop (fig. 5.12) and Wollaton while at Hardwick this was abandoned. It may have been the peculiarity of the program in Bess's house that first enabled him to make the change, as Bess did not keep a hall in the traditional manner (her officers and gentlewomen ate in the low great chamber and paved dining room on the upper floor) and, as a woman, she participated less directly in the rituals of service specifically focused on it.[48] The new hall at Hardwick thus functioned more as a common room than did those at either Worksop or Wollaton, where male heads of households were more strongly identified with the conventions of military planning and behavior.

These traditions were fast dying out; ten years later the closed and convoluted route to the hall would seem outdated and old-fashioned. Nevertheless, at Wollaton they remained, bearing witness to the end of an era and to the painful uncertainties that accompanied the transition to a new way of life.

6

Fame and Changing Fortunes

Willoughby's Glory

For Sir Percival and Lady Bridget (plates 4 and 5 in gallery) inheriting
the great house at Wollaton proved to be a mixed blessing. At the
time of Sir Francis's death, the couple had been living at Middleton
in Warwickshire, but they were soon entreated to return. In a letter
to Bridget Willoughby, Robert Aldridge, the chaplain at Wollaton,
wrote to remind her that the estate was "the ancient seat of the
Willoughbys, that it was the most fruitful seat which she had: the
best stored with all sorts of provision (which was a conveniency that
they should consider, being both given to hospitality) and that in
regard it had been lately built by her father at great expense and
was now termed Willughby's Glory, would, if not dwelt in, soon be
termed Willughby's Folly."[1] Aldridge "begged that she would not
think herself at home when she was not at Wollaton."

The estate was no longer sufficient to support a large household or
a lavish lifestyle. Nevertheless, Bridget and Percival chose to return
there soon after her father's death. They entertained in grand style
when necessary, but they conserved resources by careful management
and by spending most of their time in other houses that were less expensive to run. At Wollaton their industry was rewarded by a visit
from Queen Anne and her son Prince Henry on their progress south
from Scotland in 1603.[2] Undoubtedly this visit taxed the Willoughbys'
already weakened finances, but the honor to the family made up for
the expense. The royal visit was an event that Sir Francis had hoped
for but never lived to see; it came after both he and the sovereign he
built for were already dead.

Wollaton fared well under the careful administration of Bridget
and Percival Willoughby. Writing in 1610, Thomas Ridgeway, their
son's father-in-law, reported on his recent visit to the estate:

> At Wollaton (to my comfort) I saw the miracle, and true model
> indeed, of a most perfect and well-shaped house, none in England
> better, unless greater, and yet if this were greater it were the
> worser. The gate-house, curtelages [courtyards], gardens, orchards,

stables, etc., a very little time (joined with Sir Percival's great care
and exquisite judgement in contriving) will easily and delight-
somely produce, by God's good help . . . I never saw so many
windows so sound, and so well kept . . . Even now we are at
Middleton (a delicate seat and a delightful house). . . . I will say
no more, but all that I saw was very good (notwithstanding the
apparent marks of a mother-in-law within doors). God's name be
praised for all, and both you be ever thanked by me and mine.[3]

His description suggests that despite the strains and hardships of
the past decade very little had been altered at Wollaton since Sir
Francis's death. The fabric of the house remained essentially the
same, yet this apparent continuity masked fundamental changes in
the lives and attitudes of its occupants.

Unlike their parents, Percival and Bridget Willoughby lived a life
that was much more like that of ordinary gentry families and much
less like that of the great nobility.[4] Thus the household at Wollaton
ceased to be the impressive ceremonial showplace that Sir Francis
had imagined, taking his cue from the Court and its powerful attendants. Now it seemed more private, more like a home. To begin
with, the household was no longer exclusively a man's world in which
women were isolated figureheads. In domestic matters, Lady Bridget
acted in partnership with her husband, and their household was
largely free of the sorts of petty intrigues and disputes that had so
troubled her parents' lives. In part this was the result of the personalities of the people who lived there: Percival and Bridget had always
treated each other with a love and kindness that was lacking in Sir
Francis's marriage.[5] The couple's life was not free of discord, but it
was taken in stride. More important, the things they argued about—
domestic concerns and the discipline of their children—were not the
same as those which so bitterly divided Sir Francis and his wife. Their
differences were not profound disputes but the predictable squabbles
of everyday domestic life.

Many of Lady Bridget's letters to her husband reveal a mild manner and a sense of humor that would have been foreign to her parents. Even when financial troubles gave her cause for concern, she
wrote with affection:

she writ that her father was with her [at Middleton] and no small
resort of company to the house, which occasioned great charges,
and tho he had left with her those that could do all things well, yet
she presumed they could not make money, for which reason she
desired if he did not come soon himself that he would send her
what she needed, and wheras he used to say that a wife and a house
were not furnished in a month, he mistakes her: for on these accounts she had no cause to grieve.[6]

Bridget seems to have acted as mistress of her own household; un-like her mother, she did not have to contend with an army of ser-vants and officers but surrounded herself instead with a small group of men and women of her own choosing. A list of household members at Wollaton in 1598 names forty-six people, but these included the master and mistress, their children, Percival's brother Edward Willoughby and Winifred, his wife (Bridget's sister), as well as a number of other family members; fewer than twenty of the men named were household servants, and of these, eight were listed as "waiters."[7] Clearly, then, the household was close-knit, clearly di-vided by class status, and firmly under the control of its mistress.

Most of the correspondence exchanged by Bridget and her hus-band related to the running of the household and the education and marriage of their children.[8] In a letter of 1612, she wrote to her hus-band in London asking him to send her down "fruit, spice, oranges and lemons and a barrell of olives."[9] Percival sent notes to his wife with news of his difficult financial dealings in town and of his political career (he was Member of Parliament for Tamworth in Warwick-shire), asking for her forgiveness for his long absences.[10]

The difficulties between them appear to have been quickly re-solved—at least in comparison to the ongoing battles of Lady Bridget's parents. At times she wrote somewhat caustically, asking him "to make her acquainted with his affairs, and not leave her to guess"; elsewhere she might blame his servants for his difficulties or complain that she should be better provided for, "having hardly a servant at home, and instead of usefull people, [a] store of children and dogs."[11] His responses were good-humored and temperate.

Writing in the early eighteenth century, Cassandra Willoughby ex-pressed the greatest respect for her great-grandmother: "She seems to have had a very good understanding, and to have acted with great dis-cretion in those unhappy differences between her father and mother, and Sir Percival and her father. She appears to have been a lady fit for business and very well able to grapple with those difficulties which their perplexed affairs often brought them under."[12]

These were the qualities that Cassandra's own generation admired; although separated from Lady Bridget by more years than separated Lady Bridget from her mother, Cassandra's world was more like that of her great-grandmother than it was different. Both women were frugal and efficient mistresses at Wollaton who considered the house—and not London or the Court—their home and proper sphere. A sig-nificant shift had occurred in the short time since the deaths of Lady Elizabeth and Sir Francis—and this change was already felt in Bridget's lifetime. While Bridget was mistress of the Wollaton household, its numbers were reduced and many traditional rituals abandoned. For her, it seems, the care of her husband and children were enough; she knew what was expected of her and, with the image of her unhappy parents never far from her mind, she spent her days at Wollaton, managing the household and raising her children.

Despite these changes in daily life, the house itself changed little. The great hall and two magnificent great chambers were occupied by the family and their servants from day to day. While the lavish entertainments planned by Sir Francis in the 1570s were no longer held here, the house nonetheless continued to be used. More women and children filled the large rooms than Sir Francis could have imagined, and much of his son-in-law's business was transacted away from the house, in London. In place of the officers and servants who were to occupy the small rooms in the corner towers, children, their tutors, and nurses had the run of the house. No doubt many small rooms remained empty, used only for storage.

Lady Bridget and her husband raised their children at Wollaton and lived together in the house until her death in the mid 1620s. In the years following, the great house was quiet and in shadow, inhabited only by its aging owner and his servants. In 1633, Sir Percival wrote to his brother, complaining "of the decays of his weather beaten cottage and carkas, that his hands tremble, his leggs totter, his hearing fails, his eyes grow dim so that he can make but little use of his books which are his best friends. His head . . . was grown heavy and dull, and his memory very weak, and all the faculties of his body were decaying."[13]

He had lived at Wollaton for fifty years; his children were all married and had moved away. This was the beginning of the end. Although Sir Percival had put considerable effort into maintaining the great house, keeping up the estate, and adding new sculpture and furnishings to the building, he now found the "decays of his weather beaten cottage" overwhelming. Late in 1641, a fire destroyed parts of the gallery and great chamber, yet only the necessary repairs were made.[14] Sir Percival, who was clearly ill and nearing death, could see no further reason to pour money into the old house; he died a year later, in 1643.[15] Wollaton was then closed up and abandoned. It was to remain empty for the next forty-four years.

Cassandra Willoughby's Stewardship: 1687–1713

A new generation saw the house with different eyes. "It was about midsummer 1687," wrote Cassandra Willoughby in her *Account of the Willughby's of Wollaton*, "that my brother sent his coach with several servants to fetch me from Wanstead to him at London, and from thence we made . . . our way to Wollaton." Thus she recalled how these two "young creatures"—her brother Francis was only nineteen and she just seventeen years old at the time—excitedly set out on what would prove to be the most serious mission of their lives: to take possession of the large Elizabethan house and estate at Wollaton that had for years been left neglected and improperly managed by their stepfather Sir Josiah Child.[16] Stopping briefly at Wendy in Cambridgeshire to receive their aunt's blessing, the pair made their way to their family's ancestral home. Then, as now, their first view of the house must have been breathtaking. For Cassandra, this was to be the beginning of an involvement that would occupy her attention for years, but at that moment she knew only how excited and proud she was that her elder brother had asked her to live with him and manage his household: "This proposal I was much delighted with, thinking it would be no small pleasure for me to be Mistress of Wollaton, and to do whatever I had a mind to, believing that such a government must make me perfectly happy."[17]

At Wollaton they found the house in disrepair, the gardens uncared for and overgrown. On their arrival Cassandra and her brother discovered "heaps of rubbish" left over from the fire and very little furniture or "necessaries" with which to begin to set up house.[18] Barred by their stepfather from removing anything from their mother's jointure house at Middleton, they started from scratch, embarking on the long process of bringing the house back to life.

Francis Willoughby died in September 1688 at the age of twenty.[19] A younger brother, Thomas, aged sixteen, thus became the heir; he was then at Cambridge, but he quickly put aside his university studies to take up his brother's cause and personally direct the management of the Wollaton estates. Again Cassandra was asked to play the role of housekeeper, a responsibility which she resumed with obvious enthusiasm.

Now the renovations began again in earnest. Cassandra's *Account* contains a lengthy description of the daily routine which was followed in the house. She recalls that "college hours" were kept at Wollaton; this meant that each morning Cassandra, her brother Thomas, and his tutor Dr. Man, a fellow of Jesus College who had accompanied him from Cambridge, would rise at 5 A.M., at which time the two men would repair to the library for three hours of lessons.[20] Prayers began between 8 and 9 o'clock and were required of the whole household: "such servants as were not at prayers," wrote Cassandra, "and could not give just reason for their absence, were to fast till dinner." It was she, or her brother, who meted out punishment to any member of their "family" who did not conform to the rules.

6.1. (opposite page) Jan Siberechts, *Wollaton Hall,* 1697 Yale Center for British Art, Paul Mellon Collection.

After breakfast, the young master and mistress wandered among the workmen who were repairing the building and restoring the gardens. With the help of Dr. Man and his colleague Mr. Pratt, formerly of the Chelsea Physick Gardens, Thomas oversaw the design and installation of a garden of botanical specimens, a project of particular interest to him. According to the *Account,* "the garden which formerly belonged to the house was (after the fashion of those times) but a little piece of ground, in which was the plan of the house planted with box trees." This was replaced by new plantings, and the entire area was landscaped according to current fashion. Views of Wollaton Hall by Jan Siberechts (fig. 6.1) and by Kip and Knyff (fig. 6.2) in the late 1690s show formal parterres on the southeast side of the garden next to a substantial greenhouse. There was also a newly planted "wilderness," a "ha-ha," and, adjacent to the house itself, a bowling green where the young brother and sister might entertain their guests on pleasant spring or summer evenings[21] (see plate 7).

Inside the house the workmen were busy. Carpenters and plasterers remodeled the principal rooms and repaired the damage left over from the fire. Artists were called in to decorate the walls with paintings; Laguerre and Thornhill devised large mythological murals for the north and south stairwells.[22] Old furnishings were replaced by new ones purchased by Cassandra in London; suites of upholstered chairs and elegant hangings now ornamented the rooms.[23] Soon the house began to reflect the aspirations of its young owners and the current fashions of the times.

As housekeeper, Cassandra's principal duty, besides the supervision of the servants, was to keep the furniture and fittings in good repair. Thus in her *Account* she recorded that, following her consultations with the workmen, she would work on "such furniture as needed to be altered and mended in the house" while her brother read to her "from some diverting book." After dinner, these activities might be resumed or perhaps company would arrive; evenings were spent taking exercise in the garden or riding out to enjoy the surrounding Nottingham countryside. Cassandra was often permitted to accompany her brother if he spent the day hunting.[24] Whatever their activity, it was ended by 10 o'clock when a bell rang, summoning the family together once again for prayers before bed.

Despite "this mighty regular course of life," Cassandra enjoyed considerable freedom as the young mistress of Wollaton Hall.[25] Her father, Francis Willoughby, had been an eminent natural scientist, and founding member of the Royal Society, whose intellectual curiosity and status in his field provided his children with an inheritance that included both a large library and a substantial collection of "curiosities." More important, perhaps, since the father had died when

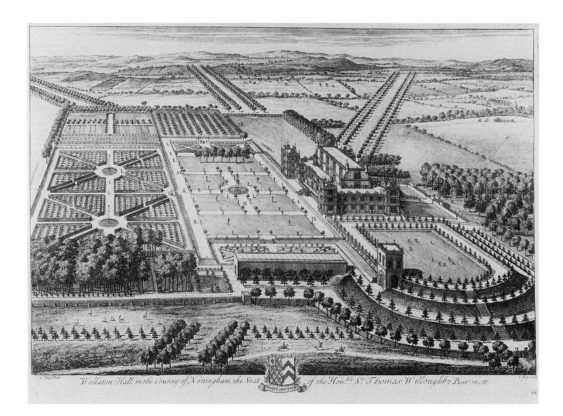

Wollaton Hall in the County of Nottingham the Seat of the Hon.ble Sr Thomas Willoughby Baronett

6.2. J. Kip and L. Knyff. *Wollaton Hall,* from *Brittania Illustrata,* 1707. Photo reproduced by permission of the British Library.

the children were quite young, was the legacy of a supportive circle of friends and correspondents who encouraged them in their studies.[26] Though she was not educated at a university as her brothers had been, Cassandra was nevertheless included in virtually all the activities at Wollaton, with the exception of Thomas's lessons with his tutor. When the lawsuit challenging Sir Josiah Child was finally settled in their favor, for instance, the brother and sister rode at once to Middleton to claim their father's belongings. His collection of books and specimens were packed up, unpacked, and installed at Wollaton by both of them together, as Cassandra described:

> There were also a fine collection of valuable medals and other rarities which my father had collected together with dryed birds, fish, insects, shells, seeds, minerals and plants and other rarities which had lain neglected at Middleton from the time that my mother had married Sir J.C. and left the house. All these we removed, and when we had them at Wollaton it was a vast business for us to clean, label, and put them in order, which we were fain to do ourselves, fearing the servants might make mistakes, and pull such tender curiosities to pieces.[27]

In London, as well, they spent all their leisure hours in each other's company. Both were entertained by Mr. Flamstead at Greenwich and saw his "astronomical instruments" in the Royal Observatory, both viewed Mr. Charlton's famous collection of "rarities."[28] Thus Cassandra was able to enter a world of books and ideas generally closed to young women.

Had she remained at home with her mother, few of these opportunities for learning would have been open to her now that it was no longer considered fashionable or necessary to educate young girls, and if she had married early instead of remaining single until the age of forty-three (she married her cousin, James Brydges, first Duke of Chandos in 1713) she would have had to give her attention to her husband and children instead of to her own interests. As it was, Cassandra's peculiar status as the young mistress of her brother's household at Wollaton gave her the opportunity to furnish and decorate a major country house at a very young age and left her time not only for needlework and ordinary household duties but also to read, to write letters, to catalogue her father's collection, to entertain friends, and to visit other country houses throughout England.[29]

Cassandra Willoughby's curiosity eventually led her to the family papers in the library at Wollaton, and it was there that she found her most passionate employment. In December 1702 she began writing the history of her family.[30] Working through the huge family archive of legal, genealogical, and personal documents, she began her chronicle with a narrative of fourteenth- and fifteenth-century marriages, births, and deaths, adding short descriptions of the outstanding deeds of her ancestors.[31] She said little about political events in her chronicle. Although Cassandra turned to the works of Thoroton, or Dugdale, or to Baker's *Chronicles of the Kings of England* to provide her with official, scholarly accounts of her ancestors' accomplishments, she extracted the minutiae of daily life from the many personal papers with the instinctive voracity of a woman whose own personal concerns lay with these private domestic affairs and not with high-level events. She wrote about the price of woodcocks, claret and beef, about the comings and goings of children and servants, and about her ancestors' successes and failures in courtship and marriage. These were the things that interested her.

Unfettered by romanticized reverence for the Elizabethan period, Cassandra was able to hold her sixteenth-century ancestors at arm's length and subject them to a careful inspection. Perhaps something of her father's empiricism had been acquired by this extraordinary young woman as she learned to categorize and analyze her observations. But her feeling for her subject matter was not without its lighter side, as she revealed in a passage describing her first Christmas at Wollaton:

> At Christmas my brother invited all his neighbours and some of his acquaintance from London to keep the Holy days with us, when my brother diverted himself and company in a very cheerful and

innocent manner—a little play, some dancing—and to make that the more comical he made an old wardrobe of short coats, ruffs, farthingales, etc. to be brought out to dress some of the company in the same manner as some of the family pictures in Wollaton parlour are dressed, which helped to add to the mirth.[32]

It was to be precisely these same odd-looking people who would come to life in the pages of her history.

Cassandra Willoughby was not interested in architectural history as such. The archive at Wollaton contained a series of building accounts and inventories which she passed over quickly. For her, Wollaton was the place where she lived, a home which required daily attention. While she could acknowledge its importance as architecture, she paid little attention to this aspect of its history. Her only description of Wollaton is included almost incidentally in another discussion. A chance reference to Sir Francis's "building" in a letter from his sister Lady Arundell inspired the following explanation:

The building which Lady Arundell means was, I believe, Wollaton new house. The old hall was built near the church. What now remains of that old building is turned into three or four farm houses, of which one is about a quarter of a mile from the rest, which was the dairy house to the old hall. The new house is placed upon a hill about half a mile from the old hall, from whence there is a very noble prospect of the country round it. One side of the house looks upon the castle and town of Nottingham, from another there is a fine view of Clifton House and gardens, the seat of Sir Gervas Clifton; from the other sides of the house there is the prospect of several houses and little villages, and each corner and middle of the house pretty near point to churches that are about two or three miles off. The house itself is a very noble pile of building, but it being less easie to describe it by writing then by drawing, I design to place at the end of this book a draught and a plan of it, and shall therefore only mention here the Sir Francis Willughby began the building, A.D. 1580, and finished it A.D. 1588. The master workmen which built the house he sent for out of Italy, as also most of the stone figures which adorn the house. All the stone which it is built with was brought from Ancaster in Lincolnshire by the people who dwelt there, and who exchanged their stone with Sir Francis for his coal, which they carried back from Wollaton. But notwithstanding the stone and its carriage cost nothing but the return of cole which Sir Francis made for it, and that at that time labourers' wages was very small, yet it appears by a very particular account of the building, which still remains in the library, that the building of that house cost Sir Francis Willughby four-score thousand pounds.[33]

This description clearly contains numerous errors. Here Cassandra was hampered by her own generation's strong prejudice in favor of

Italian art and artists and against English craftsmanship. Yet, as we have seen, there was also a grain of truth in her statement.

Family lore incorporated hearsay and the speculation of "experts" into its stories. For example, Robert Thoroton's *Antiquities of Nottinghamshire* contained a mention of Wollaton which bears an obvious resemblance to Cassandra's statement about it: ". . . that stately Pile, the House at Wollaton, the stone whereof was all brought from Ancaster in Lincolnshire by the people of those parts, who then fetch'd coles from Wollaton, which they had for their labour, which still remains a conspicuous monument of the family and estate."[34]

Deferring to Thoroton's expertise, Cassandra incorporated his text into hers. Where he got his information is a mystery: the accounts show that the stone did indeed come from Ancaster, but no exchange of stone for coal is recorded. Cassandra pointed to "a very particular account" as the source of her information, but some of it obviously came from Thoroton, whom she relied on heavily elsewhere. How she arrived at the figure of £80,000 for the total cost of the house is equally unclear. While the accounts reveal that the building was extremely expensive, the evidence suggests a total more like one-tenth of Cassandra's figure. Here again Cassandra seems to have deferred to family legend or let her contemporary sense of monetary values overshadow her reading of the documents.

Under Cassandra Willoughby's stewardship the house at Wollaton flourished. She replaced the old furnishings left by her great-grandparents with new pieces acquired in London. She had the house redecorated and the gardens changed to suit current taste. Most important, the house was a place where she and her brother could entertain, a "country seat" to which they could return while away from London. Although no documents describing the resident staff at Wollaton during this period survive, we know that households were becoming smaller. Even at the magnificent palace of Canons, built by Cassandra and her husband as Duke and Duchess of Chandos, the household numbered only ninety, including a resident orchestra of sixteen. Virtually all of these men and women were engaged in the business of maintaining the house and its occupants; they were domestic servants in the modern sense.[35] The Duke and his associates transacted their business in town.

Reflecting the change in fashion, Cassandra commented on Sir Francis's unhappy household:

> It was the fashion of those times for families of distinction to maintain as their retinue in their own familys and to be ready to attend them upon any occasion many gentlemen who were really born so and who looked upon it to be no disgrace to be retained by the great families then in England but rather the contrary, for it was

then usuall for gentlemen to get their sons placed in a man of qualitie's house . . . of this sort of gentleman Sir Francis Willughby always retained a great number. . . .[36]

According to Cassandra, it was these gentleman servants who disrupted the household, creating "unhappy divisions" between Sir Francis and his wife, and later between him and his children. Their goal in this was only their own profit. She called her ancestor "a man of great piety and learning . . . of a very mild, sweet disposition, and a lover of hospitality, but a little too apt to be imposed on by stories from his servants." For Cassandra, Lady Willoughby was "a woman of wit and virtue, but of a turbulent spirit and ungovernable passions."[37] Their problem, as she saw it, was the disorderliness of their household, a condition brought on by the presence of too many people who served their own rather than their master's interests. Under her own good stewardship, the estate would not have fallen into such a "shattered condition" as it did at the time of Sir Francis's death.

In the 1690s, Wollaton once again became the magnificent country seat that Sir Francis had intended it to be. And once again conditions favored the building of houses by the gentry and aristocracy. Wollaton and Middleton were both restored; in the 1720s Cassandra's husband built the great house at Canons and restored Shaw Hall in Berkshire, while her stepbrother Richard Child hired Colin Campbell to build a Palladian showplace at Wanstead.[38] With these building activities a new life began for Wollaton and for other houses of its time. For almost one hundred years the house had been able to accommodate the rapidly changing fashions of its occupants, providing flexible spaces in which a variety of activities—from the formal service of Sir Francis to the relative informality of occasional visits by Cassandra's parents and their families—could all take place. With the end of the seventeenth century, however, came changes too great for the old house to accommodate. These were both social and stylistic; for a generation raised on the baroque, Wollaton seemed peculiar and old-fashioned. Thus, the new generation of Willoughbys thoroughly remodeled the house and the young mistress turned her attention to the "old papers" in the library. For her, both the old house and its builders were the stuff of history. Living at Wollaton, she could bring the house into the present with her skills as a housekeeper. With her ancestors all around her—these faces in the old pictures and unruly writers of the letters she pored over day after day—she was able to bring them back to life in the pages of her *Account.*

The Family Home: 1713–1924

For the generations which followed, Wollaton Hall would serve a variety of purposes: family home, country estate, Elizabethan relic. Its popularity rose and fell with the tide of fashion. For the late eighteenth century, the house had the appeal of an ornament in a picturesque landscape: a 1790 edition of Thoroton's *Nottinghamshire* illustrated it with gardens in the style of Capability Brown (fig. 6.3) and it attracted attention as a notable example of truly English (rather than Italianate) architecture. In his "Essay on the Picturesque" (1794), for example, Uvedale Price took up the question of the relative merits of variety and uniformity in design, using Wollaton as an example. According to him, variety in massing made a building more interesting and gave it an importance which neoclassical buildings lacked:

> The effect of this principle struck me very much at Wollaton, a house which for the richness of its ornaments in the near view, and the grandeur of its masses from every point, yields to few, if any in the kingdom. But it is still more striking when contrasted with the neighboring castel (as it is called) of Nottingham. This is a long, square house of the Italian style, built in a high commanding situation overlooking the town. The long unvaried line of the summit, and the dull uniformity of the whole mass, would not have embellished any style of landscape; but such a building, on such high ground, and its outline always distinctly opposed to the sky, gives an impression of ridicule and disgust. The hill and the town are flattened by it; while the comparatively low situation of Wollaton, is so elevated by the form of the house that it seems to command the whole country round it.[39]

The effect of such criticism was to increase awareness of Elizabethan houses and inspire new pride in them, but many were soon subjected to "improvements" in the Elizabethan style.

Wollaton was one of many houses, including Longleat and Chatsworth, in which a campaign of renovation at the turn of the nineteenth century greatly altered the interior, leaving the outer walls intact. These changes were far more extensive than any undertaken in the earlier period. To neoclassical tastes, the cramped spaces and dark wood of earlier houses seemed hopelessly old-fashioned. In his *Architectural Antiquities of Great Britain* of 1809, John Britton described the "alterations" planned by Lord Middleton for "the conversion of the interior . . . to the present, and more comfortable modes of domestic life." These included: (1) enlarging the north entrance; (2) knocking down walls of two small rooms on the east side to form the new library; (3) cutting through the wall of the great hall to open up a passage directly from the front door; (4) enlarging the saloon; and (5) improving communication between the service areas in the basement and the upper parts of the house.[40] A plan showing the proposed changes accompanied the text; they closely match the alterations which were carried out (fig. 6.4).

The architect principally responsible for these changes was Jeffry Wyatville.[41] He seems to have worked at Wollaton at various times between 1804 and the mid 1830s, completing a number of significant alterations during this long span of time. In addition to the projects noted above, Wyatville constructed a service wing on the west side of the house in 1823 (fig. 6.5), which was intended to form an independent unit virtually separate from the main house itself. This change in the plan of the house widened the gap between the servants and served population at Wollaton still further. The construction of a new brick stable block and estate offices (fig. 6.6) in 1779 had removed most of the estate's business and management activities from the main house itself, and now the withdrawal of the family into the private and personal realm was complete.[42]

In 1831, the sixth Lord Middleton instructed Wyatville to design new paneling to replace the elaborate Elizabethan woodwork in the hall, citing the danger of fire and the threat posed by anti-Reform Act rioters.[43] Wyatville submitted a drawing, still in the Middleton Collection (fig. 6.7), showing two variants. Middleton chose the one which he thought would "light better and be nearer the old panels in the former wainscot".[44] This paneling still exists in the hall; it is capped by a doric frieze matching that on the screen, to which a balustrade was added (fig. 6.15). Middleton also instructed Wyatville to remove the paneling in the saloon (the old parlor on the ground floor) and "to fit up the Room in character with the rest of the building." Thus the saloon was extended over the stairs to the garden and given a neo-Elizabethan plaster ceiling and French doors leading out to the garden (fig. 6.8). Wyatville's presentation drawings (figs. 6.9–10) showed the house before alterations, perhaps as part of an earlier scheme to minimize new construction.

The paintings by Laguerre and Thornhill in the stairwell had been restored by J. F. Rigaud, R.A. in 1807; these were retouched by a "Mr. Brown" in 1835.[45] Other alterations included reglazing (but probably not recutting) windows and removing the leads and small panes, placing classicized surrounds on doors throughout the building, adding the swan-neck chimneys to the corner towers and repairing others throughout the house, repainting the hall ceiling, and rebuilding the Prospect Room above it to ensure soundness of construction and to make it look more modern[46] (figs. 6.11–12).

WOLLATON HALL,

The Seat of the Right- Hon:ble Lord · Middleton

Published by J. Throsby, Nottingham, Nov 5.ᵗʰ 1796. Sold by W.ᵐ Miller, N.º 16 Old Bond St. London.

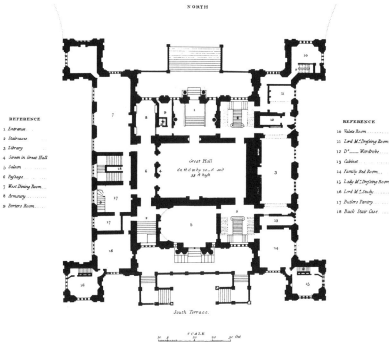

NORTH

REFERENCE

1 Entrance
2 Staircases
3 Library
4 Screen in Great Hall
5 Saloon
6 Passage
7 West Dining Room
8 Armoury
9 Porters Room

REFERENCE

10 Valets Room
11 Lord M.ᵈˢ Dressing Room
12 D.º ___ Wardrobe
13 Cabinet
14 Family Bed Room
15 Lady M.ᵈˢ Dressing Room
16 Lord M.ᵈˢ Study
17 Butlers Pantry
18 Back Stair Case

Great Hall
60 ft 6 in by 30 ft and 50 ft high

South Terrace.

SCALE
10 ft 20 30 feet

6.3. *Wollaton Hall, from John Throsby, Thoroton's Antiquities of Nottinghamshire, 1790.*

6.4. Wollaton Hall: Plan of the Ground Floor, from John Britton, *Architectural Antiquities of Great Britain.* 1809. Vol. II.

6.5. Wollaton Hall:
West Facade and
Service Wing.

6.6. Aerial View of
Wollaton Hall and
Stables. Photo by Jon
Jayes, Nottingham.

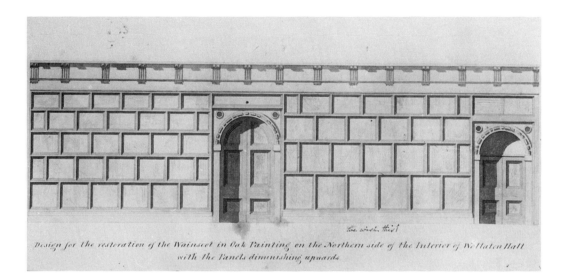

Design for the restoration of the Wainscot in Oak Painting on the Northern side of the Interior of Wollaton Hall with the Panels diminishing upwards

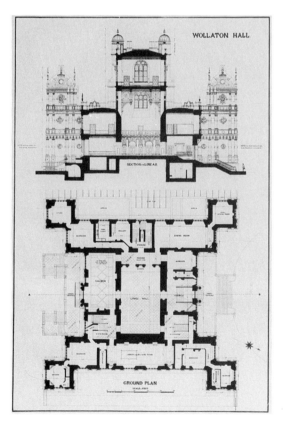

WOLLATON HALL

GROUND PLAN

6.7. J. Wyatville, *Design for Wainscot.* University of Nottingham. Middleton Collection. By courtesy of Lord Middleton.

6.8. P. K. Allen, *Wollaton Hall. Plan and Section,* from *The Builder,* 13 April 1889.

6.9. J. Wyatville, *Wollaton Hall: East Front.* Yale Center for British Art, Paul Mellon Collection.

6.10. J. Wyatville, *Wollaton Hall: South Front.* Yale Center for British Art, Paul Mellon Collection.

6.11. Wollaton Hall:
The Ceiling in the
Prospect Room.

6.12. Wollaton Hall:
Wall Niche in the
Prospect Room.

6.13. The Gate Lodge. Photo by Jon Jayes, Nottingham.

6.14. The Camellia House, Wollaton Hall. City of Nottingham.

6.15. Wollaton Hall:
The Hall, ca. 1902.

6.16. Wollaton Hall:
The Drawing Room
(North Great Cham-
ber), ca. 1902.

6.17. Ladies at the Grand Fancy Bazaar, Wollaton Hall, 1884. Photo reproduced by permission of the Nottinghamshire County Library Service.

6.18. Wollaton Hall: Early Museum Displays in the Hall. Photo reproduced by permission of the Nottinghamshire County Library Service.

While some of the more destructive schemes—like cutting away the screen in the great hall or placing flying buttresses between the roof terrace and the Prospect Tower—were abandoned, this period of intensive rebuilding clearly altered the character of the house, wiping away all but the faintest traces of the original on the interior.[47] With the building of the new gate lodge (fig. 6.13) and the iron and glass Camellia House in 1823 (fig. 6.14), the transformation of the old house into a fashionable nineteenth-century country estate was complete.[48] Now the house not only had all of the conveniences of a modern structure but also the appeal of its picturesque past. Such was the popularity of the style at mid-century that the house was copied twice: first by Paxton and Stokes at Mentmore (in the 1830s) and later by Charles Barry at Highclere.[49]

Over the course of its history, Wollaton had changed to suit the needs of its various occupants. Rather than see the house as static and unchanging, each generation had refurnished, redecorated, and remodeled to make the rooms conform to current fashion. According to an account written by Lady Middleton in 1902, the "dining room" (the old south great chamber) had been temporarily partitioned to form "small closed cubicles for bachelors."[50] Victorian armchairs, occasional tables and bric-a-brac now graced the great hall (fig. 6.15) and drawing room (fig. 6.16), the former north great chamber. Yet reminders of the past were everywhere. Just as Cassandra and her brother put on the old clothes that they found at Wollaton and jokingly pretended to be their own Elizabethan ancestors, so too did the ladies of the Willoughby family and their friends dress up as figures from the past for the Grand Fancy Bazaar in 1884 (fig. 6.17). For those who lived at Wollaton, then, the past and the present existed side by side.

The economic pressures of World War I and the difficulties of maintaining a large country estate in the twentieth century brought Wollaton's history as a private family home to an end in 1924. And once again the house was adapted to a new use: sold to the city of Nottingham together with its extensive grounds and gardens, it became a Museum of Natural History (fig. 6.18) and a public park. In this new capacity it continues to be a showplace, filled with visitors who marvel at its great size and variety.[51]

Conclusion

The history of Wollaton Hall presented here conforms to many of the patterns previously established by research in social and architectural history. To begin with, the innovative doubling of the great chambers, combined with the overall increase in the size and importance of the rooms on the upper floors, parallels a trend toward greater privacy and specialization of function in English domestic architecture at all levels of society. In his studies of cottages and farmhouses built during this period, for instance, W. G. Hoskins noted both an increase in the numbers of structures erected and also a marked tendency on the part of renovators to put their money into making smaller, more defined spaces out of larger ones: subdividing halls, partitioning great chambers, and adding chambers on upper floors.[1] A desire for greater privacy was the motive. Among the upper classes, these developments were matched not only by an increase in the numbers of monumental country houses, but also by a gradual and generalized retreat into the confines of spaces with limited access—open only to the family, the married couple, or the individual.

The strength of the Elizabethan economy during the 1570s and 1580s made these changes possible. Whether it was the project of a prosperous yeoman farmer or of an entrepreneur of enormous wealth like Sir Francis Willoughby, the decision to build a new house required both ample capital and the luxury to invest it in architecture.[2] During the first half of Elizabeth's reign, economic conditions favored such schemes. For Willoughby, as for the average cottage builder, financial security was in part the result of the growing agricultural economy of these years, although his profits were vastly increased by successful coal-mining operations. But for all classes the investment involved risks: for farmers, house building absorbed whatever sums could be raised over the course of four or five good seasons; for a man like Willoughby, the outlay of capital was proportionally large.

The 1590s brought economic hardship and a slump in building activities throughout England.[3] As we have seen, Willoughby's own finances were completely destroyed during this period. In his case, debt and desperation were exacerbated by the fluctuations of his own poor investments, but like others, his fortunes were tied to the land

and to the economy as a whole. Even the remarkably solid empire of Bess of Hardwick suffered serious setbacks (a twenty-five percent reduction in land-based revenue) during the middle years of the decade).[4] Her building activities continued unabated, but as we have seen, Willoughby—and later his heirs—had to scramble to maintain even a semblance of their former grandeur. Their family fortunes only fully recovered in the second half of the seventeenth century, a development again paralleled by an overall strengthening of the economic situation of the landed gentry. This economic growth produced the momentum that made the rebuilding of Wollaton Hall in the 1690s possible.

In the area of social history, one fact stands out: Wollaton was built to accommodate a form of household organization which was soon to become outmoded and, not long afterwards, to be virtually extinct.[5] Few great households, even those of the most powerful nobles, would later dispense hospitality and adhere to the ancient rituals of service in the way that Willoughby had done in the 1570s. The reasons for this are various, but economic changes surely rank high among them. Diversification of the economy and the growth of both commercial and professional activity in the towns (notably London) combined to offer attractive opportunities to the younger sons and lesser gentry who had formerly made up the core of the upper servant staff in large households. Moreover, large landowners now demonstrated their power not through maintenance of private armies but by hiring lawyers and skilled, nonresident agents devoted to the maintenance of their employers' estates. Thus, even if the reverses of the 1590s had not undermined the structure of the household at Wollaton, it is likely that the next generation would have limited the numbers of officers and servants, and adjusted their duties, to bring these into line with current practice.

The complex issue of relationships between women and men remains somewhat more elusive. In broad outline, Wollaton parallels the general trend in household structure: male-dominated Elizabethan households in which women formed only a small and—it must be admitted even in the best circumstances—rather alienated group gave way in the course of the seventeenth century to households in which women were not only more numerous but, at the top of the hierarchy at least, more powerful through their identification with domestic administration. This was, to be certain, predicated on significant conditions: first, on the separation of public and private activities which had formerly taken place under a single roof; and second, on the contemporaneous investment of the private sphere—that of the home, the family, and personal life—with new value.[6]

Thus, in our own example, we can recognize that Wollaton in the 1690s had become a place primarily for country entertainments and social gatherings where men and women mixed informally; it was quite separate from the world of business and law in London, and social life there was different from that which took place in the city. Over this world Cassandra Willoughby reigned in the early years as its mistress and "housekeeper," a position now more clearly defined and identified with women. Following her brother's marriage, Cassandra worked in the library at Wollaton and traveled frequently.[7] At the age of forty-three she became Duchess of Chandos, and entered one of England's most substantial households. Yet Canons, the palatial suburban house which she and her husband built in the 1720s, was staffed by an assemblage of men and women that Sir Francis would have found strangely informal and small in number. For Cassandra, however, the changes represented a significant improvement over the life of the Elizabethan great household; at no time was she marginalized in the way that her ancestor Lady Elizabeth had been.

As a group, the married couples whom we have looked at seem typical of their time, but ultimately it is their diversity rather than any marked trend in one direction or another which characterizes them. Some were able to form successful relationships, others were thwarted in this; some were genuinely enamored of their spouses, others remained distant and embittered. This pattern of widely differing experience—one might even call it patternlessness—seems to fit with other evidence for upper-class marriages in the late Tudor and Stuart periods.[8] The danger and difficulties in attempting to correlate the free choice of a partner with the success or failure of marriage are perhaps most poignantly summed up in our own example by a comparison between the dismal failure of the marriage of Sir Francis and Lady Elizabeth and the overwhelming success of that between Sir Percival and Lady Bridget. The former, as we have seen, was freely chosen, the latter, arranged.

Yet the evidence is conclusive on one point: where expectation—of property, of mobility, of power within the household—differed significantly from the reality that was experienced, the result was disaster. It appears that two areas of particular uncertainty caused problems: the first concerned the transfer of property, and the second concerned the relative status of upper-class women in their own households. Both were exacerbated by shifting power relationships within the society at large. Thus, ambiguity in the land law and new economic opportunities placed added weight on personal abilities and private manipulations, heightening competition between those who stood to gain or lose from the favor of wealthy landowners. New criteria, such as education and success in business or the professions, created ambiguities in an already uneasy balance of power between men and women of different classes. Those who entered the marriage bond with different expectations from their partners of where they would stand in the household hierarchy were destined to meet with resistance from all other parties concerned. Further, in a period which witnessed such widely divergent views on women and the home as this one did—with the example of the Queen placed side by side with the stock figures of the shrew and the temptress, or indeed, with the figure of the virtuous mother and wife patiently attending to her family in the home—there were bound to be uncertainties in the ordering of relationships as complex as those within the hierarchy of a large and fully staffed household.

The removal of the household officers from the home and their gradual replacement by professional agents was thus a significant occurrence. The smaller, family-based household was obviously much easier to manage, and it had the advantage of assigning separate and respected roles to men and women. Successful and close personal relationships were obviously possible at all levels of society, but they were particularly difficult where economic tensions exacerbated the inevitable problems of personal life. The restructuring of the large household may have been, in part, a response to this fact.

Finally, by placing the evidence of social and economic conditions within the Willoughby household side by side with developments in architectural design, we can recognize important relationships between the two. Smythson's impulse to experiment with the centrally planned villa-types newly exported from the Continent was clearly tied to Willoughby's rather ambivalent program: thus, at Wollaton, one floor of the house looks backward to traditional English planning while the other looks forward to the classicized designs of the mid seventeenth century. The hall, screens, and screens passage were the symbolic (if no longer the real) center of life at Wollaton, and thus they were featured in plan and expressed flamboyantly on the exterior by a high, bartizaned tower. Yet up the two grand flights of stairs all was changed: the great chambers and withdrawing rooms to the north and south matched each other perfectly in an exquisite display both of fashionable classicizing planning and the conspicuous consumption of space. With the gallery, Prospect Room, and rooftop terraces, there was ample room to impress and entertain visitors according to the conventions of London and the Court. The carefully laid out gardens below extended the house beyond the confines of its walls, embracing nature itself with the ever-longer reach of Willoughby's administration.

At Wollaton, the demands of the program were different from that of any house that preceded or followed it. Both Willoughby and Smythson had been raised in a visual environment in which the regular rhythms of columns and entablatures were still novelties, where the power of the landowner was still communicated by the strength and height of the walls of his castle and the numbers of men he kept in his household. But this was also a period of transition: the castle form had taken on almost mythical significance, and the tales of knights and heroes who lived in them were elaborated with the gusto and self-consciousness typical of a revival movement. At Court, Willoughby discovered sham castles more fantastic than those which he or his architect had ever seen, stage sets which sprouted turrets and towers as quickly as painters and carpenters could imagine them and put them up. These images he brought home to Wollaton, giving his architect free rein to devise a building in which the *idea* of a castle would shine forth with all the immediacy and excitement of the courtly artist's fantasies. To this the novelty of classical Orders and a sculptural program of gods and heroes were added, for Willoughby saw himself as the educated gentleman-knight, the man who served as a justice and as sheriff of his shire, who dispensed hospitality to his friends and neighbors in a style of which his grandfather would have been proud. He was the man of power, but a cultured man who read Virgil and Cicero for pleasure in his library study. He was the head of a large household, the father and husband whose family made him proud. Wollaton was to be a monument that would say all of this, and a home in which Willoughby imagined his descendants living for generations as his ancestors had lived at the old hall in the village. Smythson took the challenge of this complex man's ideas, designing a house which stood proudly on its hilltop, proclaiming its owner's indominable but curious spirit to all who saw it. For his part, Willoughby could look out from its high tower at the countryside around him, escaping if only for a moment the pressures that made the world below such a difficult place in which to live.

Appendix A
The Willoughby Household
Orders of 1572

Item that Foxe supply the place of the usher, whose office is first of all to see that the hall be kept clean and that his groom sees no doggs come there at all. He is diligently to have good regard of every person that comes into the hall, to the end that if they be of the better sort, notice may be given to the master, or some head officer that they may be entertained accordingly. If of the meaner sort, then to know the cause of their coming, and to give advertisement over, to the end they may be dispatched and answer'd of their business, provided always that no stranger be suffered to pass without offering him to drink, and that no rascall or unseemly person be suffer'd to tarry there. The covering of the boards [tables] doth appertain to the under-butler.

Upon intelligence given from the clerk or the cook that meat is ready to be served, he is with a loud voice to command all gentlemen and yeomen to repair to the dresser. At the neither [sic] end of the hall he is to meet the service, saying with a loud voice, "Give place, my masters," albeit no man be in the way, and so to goe before the same service untill he come to the upper end of the hall, carrying a little fine rod in this hand, which at all other times he is to carry in his bosom, whereby he is to be known of all strangers to be the usher. He is also to appoint some one yeoman, at his discretion, in the winter time to carry the torch before service in the night time. The dining chamber being served, he is to place in the hall in dinner and supper time all noblemen's men which be fellows together, and all gentlemen according to every of their master's degrees, but before their placing and sitting down, he is to give notice unto the clerk that so many mease are to be provided for, but in that matter the diligence of the clerk is no less required then the usher, to the end that they may both to the master's worship see the same very well served, according to their degrees and number of the strangers there.

If any great press of strangers shall be, then three or four of the meanest sort of servants, as namely the slaughterman, the carter, and some of the best grooms of the stable, or such like, are to be appointed by the usher to attend in t'hall. If no strangers be, then the grooms of the stable, and the allowed pages and boys in the house, to attend upon the first dinner, and they to have the remainder thereof, with some little help out of the kitchen, as the usher shall see cause. And likewise the pages at the latter dinner to attend upon the gentlemen and yeomen, and the remainder of the meat at [sic] after both the dinners and suppers, presently by the usher to be put into the almes table, which is always by him to be kept safely locked, to be distributed among the poor such days as shall be appointed. Imediately after supper, if there be any strangers, the usher is with a loud voice to command all yeomen waiters to attend upon the buttery hatch, for the serving of [. . .].

All disorders in the hall are by the usher to be reformed, and if there shall be any stubborn persons, he is to expell them out of the hall, and to command all men at dinner and supper time (if any great noise shall be) to keep silence, saying with a loud voice, "Speak softly, my masters." His part is also to walk up and down the hall, and especially in the time of the first dinner or supper, and only to call and to command the buttler, the pantter, and such as be attendents to bring or fetch any thing that shall be wanting, but not in any wise to doe any service himself, otherwise than diligently to look to the tables. The benefit of the play in this as in many places doth belong to the buttler, but in most unto th'usher. He is diligently to see that no meat filched forth of the chamber be brought into the hall, nor yet to suffer any waiter to abide in the hall during the time their master is at dinner or supper, nor is he to suffer any filchen through the hall from the buttery, kitchen, or such like places. For he is an officer of great trust and credit, and next to the usher of the great chamber (if any be) in degree, above either cooke, butler, yeomen of the chambers, or porter.

Penne being appointed for the buttery, his office is ever to keep clean and sweet his buttery, and likewise his plate and cups, making sure every day to have fresh and clean water, and for the most part twice a day to wash the same withal. His jacks appointed for the hall are to be kept from furring and unsweet savour. His office with th'aid of an under-buttler is to keep the great chamber clean, to make fires there, and to provide for lights in due season, and to cover the boards and cupboards there, having very good regard to the cleanes of his linen, and likewise to provide for cards and dice, whereof he is to have the profit.

The under-butler is to cover the boards in the hall. He is to suffer no household servant to remain tipling, or to be at all in the buttery; but whosoever is disposed to drink to be served at the hatch, and so to depart. Neither is he to suffer any stranger to come in the buttery, other then such as shall be of worship or good reputation, and they to be brought in either by some of their officers, by th'usher of th'hall, or else by some discrete gentleman or yeoman, for their better entertainment, according to their degrees and credit. He is to foresee that no breakfast, afternoon meats, nor hancks after supper be had or made there, or if any household servant by reason of his business come after dinner and is to have some meat, he is to be served in the hall and not in the buttery. But if any stranger of credit in like case come, he is by th'usher or some other discrete servant to be had into the buttery and not to be served in the hall.

The butler is also to use good discretion in serving forth of the bread and beer to the houses of office, as to the kitchen, the bakehouse, the nursery, and such like, that he, understanding the allowed number there, may so serve them, as it neither be with want nor yet with over great excess. He is to foresee that his broken beer be safe, and clean kept in sweet vessels for the poor. The buttery door ought not without speciall cause to be set open till eight of the clock in the morning, and then so to stand till it be nine, and from thence to be shut again till between ten and eleven, and then to remain open till all dinners be done, and so after dinner and supper be done to be shut again till between two and three, and then after half an hour or thereabouts to be made fast till five, and so to remain open till nine, and after by no means to be opened that night without speciall cause. The discretion of that officer is to foresee that no filching of bread or beer be suffer'd, nor yet any want where reason doth require may be greatly both for his master's profit and worshipp, for it is an office both of good credit and great trust.

Appendix B
Building Accounts and
Related Documents:

Middleton Collection, University of Nottingham Library

Mi A 60/1   March 1582–March 1583.
Mi A 60/2   Summary of Household Payments (including Building) 1583.
Mi A 60/3   November 1584–November 1585.
Mi A 60/4   Summary of Building Payments 1584–85.
Mi A 60/5   March 1586–March 1587.
Mi A 60/6   April 1587–March 1588.
5/165/129   Glass Measured at the New Hall (22 November 1587), signed by Robert Smythson.
Mi A 70 (205) Estate and Household Accounts 1591: New doors and roof work at the new Hall. Erection of Henry Willoughby Monument, St. Leonard's Church, Wollaton.
5/171/56   Power of Attorney: Henry Willoughby to Robert Smythson (February 1602).
Mi A 80 (205) Estate Accounts 1603: Building works associated with the visit of Queen Anne and Prince Henry.
Mi A 90a   Building Accounts 1641–42: Repairs to the gallery and hall following the fire of November 1641.
Mi P 3 A-K   Early Nineteenth-Century Drawings of Wollaton Hall and Lenton Lodge, by C. S. Smith, J. Wyatt, J. and J. C. Buckler, C. Chouler.

Notes

Introduction

1. A. C. Wood, *The Continuation of the History of the Willoughby Family By Cassandra Duchess of Chandos* (Eton, Windsor, 1958), 125 and Middleton Manuscripts Collection [hereafter as Mi] LM 27, f. 137.

2. Although the two variant spellings "Willughby" and "Willoughby" were used interchangeably up to the mid eighteenth century, the latter version has been adopted throughout this study. The first volume of Cassandra's *Account* (Mi LM 26) was published in part by the Historical Manuscripts Commission, *Report on the Manuscripts of Lord Middleton Presently at Wollaton Hall* (London, 1911). The second volume (Mi LM 27) was published by Wood, in the *Continuation* (as in note 1 above).

3. See A. T. Friedman, "Portrait of a Marriage: The Willoughby Letters of 1585–86," *Signs: Journal of Women in Culture and Society* 11, no. 3 (Spring 1986): 542–55. The letter is in the British Library, Lansdowne 46, no. 31; it is discussed by Cassandra in Mi LM 26, f. 126v–27v.

4. C. Geertz, "Art as a Cultural System," in *Local Knowledge: Further Essays in Interpretive Anthropology* (New York, 1983), 94–120. The discussion of historical time owes a great deal to Fernand Braudel's work; see "History and the Social Sciences: The *Longue Durée*," in *On History*, trans. by S. Matthews (Chicago, 1980), 25–54.

5. For detailed bibliographies of works about this period, see D. M. Palliser, *The Age of Elizabeth: England Under the Later Tudors 1547–1603* (London and New York, 1983), and L. Stone, *The Family, Sex and Marriage in England 1500–1800* (London, 1977).

6. The attitude is widely expressed; a particularly striking example is R. Wittkower, "English Neoclassicism and the Vicissitudes of Palladio's *Quattro libri*," in *Palladio and Palladianism* (New York, 1974), 73–94.

7. For an overview of the period sympathetic to the Elizabethan and Jacobean styles, see J. Summerson, *Architecture in Britain 1530–1830* (Harmondsworth, 1970).

8. The Middleton Collection was given to the University of Nottingham after the sale of Wollaton Hall in 1924 and the breakup of the old muniment room. The name of the collection is taken from the title given to Thomas Willoughby when he was elevated to the peerage in 1712.

9. See Summerson, *Architecture in Britain*; as in note 6; E. Mercer, *English Art 1553–1625* (Oxford: The Clarendon Press, 1962); and M. Girouard, *Robert Smythson and the Elizabethan Country House* (New Haven and London, 1983), and *Life in the English Country House: A Social and Architectural History* (New Haven and London, 1978).

10. E. Mercer, "The Houses of the Gentry," *Past and Present* (1954):

11–32. See also N. Elias, "Structure of Dwellings and the Structure of the Society," in *The Court Society* (New York, 1983); originally published at Darmstadt, 1969.

11. C. Geertz, "Blurred Genres: The Refiguring of Social Thought," in *Local Knowledge,* as in note 4 above. The implications of focusing on individual cases, by contrast, are discussed by L. Stone, "The Revival of Narrative," *Past and Present* 85 (1979):3–24.

12. The case for the study of "women's history" is eloquently presented by N. Z. Davis in "'Women's History' in Transition: The European Case," *Feminist Studies* (Spring-Summer, 1976):83–103.

13. This view has been put forward by a number of historians, among them Lawrence Stone, who described the high incidence of marital breakdown among the aristocracy in his *The Crisis of the Aristocracy 1558–1641* (Oxford, 1965), 661ff. See also his *The Family, Sex and Marriage in England,* as in note 5 above, esp. 195ff.

14. L. Jardine, *Still Harping on Daughters: Women and Drama in the Age of Shakespeare* (Totowa, NJ, 1983); the work includes a useful bibliography.

15. K. Wrightson, *English Society 1580–1680* (London, 1984), chap. 4, stresses the different experiences recorded by diarists and letter-writers and the importance of interpreting these in terms of economic status and individual temperament (or luck).

16. The difficulties of approaching this problem are discussed by Wrightson, as in note 15. See also R. Masek, "Women in the Age of Transition 1485–1714," in B. Kanner, ed., *The Women of England From Anglo-Saxon Times to the Present* (London, 1980), 138–82.

17. See G. Wekerle, R. Peterson, and D. Morley, eds., *New Space for Women* (Boulder, CO, 1980); and C. R. Stimpson et al., eds., *Women in the American City* (Chicago, 1981).

18. S. Ardener, "Ground Rules and Social Maps for Women: An Introduction," in *Women and Space* (Oxford, 1981).

19. The complex and extensive literature on this subject is summarized in Palliser, *The Age of Elizabeth,* as in note 5 above; see also J. H. Hexter, *Reappraisals in History* (Chicago, 1979).

20. See W. G. Hoskins, "The Rebuilding of Rural England 1570–1640," *Past and Present* 4 (Nov. 1953):44–59; and Girouard, *Life,* as in note 9 above.

21. M. Baxandall, *Painting and Experience in Fifteenth-Century Italy: A Primer in the Social History of Pictorial Style* (Oxford, 1972), esp. part 2.

22. For a detailed discussion of this point, see J. Berger, *Ways of Seeing* (Penguin Books, 1972).

23. E. Gombrich, *Art and Illusion,* 5th rev. ed. (Oxford, 1977).

24. Gombrich, *Art and Illusion,* 53.

25. Ibid.

26. E. Gombrich, "Zum Werke Giulio Romanos," *Jahrbuch der Kunsthistorisches Sammlung in Wien* 8 (1934); 79ff; and 9 (1935), 121ff.

27. For two different views on this question, one primarily psychological, the other semiotic, see K. C. Bloomer and C. W. Moore, *Body, Memory and Architecture* (New Haven and London, 1977) and U. Eco, "Function and Sign: Semiotics of Architecture," in *Structures Implicit and Explicit,* edited by J. Bryan and R. Sauer (Philadelphia, 1973).

28. The work of Lawrence Stone perhaps best exemplifies this genre.

See, for example, L. Stone and J. F. Stone, *An Open Elite? England 1540–1800* (Oxford, 1984).

Chapter 1

1. W. Camden, *Brittania*, trans. by E. Gibson (London, 1695), 482.

2. M. Girouard, *Life in the English Country House*, chaps. 2 and 3. See also L. Stone, *The Crisis of the Aristocracy* (Oxford, 1965), 547ff.

3. See D. Cressy, "Describing the Social Order of Elizabethan and Stuart England," *Literature and History* 3 (March 1976), 29–44, and L. Stone, "Social Mobility in England 1500–1700," in *Seventeenth-Century England: Society in an Age of Revolution*, edited by P. S. Seaver (New York, 1976), 26–70. In *The Age of Elizabeth: England Under the Late Tudors* (London, 1983), 69 ff., D. Palliser described how precedence among the gentry went to "knights whose military origin was fading"; his discussion of social mobility in the period (chap. 3) is excellent.

4. N. Hart, "State Control of Dress and Social Change in Pre-Industrial England," in *Trade, Government and Economy in Pre-Industrial England: Essays Presented to F. J. Fisher*, edited by D. C. Colman and A. H. Johns (London, 1976), 132–65.

5. R. A. Brown, *English Castles* (London, 1976). The use of rooms in medieval houses and castles is discussed by Girouard (as in note 2 above) and by P. A. Faulkener, "Castle Planning in the 14th Century," *Archaeological Journal* 120 (1963):215–35.

6. The household accounts from 1572 to 1575 (Mi A 57) are discussed below.

7. In the mid thirteenth century an estate at Willoughby-on-the-Wolds was purchased by Ralph Bugge, a merchant of Nottingham who changed his name to Willughby (or Willoughby; both spellings were used). Other principal acquisitions were by marriage. The first, in the early fourteenth century, was the marriage of Richard de Willughby to the daughter of Richard de Mortein, which brought the Nottinghamshire estates of Wollaton and Cossall. The second was the marriage of Hugh Willughby to Margaret Freville in ca. 1435, which brought estates in Warwickshire, including the manors of Middleton, Whitnash, and Wiken (near Coventry), among others. The first member of the family to live at Wollaton was Richard Willughby (d. 1471) who was buried at St. Leonard's church in the village. The most complete history of the family is R. S. Smith, "The Willoughbys of Wollaton 1500–1643, with special reference to mining in Nottinghamshire" (Ph.D diss., University of Nottingham, 1964). Much of the early history presented here is drawn from this excellent detailed account. See also J. C. Holt, "Willoughby Deeds," A *Medieval Miscellany for Doris Mary Stenton, Pipe Roll Society*, n.s. 26 (1962):167–75. In the Middleton Collection see Mi LM 13, "Notes by Francis Willoughby, F.R.S. on the history of his family."

8. *Middleton*, 327–87. See also A. Cameron, "Sir Henry Willoughby of Wollaton," *Transactions of the Thoroton Society of Nottinghamshire* 74 (1970):10ff.

9. *Middleton*, 132, 136, 140, 335, 510–11. This man died childless in 1548, leaving his lands to Sir Henry Willoughby.

10. For further information on Sir Hugh Willoughby, see Richard Hak-

luyt, *The Principal Navigations . . . of the English Nation*, vol. 1 (London, 1589), 59–70; E. G. R. Taylor, *Tudor Geography 1485–1583* (London, 1930); *Middleton*, 511; and DNB, "Hugh Willoughby."

11. *Middleton*, 518. Anne Grey was a Lady in Waiting to Mary of France (see note 19 below).

12. For Kett's Rebellion, see S. T. Bindoff, *Ket's Rebellion 1549* (London, 1949) and D. MacCulloch, "Kett's Rebellion in Context," *Past and Present* 84 (1979):36–59.

13. For enclosures see I. S. Leaden, ed., *The Domesday of Enclosures in Nottinghamshire, 1517, Thoroton Society Record Series*, vol. 2 (1904), 39ff, and Mi 177/137 (relating to Sir Francis Willoughby's enclosures). For early coal and wool profits see R. S. Smith, "The Willoughbys" (as in note 7 above), and J. U. Nef, *The Rise of the British Coal Industry*, 2 vols. (New York, 1932).

14. See G. E. Mingay, *The Gentry: The Rise and Fall of A Ruling Class* (London, 1976). For a balanced view of economic change in this period, see J. H. Hexter, "Storm over the Gentry," in *Reappraisals in History*, 2d ed. (Chicago, 1979) 71–116, and Palliser, *Age of Elizabeth* (as in note 3).

15. Sir Henry Willoughby's will is Mi 6/179/35a.

16. See J. Hurstfield, *The Queen's Wards: Wardship and Marriage under Elizabeth I* (Cambridge, 1958) and H. E. Bell, *An Introduction to the History and Records of the Court of Wards and Liveries* (London, 1953).

17. DNB, "Henry Grey."

18. J. Venn, *Alumni Cantabrigiensis* (London, 1922), part I, I, vi, and W. P. Baildon, ed., *Records of Lincolns Inn* (London, 1897). Mi A 31 records a payment of 1553 to "the clarke of the signett" for writing a seal of license for Thomas Willoughby to "goe over the seaez to the universitye of Parys to studye," but he does not seem to have gone since he is recorded at Lord Paget's in the same year.

19. *Middleton*, 520–21; Mi A 31, 32. The household is described in C. Goff, *A Woman of the Tudor Age: Katherine Willoughby Duchess of Suffolk* (New York, 1930) and E. Reed, *My Lady Suffolk: A Portrait of Catherine Willoughby, Duchess of Suffolk* (New York, 1963), esp. 204–5.

20. For the education of Lady Jane Grey, see R. Ascham, *The Schoolmaster, 1570*, edited by L. V. Ryan (Ithaca, 1967); J. Kamm, *Hope Deferred: Girls Education in English History* (London, 1965), chap. 3, gives a survey of the period.

21. Mi A 32.

22. See Friedman, "The Influence of Humanism on the Education of Girls and Boys in Tudor England," *The History of Education Quarterly* 25, nos. 1 and 2 (Spring/Summer 1985), 57–70. Both M. L. King, "Book-Lined Cells: Women and Humanism in the Early Italian Renaissance," in *Beyond Their Sex: Learned Women of the European Past*, edited by P. Labalme (New York, 1980), 66–90, and C. Jordan, "Feminism and the Humanists: The Case of Sir Thomas Elyot's *The Defense of Good Women*," *Renaissance Quarterly* 36, no. 2 (Summer 1983):181–201, contain excellent discussions of educational theory that served to reinforce accepted notions of male and female roles. The classic article on this issue is J. Kelly-Gadol, "Did Women Have a Renaissance?," in R. Bridenthal and C. Koonz, eds., *Becoming Visible: Women in European History* (New York, 1977), 137–64.

23. Mi A 31, 32. In Medley's will (Mi 7/183/12) he stipulates that his

books should be divided between his sons, except the English books, which would go to his wife.

24. See J. L. Vives, *The Instruction of A Christian Woman*, trans. by R. Hyrde (London, 1540). This was first published in 1523.

25. See below, chapter 3.

26. In vol. 3 of the *Lisle Letters*, edited by M. St. Clair Byrne (Chicago, 1981), 75ff, there is similar evidence to show the differential educations of children depending on their place in the family: the youngest son was trained for a career in diplomacy. See also L. Stone, "The Educational Revolution in England 1560–1640," *Past and Present* 28 (July 1964): 40–80, and J. H. Hexter, "The Education of the Aristocracy in the Renaissance," in *Reappraisals* (as in note 14), 45–70.

27. Mi A 32, f.36.

28. *Middleton*, 521, n.1. Medley was in the tower from 26 February 1554. His house at the Minories had been searched a month earlier by Bishop Gardiner, *Chronicle of Queen Mary*, Camden Society 66 (1850), 185.

29. *Middleton*, 521.

30. Mi A 31, f. 10r and Mi 6/171/8-9. See also *Middleton*, 523.

31. Mi A 32, f. 49. See also J. Nichols, *Progresses and Public Processions of Queen Elizabeth* (London, 1823), 12–31.

32. Mi A 32, ff. 41, 47, 54.

33. Mi A 32, ff. 54–57. The school at Walden is discussed by A. F. Leach, *English Schools at the Reformation 1546–48* (New York, 1896), 62–63, and J. Simon, *Education and Society in Tudor England* (Cambridge, 1966), 230. Francis Willoughby's schooling is discussed by T. W. Baldwin, *William Shakespeare's small Latine and lesse Greeke*, vol. 1 (Urbana, 1944), 375–79. See also K. Charlton, *Education in Renaissance England* (London, 1965), 93ff.

34. This emphasis on language and its effects is discussed by F. Caspari, *Humanism and the Social Order in Tudor England* (Chicago, 1954), 7ff.

35. Mi A 32, f. 65.

36. *Middleton*, 284, papers calendared by W. H. Stevenson as "Charges by Sir Francis Willoughby as Justice at the Quarter Sessions, noticeable for their Latin quotations and for their sententious style . . ." (MiO 2, 15–18).

37. Willoughby's notebook of lute music from ca. 1565 survives (Mi LM 16). Mi A 57, f.31v and *passim*.

38. *Middleton*, 528–29.

39. Mi A 32, f. 68. There were a number of Dr. Carrs in Cambridge in these years. T. Baldwin (as in note 33) maintains that the account refers to Nicholas Carr of Trinity. Others included Richard Carr, the Master of Magdalene College. See J. Mullinger, *The University of Cambridge* (London, 1873–74).

40. *Middleton*, 524.

41. Mi A 32, f. 24.

42. Mi 6/171/10 (custody of Francis Willoughby to Sir Francis Knollys).

43. Francis Willoughby's will of 1572 directs his executors to place his accounts at Jesus College, Cambridge, suggesting a possible connection. For Knollys, see DNB, "Francis Knollys."

44. Mi A 31, f.24r.

45. Mi 6/178/49; see also Mi 6/171/15: a license to assign custody of the ward.

46. *Middleton*, 525.

47. *Middleton*, 525–26.

48. For Littleton, see *Collins Peerage of England . . . augumented by Sir Egerton Brydges*, vol. 8 (London, 1812), 333; Victoria County History, *Worcestershire* (London, 1971), 327, 341, n. 41.

49. *Middleton*, 528.

50. Willoughby wrote that Littleton "required a very reasonable jointure and the settlement of but one-third part of his estate upon heirs male by her" (*Middleton*, 527).

51. See below, chapter 3. *Middleton*, 529, quotes a letter from Littleton apologizing for his failure to pay a sum he owed to Willoughby; this is the first indication of trouble.

52. *Middleton*, 527–28.

53. *Middleton*, 528. The letter was sent from Wilton.

54. Nichols, *Progresses*, vol. 1, xviii and 418ff.

55. Nichols, *Progresses*, vol. 1, 431–32.

56. Nichols, *Progresses*, vol. 1, 498.

57. See F. Yates, "Elizabethan Chivalry: The Romance of the Accession Day Tilts," *Journal of the Warburg and Courtauld Institutes* 20 (1957):4–25. This tradition and its relevance to architecture are discussed by M. Girouard, "Elizabethan Architecture and the Gothic Tradition," *Architectural History* 6 (1963):23–40. See also R. Strong, *The Cult of Elizabeth* (London, 1977). For Willoughby's fencing lessons see Mi A 57, f.6r.

58. Nichols, *Progresses*, vol. 1, 459.

59. *Middleton*, 538.

60. Ibid. Even the powerful Nicholas Bacon was unsettled by the prospect of a royal visit, writing to Burghley in haste to ask him what to do if the Queen visited his house; see Robert Tittler, *Nicholas Bacon: The Making of a Tudor Statesman* (London, 1976), 146–47.

61. W. C. Metcalfe, F.S.A., *A Book of Knights* (London, 1885), 129.

62. For a discussion of these terms and of Willoughby's investment activities, see Joan Thirsk, *Economic Policy and Projects: The Development of a Consumer Society in Early Modern England* (Oxford, 1978), 1–7, 27ff., 39.

63. R. H. Tawney, *The Agrarian Problem in the Sixteenth Century* (London, 1912), 192. For other investments made by Francis and Percival Willoughby, see Smith, "Sir Francis Willoughby's Ironworks 1570–1616," *Renaissance and Modern Studies* 11 (1967):90–140, and *idem*, "A Woad Growing Project at Wollaton in the 1580s," *Transactions of the Thoroton Society* 65 (1961):24–34, and *idem*, "Glass-making at Wollaton in the Early Seventeenth Century," *Transactions of the Thoroton Society* 66 (1962): 24–34.

64. R. S. Smith, "Huntingdon Beaumont Adventurer in Coal Mines," *Renaissance and Modern Studies* 1 (1957):115–53, esp. 119.

65. Nef (as in note 13), vol. 1, 59–60.

66. Mi 6/79/35a and Smith "Beaumont," 119–20.

67. Nef (as in note 13), vol. 2, 13. Willoughby attempted to purchase the Coleorton property in 1576 (see Smith, "Beaumont," 116).

68. *Middleton*, 494–95. See also Mi 165/92/7, a memorandum of ca. 1577 on the price of iron.

69. See R. S. Smith, "Sir Francis Willoughby's Ironworks" (as in note 63).

70. Smith, "The Willoughbys of Wollaton" (as in note 7), 46.

71. *Middleton*, 530.

72. For an overview of economic diversification and industrial production in this period, see C. G. A. Clay, *Economic Expansion and Social Change: England 1500–1700*, 2 vols. (Cambridge University Press, 1984), esp. vol. 2, chap. 8.

73. The episode is described in Smith "Woad" (as in note 63 above). The relevant mss. are Mi 5/165/97–126.

74. Thirsk, *Economic Policy*, 27–30.

75. Mi 165/5/121–22.

76. Mi 165/5/97. For the dye-house proposal, see Mi 165/5/105.

77. For the "great rebuilding," see W. G. Hoskins, "The Rebuilding of Rural England 1570–1640," *Past and Present* 4 (Nov. 1953):44–59 and R. Machin, "The Great Rebuilding: A Reassessment," *Past and Present* 77 (1977):33–58.

78. *Middleton*, 421, 432. See R. Strong, *The English Icon* (London, 1969) and J. W. Goodison, "George Gower, Serjeant Painter to Queen Elizabeth," *The Burlington Magazine* 90 (Sept. 1948):261–64.

79. *Middleton*, 432–33; in November 1574, the servant George Cam returned from London with over £16 worth of fabrics and sewing materials used for clothes for the couple, Lady Elizabeth's gentlewomen, and for the children (*Middleton*, 448–49.)

80. In 1577, an agent wrote to the Earl of Rutland, Willoughby's neighbor, to say that the Lord Chamberlain "was desirous to have [his] picture, which . . . Gower must deliver to him, though imperfect." H. M. C., *Rutland*, vol. 1, 111. For Lady Elizabeth's jewel, see D. Scarisbrick, "Trumpeting Tritons and Trinkets: Maritime Themes in English Jewelry," *Country Life* 6 (June 1985), 1621–23.

81. *Middleton*, 424, 440, 446, 447; see also Mi A 57, 6r, 35r and *passim*.

82. See E. K. Chambers, *The English Stage*, vol. 2 (Oxford, 1923), 92–95, 102, and 220–39.

83. See R. A. Fraser and N. Rabkin, eds., *Drama of the English Renaissance: The Tudor Period* (New York, 1976), 59.

84. See W. L. Woodfill, *Musicians in English Society from Elizabeth to Charles I* (Princeton, 1953), 72ff. The Willoughby accounts relating to music are published on 274–76.

85. *Middleton*, 538–40 and chapter 3 below.

86. *Middleton*, 544, 584. See also Mi O 2, and Mi O 16/7, which includes quotations from John Foxe's *Book of Martyrs* (London, 1570).

87. The shelf list, Mi I 17/1, has traditionally been dated to ca. 1660 and presumed to be in the hand of Francis Willoughby, F. R. S., Cassandra's father. Yet f.27 lists "Rays Synopsis methodicae stirpium," referring to either the first edition of 1690 or the second edition of 1696 listed in the Christie's catalogue. The large numbers of books on natural science dating from the mid seventeenth century suggest that Mi I 17/1 was drawn up when the libraries of Middleton and Wollaton were amalgamated in 1691–92. The reference to "a ms. of Mr. Willughby's Geograph" on f.21 suggests further that this list was drawn up by a librarian, perhaps Thomas Willoughby's tutor Dr. Mann.

88. See Mi O 16/7/1–3.

89. For Lumley, see *The Lumley Library*, edited by Sears Jayne and F. R. Johnson (London, 1956); for Dee, see F. A. Yates, *Theatre of the World* (London, 1969), chaps. 1 and 2. The ms. of the inventory is in the British Library (Harley 1879, ff. 20r–108r.)

90. See Sears Jayne, *Library Catalogues of the English Renaissance* (Berkeley and Los Angeles, 1956), *passim*.

91. *Middleton*, 433. For other references to books see, for example, *Middleton*, 534, where the servant called Squire recalls a conversation with Margaret Arundell preceded by "a little astronomicall talk, and [discussion] about mathematicall books in the Italian tongue." The price of books is discussed by F. R. Johnson, "Notes on English Retail Book Prices 1550–1640," *The Library* 5, no. 2 (September 1950), esp. 89–91. During this period ordinary books cost approximately one-half penny per sheet; illustrated books and music cost two or three pence per sheet.

92. *Lumley Library*, 11–12.

93. Jayne, *Library Catalogues*, 119. See also L. B. Wright, *Middle Class Culture in Elizabethan England* (Chapel Hill, 1938), 84ff.

94. Mi I 17/1, f.6. See chap. 2 below.

95. Lucy Gent, *Picture and Poetry 1560–1620* (Leamington Spa, 1981), Appendix, esp. 78–86.

96. J. Alfred Gotch, "The Renaissance in Northamptonshire," *Transactions of the RIBA*, n.s. 6 (1890):87–114. The correspondence relating to Burghley House is listed in an appendix to this article.

97. Quoted by Conyers Read, *Lord Burghley and Queen Elizabeth* (London, 1960), 216.

98. Ibid. See E. S. Hartshorne, *Memorials of Holdenby* (London, 1868), 13–16.

99. Historical Manuscripts Commission, *Tresham Papers*, vol. 55, part 3 (London, 1904).

100. *Tresham Papers*, xxxiv.

101. For tombs, see N. Llewellyn, "John Weever and English Funeral Monuments of the Sixteenth and Seventeenth Centuries (Ph.D. diss., University of London, The Warburg Institute, 1983).

102. See L. Gent, *Picture and Poetry*, Appendix.

103. *Tresham Papers*, lv.

104. J. Summerson, *Architecture in Britain, 1530–1830* (Harmondsworth, 1970), 42–48. See also W. G. Clark-Maxwell, "Sir William Sharrington's Work at Lacock, Sudeley and Dudley," *Archaeological Journal* 70 (1913):176–82 and W. Simpson, "Dudley Castle: The Renaissance Buildings," *Archaeological Journal* 101 (1944):119–25. See also Summerson, "The Building of Theobalds 1564–1585," *Archaeologia* 97 (1959):107–26. For Hill Hall, see P. J. Drury, "'A Fayre House Buylt by Sir Thomas Smith': The Development of Hill Hall, Essex, 1557–81," *Journal of the British Archaeological Association* 136 (1983):98–123. Drury shows that Smith was the author of the design and that foreign craftsmen were used in the execution of ornamental details.

105. Girouard, *Life in the English Country House*, chap. 1.

106. See Girouard, "Elizabethan Architecture," as in note 57.

107. J. Hodson, "The First Wollaton Hall," *Transactions of the Thoroton Society* 72 (1968):59–67. The relevant inventories are Mi I 2; 3/1; 36 and 37.

108. Oliver, *Collections Illustrating the History of the Catholic Religion in Cornwall, Devon, Dorset, Somerset, Wiltshire and Gloucester* (London, 1857), 75–77, and J. A. Williams, *Catholic Recusancy in Wiltshire* (Catholic Record Society, 1968). Matthew Arundell's son was a Catholic whose activities were a source of embarassment to his parents at Court.

109. Girouard, *Smythson*, chap. 2.

110. Girouard, *Smythson*, chap. 1.

111. Girouard, "Elizabethan Holdenby," *Country Life* (Oct. 18, 1979), 1286–89; and (Oct. 25, 1979), 1398–1401.

112. D. Durant, "Wollaton Hall—A Rejected Plan," *Transactions of the Thoroton Society* 76 (1972): 13–17.

113. *Middleton*, 429 (Mi A 57).

114. For family history and antiquarianism in the period, see J. G. Mann, "Instances of Antiquarianism in Medieval and Renaissance Architecture," *Archaeological Journal* 89 (1932): 254–74. See also M. Aston, "English Ruins and English History: The Dissolution and the Sense of the Past," *Journal of the Warburg and Courtauld Institutes* 36 (1973): 231–55.

115. Mi 2/76/3–16, April 1626.

Chapter 2

1. *Middleton*, 565–6 [Mi LM, 128–29].

2. A drawing by her in the Stowe Collection at the Huntington Library was identified by C. H. Baker as Throseby Hall [STB Box 1 (45)]. See C. H. and M. I. Baker, *James Brydges, First Duke of Chandos* (London, 1949), 410.

3. Sheila M. Strauss, *A Short History of Wollaton and Wollaton Hall* (Nottingham, 1979), 44. Strauss reports that on either side of the dovecote's door are the initials "FW," spelled out in darker colored bricks. An existing cottage at Wollaton village may also be a part of the old manor house complex.

4. These include inventories (Mi I 2, 1550) and accounts (Mi A 53, 56, 57, 77), which have been studied by J. H. Hodson, "The First Wollaton Hall," *Transactions of the Thoroton Society* 72 (1968): 59–67. The material presented here draws heavily on his reconstruction of the hall.

5. Hodson, 59. The first member of the family to live at Wollaton was Richard Willoughby; he died in 1471 and was buried at St. Leonard's Church.

6. Hodson, 62.

7. See R. W. Brunskill, *Illustrated Handbook of Vernacular Architecture* (London, 1970).

8. Hodson, 62. See Mi I 2 (published in *Middleton*, 474–85). See also Girouard, *Life in the English Country House*, 54.

9. *Middleton*, 478.

10. Girouard, *Life*, 32–40, discusses the traditional arrangements of halls and service areas in medieval houses.

11. *Middleton*, 474–75.

12. *Middleton*, 483.

13. For the orders see *Middleton*, 538–41; for the account see *Middleton*, 421–51 (Mi A 57); for the list of household members see *Middleton*, 541–42. The letters can be found throughout Cassandra's *Account* (*Middleton*, 504–610 and Mi LM 26).

14. Household orders and their implications for architecture are extensively treated in Girouard, *Life*, chaps. 2–4; the principal documents are listed and annotated in an appendix to that work. The most relevant for the present discussion are: "R. B.," *Some Rules and Orders for the Government of the House of an Earle, set down by R. B. at the instant request of his loving frende M. L.* (hereafter as "R. B.") (London, 1821); Joseph Banks, ed., "A Breviate Touching the Order and Government of a Nobleman's House, etc." (hereafter as Banks, *Order*), *Archaeologia* 13 (1800): 315–89, S. D. Scott, ed., "A

Book of Orders and Rules of Anthony Viscount Montague in 1595 (hereafter as *Montague*), *Sussex Archaeological Collections* 7 (1853–54):173–212; see also Thomas Percy, ed., *The Regulations and Establishment of the Household of Henry Algernon Percy, the Fifth Earl of Northumberland at his Castle of Wresill and Lekinfield in Yorkshire* (hereafter as *Northumberland*) (London, 1770).

15. See Mi A 57, ff. 34r and 76v; he is not to be confused with Geoffry Fox, an officer in the household during the 1580s and 1590s (see *Middleton*, 452, 574, 580). There is a reference in Sir Henry Willoughby's will to "George Willoughby, alias Fox, his [father's] bastard"; Robert and Geoffry Fox may thus have been cousins of Sir Francis.

16. According to R. B., the usher of the hall had two parts of the profit of the box in the hall, the groom one-third; in the great chamber it was divided between the yeoman and groom, "but the box in the withdrawing chamber or gallery belongeth to the groomes of the bedchamber, who are to keepe faire these rooms" (26–27).

17. *Middleton*, 533–35, 547–48, 551–53. For a discussion of patronage and its effects on social systems, see Werner L. Gundersheimer, "Patronage in the Renaissance: An Exploratory Approach," in *Patronage in the Renaissance*, edited by G. F. Lytle and S. Orgel (Princeton, 1981):3–26.

18. For pedigrees, see G. W. Marshall, ed., *The Visitations of the County of Nottingham in the Years 1569 and 1614*, Harleian Society 55 (London, 1871); *Visitation of the County of Warwick in the Year 1619 taken by William Camden*, edited by John Fetherston, Harleian Society 12 (London, 1877); and *Visitation of the County of Warwick in 1682 and 1683*, edited by W. Harry Rylands, Harleian Society (London, 1911).

19. *Middleton*, 330–88, 396, 399, 524. Francis Willoughby's great-aunt Alice had married a Draycot and her bedchamber at Wollaton was listed in the inventory of 1550: Mi I 2.

20. For Trussell pedigree see *Visitation of . . . Nottingham*, 28.

21. For Cludd pedigree, see *Visitation of . . . Nottingham*, 103–4; for Fisher see *Visitation of Warwick*, 32.

22. "R.B.," 6.

23. "R.B.," 11.

24. See chapter 3.

25. See *Middleton*, 374–88.

26. *Middleton*, 432, 440, 444, 447.

27. *Middleton*, 543.

28. Mi A 57, 1r, 5r, 46r, 48r, 69r (Mrs. Banister, 74v, 77r, 82v).

29. M. Pelling and C. Webster, "Medical Practitioners," in *Health, Medicine and Mortality in the Sixteenth Century*, edited by C. Webster (London, 1979), 176–77, 327–28; and D. Power, "Notes on Early Portraits of John Banister, of William Harvey and the Barber-Surgeons Visceral Lecture in 1581," *Proceedings of the Royal Society of Medicine* 6 (1912):18–35. See also DNB, "John Banister."

30. *Middleton*, 437, 442, 447.

31. "R. B.," 3–4.

32. The only women listed by "R. B.," other than the lady of the house, are the laundresses; the Northumberland regulations list two "rokkers" in the nursery, "two chambermaids for my Lady," and three gentlewomen.

33. See F. Heal, "The Idea of Hospitality in Early Modern England," *Past and Present* 102 (February 1984):66–93.

34. M. Chaytor, "Household and Kinship: Ryton in the late 16th and early 17th Centuries," *History Workshop* 10 (1980):25–60, esp. 50.

35. E. K. Chambers, *The Elizabethan Stage* (Oxford, 1923), 2 vols.

36. See A. Kussmaul, *Servants in Husbandry in Early Modern England* (Cambridge University Press, 1981), 5–6, 31–37.

37. *Middleton*, 540–41.

38. "R. B.," 9.

39. Banks, *Order*, 323. In Ellesmere 1179 and 1180 (Huntington Library), by contrast, the master and his wife seem to have equal authority in the household.

40. *Middleton*, 423 (Christmas 1572), 432–33, 446.

41. See, for example, Mi A 32, where Margaret Willoughby's education is described. Women's education is discussed at length in Friedman, "The Influence of Humanism in the Education of Boys and Girls in Tudor England," *History of Education Quarterly* (Spring/Summer, 1985), 57–70. See also R. Kelso, *Doctrine for the Lady of the Renaissance* (Urbana, 1956), and S. W. Hull, *Chaste, Silent and Obedient: English Books for Women 1475–1640* (San Marino, 1984).

42. J. H. Markland, "Instructions of Henry Percy, ninth Earl of Northumberland to his son Algernon Percy . . ." (hereafter as "Instructions"), *Archaeologia* 27 (1838):306–58, esp. 318.

43. "Instructions," 330–31.

44. "Instructions," 340.

45. See chapter 1 above, esp. notes 7 and 63.

46. *Middleton*, 533, where Lady Arundell assures her brother that the reason he was not appointed a justice for Nottinghamshire was that he was to serve in Warwickshire (1572). See Mi O 2, 15, 16/7, papers relating to Willoughby's tenure as a justice. W. Stevenson, in his report to the Historical Manuscripts Commission, deemed these "noticeable for their Latin quotations and their sententious style" (*Middleton*, 284). See also *Middleton*, 320, for Willoughby's papers as Sheriff of Warwickshire.

47. T. Fuller, *The Worthies of England* (London, 1662), 312. See also *Middleton*, 158–59.

48. See B. L. Joseph, *Shakespeare's Eden* (London, 1971), 121 ff.

49. *Middleton*, 423.

50. Hodson, 63.

Chapter 3

1. Lansdowne mss. 84, nos. 70 and 106; Add Mss. 25085; and Mi 2/75/3-1 through 3-10. Their suit in Chancery was dismissed in 1619 (P.R.O.: C 78/215/6).

2. *Middleton*, 525–26, 529.

3. *Middleton*, 525–27.

4. *Middleton*, 529.

5. *Middleton*, 530.

6. For Buxton, see John Jones, *The Benefit of the auncient Bathes of Buckstones* (London, 1572). Shrewsbury's house is described on f. Aiiv. Lady Elizabeth continued to visit the baths there throughout her life: in 1589, Francis Willoughby wrote to the Countess of Shrewsbury requesting the use of her horse-litter so that his invalid wife could travel from Buxton to

Wollaton (Folger Library; Cavendish Mss., xd. 428[126]). For precepts on marriage, see L. Jardine, *Still Harping on Daughters: Women and Drama in the Age of Shakespeare* (London and Totowa, NJ, 1983), chap. 4.; and K. M. Davies, "The Sacred Condition of Equality: How Original Were Puritan Doctrines of Marriage?" *Social History* 5 (May 1977):563–80.

7. *Middleton*, 536–37.

8. *Middleton*, 532.

9. Jardine, *Still Harping*, chap. 4, and I. Maclean, *The Renaissance Notion of Women* (Cambridge University Press, 1980), esp. chap. 3.

10. T. Bentley, *The Monument of Matrons*, vol. 3 (London, 1582), 69. A copy of this book was in Willoughby's library.

11. For a thorough overview of writings on women in this period, see R. Kelso, *Doctrine for the Lady of the Renaissance* (Urbana, 1956) and S. W. Hull, *Chaste, Silent and Obedient: English Books for Women 1475–1640* (San Marino, CA, 1982). A bibliography of treatises on marriage is given by Davies, "The Sacred Condition of Equality," 564 n.3. See also J. K. Yost, "The Value of Married Life for the Social Order in the Early English Renaissance," *Societas* 6 (1976):25–39.

12. Quoted by D. Durant, *Bess of Hardwick: Portrait of an Elizabethan Dynast* (London, 1977), 126.

13. Durant, *Bess of Hardwick*, 126–27.

14. H. Smith, *A Preparative to Marriage* (London, 1591), 64–65.

15. Durant, *Bess of Hardwick* (as in note 12), esp. 136–45.

16. HMC, *Rutland*, vol. 1, 188–89. Disputes between Bess and her husband over property and control of the household came to the attention of the Queen: see Lansdowne 44, nos. 12 and 13; Lansdowne 46, no. 46. Ironically, Willoughby was named to the commission (Dec. 1585) which heard evidence on behalf of the Crown (*Cal. S. P. Dom*, vol. 2, 290).

17. See M. Chaytor, "Household and Kinship: Ryton in the Late 16th and Early 17th Centuries," *History Workshop* 10 (1980):25–60, for discussion of the issue of the relationship between a woman's (and particularly a widow's) sexuality and control of her property.

18. For these cases and an extended treatment of property transfer in the period, see B. Coward, "Disputed Inheritances: Some Difficulties of the Nobility in the Late Sixteenth and Early Seventeenth Centuries," *Bulletin of the Institute of Historical Research* 44 (1971):110, 194 ff. See also M. Slater, "The Weightiest Business: Marriage in an Upper Gentry Family in Seventeenth Century England," *Past and Present* 72 (August 1976):25–54.

19. See Coward, "Disputed Inheritances" (as in note 18 above); L. Bonfield, *Marriage Settlements, 1601–1740: The Adoption of the Strict Settlement*, (Cambridge, 1983); F. Pollack and W. Maitland, *The History of English Law*, 2d ed., vol. 2 (Cambridge, 1968), 394–437; and Pearl Hogrefe, "Legal Rights of Tudor Women and Their Circumvention by Men and Women," *Sixteenth-Century Journal* 3 (1972):97–105. A. W. B. Simpson, *An Introduction to the History of the Land Law* (Oxford, 1961) is also helpful.

20. Hogrefe, "Legal Rights," 103–4. *The Diary of Lady Anne Clifford*, edited by V. Sackville-West (New York, 1928), chronicles her lifelong struggle to secure her inheritance. The case of her parents, the third Earl and Countess of Cumberland, is also mentioned (12–14). The number of couples involved in marital disputes is obviously not subject to statistical analysis. R. Greaves, *Society and Religion in Elizabethan England* (Minneapolis, 1981), 264–65, presents a list of cases in which the Queen became in-

volved: these include the Earl of Worcester (1563), the Earl of Derby (1568), and the Earl of Shrewsbury (1585). See also L. Stone, *The Crisis of the Aristocracy* (Oxford, 1965), 660–62.

21. Mi 5/168/70, 71, 77, 79.

22. *Middleton*, 531, 543.

23. *Middleton*, 543.

24. *Middleton*, 556.

25. *Middleton*, 532.

26. *Middleton*, 535–36.

27. *Middleton*, 541–42.

28. *Middleton*, 534–35.

29. Mi C 5, reprinted in *Middleton*, 152–55. For a biography of Bess, see Durant, *Bess of Hardwick* (as in note 12). The Marmion family were related to the Willoughbys. The writer's grandfather, Henry Marmion, was a bailiff on the estates in the 1530s (*Middleton*, 313–14).

30. *Middleton*, 152–54.

31. *Middleton*, 154.

32. William Wentworth, "Advice to His Son," in *Wentworth Papers*, edited by J. P. Cooper, Camden Society, 4th ser., vol. 12 (1973), 9–24, esp. 15.

33. Wentworth, "Advice," 16.

34. Wentworth, "Advice," 21.

35. J. M. Markland, "Instructions of Henry Percy ninth Earl of Northumberland to his son Algernon Percy," *Archaeologia* 27 (1838): 306–58, esp. 337.

36. Wentworth, "Advice," 20.

37. *Middleton*, 546–47.

38. *Middleton*, 547.

39. *Middleton*, 547–48.

40. Stowe Ms., STB Box 2(2), Notebook I, f. 22v; an edited description appears in Mi LM 26 and *Middleton*, 547. Henry Percy (1609) describes similar behavior and suggests some responses: see Markland, "Instructions" (as in note 35), esp. 334–35.

41. *Middleton*, 549–50.

42. *Middleton*, 552. Many couples (like the Willoughbys and the Shrewsburys) separated informally: Lady Anne Clifford recorded that her mother, the Countess of Cumberland, was received with the Court at her father's Grafton estates, but was not acknowledged as the mistress of the household (*Diary*, 10).

43. *Middleton*, 550.

44. *Middleton*, 563–64 and Lansdowne 46 no. 31, f. 61v.

45. Lansdowne 46 no. 31, f. 61v. Willoughby's reply and Lady Elizabeth's next attempt at reconciliation are in letters nos. 32 and 33.

46. Lansdowne 46 no. 31, f. 61r; this is paraphrased by Cassandra (*Middleton*, 564). The claim is repeated in Lansdowne 46 no. 33. A loose slip of paper among Cassandra Willoughby's notes and early drafts for her *Account* in the Huntington Library records the following: "William Deverell alias Willoughby son of Katherine Deverell and as she hath confessed him, ye son of Sir FW, knt of Notts, baptized, ye 4th day of March 1584. Copy out of the Register of Laughton in ye Morthing, York, and attested by Robert Barnar, Vicr" [STB Box 2(2)]. No mention is made of this document in the *Account* or elsewhere.

47. Lansdowne 101, no. 41.

48. *Middleton,* 553.

49. See B. Harris, "Marriage Sixteenth-Century Style: Elizabeth Stafford and the Third Duke of Norfolk," *Journal of Social History* 15 (Spring 1982): 371–82, where the wife is forced out of the house for her "unreasonable" objections to her husband's infidelity.

50. See I. Maclean, *The Renaissance Notion of Women* (as in note 9), esp. the conclusion; and Jardine, *Still Harping, passim.* The issue of social mobility is taken up by Stone in his "Social Mobility in England 1500–1700," in *Seventeenth Century Society in an Age of Revolution,* edited by P. S. Seaver (New York, 1976), 26–70. See also D. Cressy, "Describing the Social Order of Elizabethan and Stuart England," *Literature and History* 3 (March 1976): 29–44; J. H. Hexter, "The Education of the Aristocracy in the Renaissance," *Reappraisals in History,* 2d ed. (Chicago, 1979), 45–70; and L. Stone, "The Educational Revolution in England," *Past and Present* 28 (1964): 41–80.

51. In a letter of 1578 excerpted by Cassandra Willoughby (*Middleton,* 545–46) Lyttleton wrote to tell Elizabeth not to come to him any more for she had "forgot the duty of a daughter to him" and that he would "forget her as his daughter in every thing." In a surviving letter to her father (Lansdowne 46 no. 30), she pleads with him to take her back into his favor.

52. *Middleton,* 557–58.

53. *Middleton,* 555–56.

54. *Middleton,* 560.

55. Mi C 17.

56. For Dorothy Willoughby, see *Middleton,* 585–92.

57. *Middleton,* 592–98. For Spencer, see M. E. Finch, "The Wealth of Five Northamptonshire Families," *Northamptonshire Record Society* 30 (1956): esp. 38–65.

58. *Middleton,* 599–603. The couple eventually eloped in 1590, and they were disowned by Sir Francis as a result. She had to beg her father to allow them £ 40 a year. Winifred Willoughby's letters reveal the very different circumstances in which the sisters found themselves. In a letter of 1606 written to her sister Bridget, for example, she asks whether her daughter Bess might be considered "handsome enough" to wait upon her more fortunate cousin, Bridget's daughter.

59. *Middleton,* 603–7.

60. M. MacDonald, *Mystical Bedlam: Madness, Anxiety and Healing in Seventeenth Century England* (Cambridge, 1981), 73–74, 98–104, discusses the psychological pressures on women and suggests that this resulted in the far greater proportion of women than men (2:1) among the patients of the physician Richard Napier.

61. See L. Stone, *The Family, Sex and Marriage in England 1500–1800* (London, 1977), 136 ff.

62. *Middleton,* 536.

63. Mi LM 26, f. 77.

64. R. Burton, *The Anatomy of Melancholy,* vol. 2 (London, 1622), ii, 3. I am grateful to Nigel Llewellyn for pointing this out to me.

65. See Mi LM 26, f. 135v–136r.

Chapter 4

1. Robert Smythson's career is discussed in detail by Mark Girouard in his *Robert Smythson and the Elizabethan Country House* (New Haven and London, 1983). This book supersedes his *Robert Smythson and the Architecture of the Elizabethan Era* (London, 1966). My own treatment of Smythson owes much to Dr. Girouard's research; wherever possible, specific information and ideas are credited in these notes.

2. See Girouard, "New Light on Longleat: Allen Maynard, A French Sculptor in England in the Sixteenth Century," *Country Life* 120 (1956): 594–97.

3. For English use of pattern books, see John Summerson, *Architecture in Britain 1530–1830*, 5th ed. (Harmondsworth, 1970). Lucy Gent, *Picture and Poetry 1560–1620: Relations Between Literature and the Visual Arts in the English Renaissance* (Leamington Spa, 1981) is also very useful for its treatment of patron's libraries. Frances Yates's *Theatre of the World* (London, 1969), 1–19 probably overestimates the extent to which craftsmen and artisans used printed reference works. Nevertheless, her discussion of John Dee's preface to Henry Billingsley's translation of Euclid's *Elements of Geometry* (1570) presents an important perspective on this question.

4. See Girouard, *Life in the English Country House* (New Haven and London, 1978), chap. 4.

5. The point is often made in the literature. One of the more interesting applications of the resulting analysis is by Rudolf Wittkower in "English Neoclassicism and the Vicissitudes of Palladio's *Quattro Libri*," in *Palladio and Palladianism* (New York, 1974), 73–94.

6. See, for example, M. Baxandall, *The Limewood Sculptors of Renaissance Germany* (New Haven and London, 1980).

7. For Palladio, see Deborah Howard, "Four Centuries of Literature on Palladio," *Journal of the Society of Architectural Historians* (hereafter as *JSAH*) 39 (1980):224–41; and James S. Ackerman, *Palladio*, 2d ed. (Harmondsworth, 1976). Among the most innovative treatments, Howard Burns et al., *Andrea Palladio 1508–1580: The Portico and the Farmyard* (London, 1975) stands out for its pioneering use of social and economic history. For vernacular and traditional influence in Palladio's villa designs, see M. Tafuri, "Committenza e tipologia nelle ville palladiane," *Bollettino del Centro Internazionale di storia dell'Architettura* (hereafter as *BCISA*) 11 (1969):65–71; and M. Rosci, "Forme e funzioni delle ville venete pre-palladiane," *L'Arte*, n.s. 1 (1968):25–54. Volume 11 of the *BCISA* contains many valuable essays on the history of the villa and its typology. See also J. Ackerman, "The Geopolitics of Venetian Architecture in the Time of Titian," in *Titian, His World and His Legacy*, edited by David Rosand, (New York, 1982), 41–71.

8. See especially D. Lewis, *The Drawings of Andrea Palladio* (Washington, D.C., 1981).

9. In his *Painting in Cinquecento Venice: Titian, Veronese, Tintoretto* (New Haven and London, 1982), 28, David Rosand briefly touches on this aspect of workshop practice in Venice. Drawings also appear in the wills of English stonemasons: see, for example, Mrs. K. A. Esdaile, "The Part Played by Refugee Sculptors in England 1600–1750," *Proceedings of the Huguenot Society* 18 (1949):254–62, where William Cure's legacy of "plots and models" is discussed.

10. The complicated publication history of Serlio's treatise is explained in W. Dinsmoor, "The Literary Remains of Sebastiano Serlio," *Art Bulletin*

24 (1942): part 1, 55–91; part 2, 113–54. For Palladio's debt to Serlio, see G. C. Argan, "Sebastiano Serlio," *L'Arte* 35 (1932):198–99, and Ackerman, *Palladio*, 24–25.

11. For Serlio in France, see M. N. Rosenfeld, *Sebastiano Serlio on Domestic Architecture* (New York, 1978), 17–60, and F. Schreiber, *Die Franzosische Renaissance-Architektur und die Poggio Reale-variationen des Sebastiano Serlio* (Halle, 1938).

12. Traditional castle planning and its connection to 16th-century central planning is discussed at length by N. Pevsner in "Double Profile: A Reconsideration of the Elizabethan Style as Seen at Wollaton," *Architectural Review* 107 (March 1950):147–53. For background, see S. Von Moos, *Turm und Bollwerk* (Zurich, 1979). See also A. Chastel, "La villa en France au XVIe siècle," *BCISA* 11 (1969):255–62.

13. Illustrated in Rosenfeld, *On Domestic Architecture* (as in note 11 above).

14. Rosenfeld, *Serlio*, 42 ff., 51–53; see also C. K. Lewis, *The Villa Giustinian at Roncade* (New York, 1977). Serlio's influence on Palladio's early villas is discussed by Rosenfeld, *Serlio*, 69; see also M. Rosci, *Il trattato di archittetura di Sebastiano Serlio* (Milano, 1967), 32–35.

15. For the influence of the Low Countries and Germany, see H.-R. Hitchcock, *Netherlandish Scrolled Gables* (New York, 1980) and idem, *German Renaissance Architecture* (Princeton, 1981).

16. The drawings were catalogued and published by M. Girouard in *Architectural History* 5 (1962).

17. For an overview of garden design in the Elizabethan period, see R. Strong, *The Renaissance Garden in England* (London, 1969).

18. See Girouard, *Smythson*, 115–42.

19. In Ackerman's "Sources of the Renaissance Villa," *Acts of the XXth International Congress on the History of Art* 2 (1963):6–18, he described the sources of this type. For an updated bibliography see Ackerman, "Geopolitics" (as in note 7), p. 67 n. 22. Further discussion is included in C. Frommel, *Die Farnesina und Peruzzis architectonisches Fruhwerke* (Berlin, 1961).

20. Girouard, *Smythson*, 88–107.

21. The influence of de Vries is clear in nos. I/25 (1) through (7) in the Girouard catalogue. See also J. Vredeman de Vries, *Das Erst Buch*, 1565, and *Variae Architecturae Formae*, 1563, as noted by Girouard, *Smythson*, 90.

22. The drawing, Mi DMF 11, was originally published by D. N. Durant, "Wollaton Hall—A Rejected Plan," *Transactions of the Thoroton Society* 76 (1972):13–16. It is illustrated, with the plan from Du Cerceau, by Girouard (*Smythson*, figs. 56 and 57).

23. See Summerson, *Architecture*, 48. Variants published by Du Cerceau include nos. 36 and 44 in the *Livre d'architecture*, 1559. The influence of Italy, and specifically of Leonardo, is discussed by C. Pedretti, *Leonardo da Vinci: The Royal Palace at Romarantin* (Cambridge, 1972) and L. Heydenreich, "Leonardo da Vinci, Architect of Francis I," *Burlington Magazine* 94 (1952): 277–84. See also Rosenfeld, *Serlio* (as in note 13).

24. See Girouard, *Smythson*, 97–100, and Pevsner, "Double Profile," as in note 12.

25. A. C. Wood, ed., *The Continuation of the History of the Willoughby Family by Cassandra Duchess of Chandos* (Eton, Windsor, 1958), 134 (Mi LM 27, 148–49).

26. The use of the hall and other rooms is discussed in chapter 5.

27. There is a parallel between Smythson's reinterpretation of his sources and Palladio's own treatment of North Italian precedents. See R. Cevese, *Ville della provincia in Vicenza* (Milan, 1972); G. Mazzotti, *Palladian and Other Venetian Villas* (Rome, 1966), esp. 79–80, and M. Kubelik, *Die Villa in Veneto: Zur typologischen Entwicklung im Quattrocento* (Kastanienbaum, 1977), esp. vol. 1, 1491–92, and vol. 2, figs. 1–6.

28. See A. Palladio, *I quattro libri dell'architettura* (Venice, 1570), 65, and *passim*.

29. Mezzanines are mentioned in Palladio's description of the Villa Thiene at Cicogna (*Quattro libri*, 62), but it is improbable that Smythson paid much attention to the text, which he would in any case have been unable to read without the help of Willoughby or another translator.

30. See "The Book of Architecture of John Thorpe in Sir John Soane's Museum," edited by John Summerson, *Walpole Society* 40 (1966).

31. Also seen in contemporary examples at Kenilworth and Kirby, built in the 1570s.

32. Summerson, *Architecture*, 528–29. See also Stewart Cruden, *The Scottish Castle* (Edinburgh, 1960) and D. Thomson, *Renaissance Paris* (University of California Press, 1984), 66–67. According to Thomson, these were often used as private studies or chambers.

33. See Girouard, *Smythson*, 104–7, for the sources of the design.

34. See W. H. Hart, "The Parliamentary Surveys of Richmond, Wimbledon, and Nonsuch in the County of Surrey, AD 1649," *Surrey Archaeological Collections* 5 (1871):75–156, esp. 143 and 144. Cassandra Willoughby's *Diary* in the Shakespeare Birthplace Trust records her visit to the "Prospect Room" at Worksop.

35. See C. Wilkinson, "The New Professionalism in the Renaissance," and J. Wilton-Ely, "The Rise of the Professional Architect in England," in *The Architect: Chapters in the History of the Profession*, edited by S. Kostoff (New York, 1977), 124–60, 180–208.

36. A facsimile was published in 1922 with an informative introduction by L. Weaver.

37. Shute, *Architecture*, f. Bii v.

38. For workshop practice, see D. Knoop and G. P. Jones, *The Medieval Mason* (Manchester, 1935), chaps. 3, 5, 7.

39. The Wollaton account books for building expenses are incomplete (see Appendix B). They are catalogued as follows:
March 1582–March 1583: Mi A 60/1
November 1584–November 1585: Mi A 60/3
March 1586–March 1587: Mi A 60/5
April 1587–March 1588: Mi A 60/6
March 1588–November 1588: Mi A 60/7
Summary of household payments including building 1583: Mi A 60/2
Summary of payments 1584–85: Mi A 60/4
Another account book that lists building expenses at the new hall in 1591 is Mi A 70. For Smythson, see Mi A 60/3, f. 7r (Dec. 1584) and 9v; Mi A 60/5, f. 6v, 7r, 8r, and *passim*. The building accounts are discussed in detail by P. E. Rossell, "The Building of Wollaton Hall 1580–88," 2 vols. (M.A. thesis, University of Sheffield, 1957). See also Girouard, *Smythson*, 87–88.

40. The wages of the highest paid masons might run between fifteen and twenty pounds per year. Often this was supplemented by room and board on the site. For comparison, the yearly allowance of Lady Elizabeth Willoughby

was £ 200, a sum she complained of bitterly. See M. Airs, *The Making of the English Country House* (London, 1979), part 4, and E. H. Phelps Brown and S. V. Hopkins, "Seven Centuries of Building Wages," *Economica*, n.s. 22 (1955): 195–206, and 23 (1956): 296–314.

41. See Mi A 60/3, f. 20v, 29r; Mi A 60/5, f. 5v, 6v. Styles also appears in the will of John Hill (or Hills) (1592), a master mason who worked closely with Smythson throughout his career (Girouard, *Smythson*, 308 n. 15).

42. Mi 5/165/129.

43. Rossell, *Wollaton*, vol. 1, 24; Girouard, *Smythson*, 166–68. He also signed an inventory of bedding [Mi I, 8 (iv)] in 1596.

44. Mi 6/171/56.

45. The career of John Smythson is treated in Girouard, *Smythson*, chaps. 5–7.

46. This occurs throughout the account books. He is among the most consistent workers on the site.

47. See Mi A 60/1, f. 34v for an example of a task letter to these masons.

48. See B. Stallybrass, "Bess of Hardwick's Buildings and Building Accounts," *Archaeologia* 64 (1912–13): 347–98, for a detailed discussion of the Hardwick craftsmen. For Accres at Hardwick, see Girouard, *Smythson*, 147.

49. Girouard, "Elizabethan Chatsworth," *Country Life* 22 (November 1973): 1668–72.

50. The plasterers first appear in 1586–87 (Mi A 60/5, *passim*).

51. For Ragg, see Stallybrass, "Hardwick," Appendix 2. For Jackson, see Geoffrey Beard, *Decorative Plasterwork in Britain* (London, 1975), 17 n. 100. The original charter is in the Guildhall Library.

52. See the summary of the accounts for 1584–85: Mi A 60/4, and Mi A 60/5, f. 11v, 14r, 22r, and *passim*.

53. He is named in Mi A 60/5, f. 17r, and Mi A 70 (205), f. 16v, and elsewhere intermittently between January and March of 1592.

54. Mi A 60/5, f. 84r ff., esp. 23r; and Mi 60/6 and 7, *passim*.

55. See HMC, Rutland, vol. 2, 351, and vol. 4, 404–5. See also E. Auerbach, *Tudor Artists* (London, 1954), 177, and W. A. D. Englefield, *The History of the Painter-Stainers Company of London* (London, 1923), 57.

56. HMC, *Rutland*, vol. 1, 147; 294–96.

57. Rossell, *Wollaton*, vol. 1, 66, counted the names of only six masons and two "layers" in the registers of local parishes.

58. This is discussed in an unpublished Ph.D. dissertation by N. Llewellyn, "John Weever and the English Funeral Monuments of the Sixteenth and Seventeenth Centuries" (Warburg Institute, University of London, 1983). See also E. Mercer, *English Art, 1553–1625* (Oxford, 1962), part 6, and M. Whinney, *Sculpture in Britain* (Harmondsworth, 1964), chap. 3.

59. See Mi A 60/1, f. 34r., 35r., where Lovell is paid £ 30 at "his going to London" in September and, in December, for two stories of carved stone. This pattern of substantial payments continues. In Mi A 60/7 (1588), Stiles and seven masons are paid for working at the quarry; elsewhere he is paid in lump sums.

60. Lady Victoria Manners, "The Rutland Monuments in Bottesford Church," *Art Journal* (1903): 269–74, 289–95, 335–39. Strapwork was commonplace in English tombs and chimney-pieces of the 1580s, and ornamental motifs were freely copied and reworked. Nevertheless, the workshops were distinguished by skill in carving and design, as well as by price.

61. Girouard discusses Maynard at length in his "New Light on Longleat: Allen Maynard, A French Sculptor in England in the Sixteenth Century," *Country Life* 120 (1956): 594–97. Longleat itself is treated more fully in his "The Development of Longleat House between 1546 and 1572," *Archaeological Journal* 116 (1961): 206–22.

62. Girouard, *Smythson*, 61.

63. See J. G. Mann, "English Church Monuments 1536–1625," *Walpole Society* 21 (1932–33), 1–22, and Philip Chatwin, "Monumental Effigies of the County of Warwick," part 3, *Transactions of the Birmingham Archaeological Society* (1922): 136–38. For the Flemish presence at Burton-on-Trent, see K. A. Esdaile, "Interaction of English and Low Country Sculpture in the Sixteenth Century; with a note on the work of Joseph Hollemans of Burton-on-Trent," *Journal of the Warburg and Courtauld Institutes* 6 (1943): 80–88.

64. The tomb is illustrated in N. Pevsner, *Nottinghamshire*. See J. T. Godfrey, *Notes on the Churches of Nottinghamshire: Hundred of Rushcliffe* (London, 1887).

65. See Whinney, *Sculpture*, chapter 3; L. Cust, "Foreign Artists of the Reformed Religion Working in London from about 1560 to 1660," *Proceedings of the Huguenot Society* 7 (1901–4): 45–82; and K. Esdaile, "Some Fellow-Citizens of Shakespeare in Southwark," *Essays and Studies*, n.s. 5 (1952): 26–31.

66. See A. C. Fryer, "Monumental Effigies Sculptured by Nicholas Stone," *Archaeological Journal* 69 (1912): 229–75, and 77 (1920): 177–90.

67. This work and others contemporary with Wollaton are discussed in Friedman, "Patronage and the Production of Tombs in London and the Provinces: The Willoughby Monument of 1591," *The Antiquaries Journal* (1985): part 2: 390–401.

68. *Middleton*, 565.

69. The representation of Aristotle as an old man with a beard and tight-fitting cap goes back to fifteenth-century Italian examples. This type was reproduced in prints and reliefs showing both full face and profile. They include works by Fabio Ursino, Enea Vico, Pirro Ligorio, and at least one French example in addition to the Wollaton bust. See Frank E. Washburn-Freund, "Leonardo's Portraits and Aristotle," *International Studio* (July 1927): 28–36, 82. This reference was very kindly supplied to me by Dr. Lilian Armstrong.

70. For Charles I's visit to Wollaton in 1604, see Wood, *Continuation*, 38. For Lesueur, see Whinney, *Sculpture*, 36–37.

71. Wood, *Continuation*, 67.

72. Yet Stone's relative and a former member of his workship, Hendrik de Keyser, was living in Nottingham between 1639 and 1643. See H. J. Louw, "Anglo-Netherlandish Architectural Interchange ca. 1600–1660," *Architectural History* 24 (1981): 1–23. I am grateful to Christy Anderson for this reference. See also W. L. Spiers, ed., "The Notebooks and Account Book of Nicholas Stone," *Walpole Society* 7 (1918–19): esp. figs. 31 and 33. I am grateful to Dr. Judith Hurtig for her suggestions about Stone's work. See also Whinney, *Sculpture*, 17–19, and Mrs. Arundell Esdaile, "The Monument of the First Lord Rich at Felsted," *Essex Archaeological Society Journal*, n.s. 22 (1940): 59–67. A detailed discussion of Evesham's work is given in K. A. Esdaile, "The Gorges Monument in Salisbury Cathedral," *Wiltshire Archaeological Magazine* 50 (1942–44): 56–62. Stone's Francis Holles monu-

ment (1622) at Westminster Abbey is strikingly similar to the Wollaton sibyls.

73. See Wood, *Continuation*, 123 and 134 ff. (Mi LM 27, 135 and 148ff).

74. See C. H. C. and M. I. Baker, *The Life and Circumstances of James Brydges, First Duke of Chandos, Patron of the Liberal Arts* (Oxford, 1949), chap. 6 and 282–88; and Girouard, *Life in the English Country House,* 139–41.

75. See Girouard, *Smythson*, 88, 147.

76. The discussion which follows is elaborated in Friedman, "Tombs," as in note 67 above.

77. See Whinney, *Sculpture*, 235 n. 18.

78. Wood, *Continuation*, 67–68 (Mi LM 27, 72).

Chapter 5

1. The Chantry at Wollaton was purchased from "Rawfe Pynder, grocer, of London," in 1562 by Henry Medley (Mi A 42, f. 12 and *Middleton*, 417); for Thurland House, see J. Holland Walker, "An Itinerary of Nottingham," *Transactions of the Thoroton Society* 39 (1935): 1–4; for Willoughby's London property, see Elijah Williams, *Early Holborn and the Legal Quarter of London,* vol. 1 (London, 1927), 1083–84.

2. Mi A 69(205), *passim*.

3. Mi A 69(205), f. 19r.

4. Mi LM 26, f. 135v–136r.

5. *Middleton*, 566.

6. Mi LM 26, f. 135r; STB Box 2 (1), f. 30–31.

7. Folger Library, Cavendish xd.428, no. 126.

8. *Middleton*, 570–71.

9. *Middleton*, 568; see also p. 571 where he writes to ask her to will her property to her unmarried daughters before her death. For Spencer's involvement in the settlement of the estate, see M. E. Finch, "The Wealth of Five Northamptonshire Families," *Northamptonshire Record Society* 19 (1956) and Huntington Library, EL 6414, 6416 and STT 1837, 1838.

10. See note 14 below.

11. Dorothy Tamworth was the widow of John Tamworth; their case came before the Privy Council in 1590 when she alleged that he used unlawful means to force her to pass fines on her lands: *Acts of the Privy Council,* vol. 20, 181. See also Greaves, *Society and Religion in Elizabethan England* (Minneapolis, 1981), 259–60.

12. *Middleton*, 575.

13. *Middleton*, 576–77.

14. See R. S. Smith, "The Willoughbys of Wollaton," and Mi 2/16 "A Note of Sir Francis Willoughby's debts." The events of these years are described in numerous documents associated with the case in Chancery: see Lansdowne 84, nos. 7 and 106; Add Mss. 25.085; Lansdowne 89, nos. 4 and 59. In Lansdowne 84, no. 106, Percival Willoughby claimed that the new wife had received £ 10,000 in goods, plate, jewels, and ready money. An inventory of 1597 (6/178/80) lists £ 346/18s removed from Wollaton Hall by Willoughby's widow after his death. See also Mi 2/75/3–1 through 3–10 (a bundle of cause papers relating to the court case). For the verdict in

Chancery in the widow's (then Lady Wharton's) favor, see PRO C. 78/215/6. Both Percival and his brother were confined to the Fleet prison at various times for their debts (see Mi 49/24).

15. *Middleton*, 582.

16. *Middleton*, 582.

17. Mi 2/75/3–10.

18. *Middleton*, 582, 620–21.

19. For the use of inventories in reconstructing the furnishings and use of rooms, see Thornton, *Interior Decoration* (as in note 27 below), chaps. 1–3.

20. Inventories Mi I 6 (1595), 7 (1595), 8 (1596; 1599), 9 (1596), 10 (1596), 15 (1601), 16 (1609) (published in *Middleton*, 485–91).

21. Both Summerson (*Architecture in Britain*) and Girouard (*Robert Smythson*) mistakenly follow Thorpe's lead in placing the kitchens on the ground floor in the northwest corner.

22. Mi I 8 (iv), December.

23. The number of small rooms in the mezzanines and basement suggest that they were used both as private rooms for the upper servants and for storage of furniture, tools, and documents.

24. *Middleton*, 571–72. See also Mi 6/178/80.

25. See note 14 above.

26. Lansdowne 84, no. 106, f.2r. (see also 6/178/80).

27. *Middleton*, 168–69, 488. See P. Thornton, *Seventeenth-Century Interior Decoration in England, France and Holland* (London, 1978), 231; and Simon Jervis, *Printed Furniture Designs Before 1650* (London, 1974). The latter illustrates a range of furniture types.

28. Wood, *Continuation*, 38; Nichols, *Progresses of James I*, vol. 1 (London, 1828), 170; Mi AV 1.

29. *Middleton*, 488–89. See also Thornton, *Interior Decoration*, 157–58.

30. Mi A 60/5, f. 11r.

31. *Middleton*, 490.

32. See Thornton, *Interior Decoration*, 315–29, and Girouard, *Life in the English Country House*, 245–50.

33. Thornton, *Interior Decoration*, 52–63, discusses such sequences of rooms and their decoration. See also Girouard, *Life*, 94–100.

34. Lindsay Boynton, ed., *The Hardwick Hall Inventories of 1601* (London, 1971), 26–27; 30–31.

35. *Middleton*, 484; (Mi I 16).

36. *Middleton*, 487; (Mi I 16).

37. Girouard, *Life*, 100.

38. Ingatestone inventory, 1600 (transcribed in 1924), now in the Department of Furniture and Interior Design, Victoria and Albert Museum, London.

39. Thornton, *Interior Decoration*, 143–46.

40. *Hardwick Hall Inventory*, 27–29.

41. Girouard, *Life*, 100–103; 173–74, gives a history of galleries from the earliest times through the nineteenth century. See also R. Coope, "The 'Long Gallery': Its Origins, Development, Use and Decoration," *Architectural History* 29 (1986):43–84.

42. *Middleton*, 434.

43. Mi A 70 (205). For the Smythson drawings, see *Architectural History* 5 (1962).

44. Roy Strong, *The Renaissance Garden in England* (New Haven and London, 1979), chap. 3.

45. *The Diary of Lady Ann Clifford*, edited by V. Sackville-West (New York, 1928), 42.

46. See Wood, *Continuation*, 27–29.

47. For Hardwick, see Girouard, *Hardwick Hall* (The National Trust, London, 1976). For Charlton, see Summerson, *Architecture in Britain* (Harmondsworth, 1970), 85–86.

48. See Durant, *Bess of Hardwick* (London, 1977), 180–81.

Chapter 6

1. Wood, *Continuation*, 28–29.

2. The expenses connected with the Queen's visit are recorded in Mi Av 1. See also J. G. Nichols, *Progresses of James I* (London, 1828), 1, 170. For the visits of Duke Charles (later Charles I) in 1604 and of the Duke of Würtemberg in 1608, see Wood, *Continuation*, 38, and 42–43.

3. Wood, *Continuation*, 70.

4. An excellent discussion of marriage as viewed and experienced by men and women of different classes is included in Keith Wrightson, *English Society 1580–1680* (London, 1982), chap. 4. Here the question is asked of each social class separately, yielding valuable results.

5. See, for example, *Middleton*, 556–60.

6. Wood, *Continuation*, 26–27.

7. Mi I 11.

8. Mi 6/170/138, nos. 1–8.

9. Wood, *Continuation*, 45.

10. Wood, *Continuation*, 47 and *passim*.

11. Wood, *Continuation*, 47, 27.

12. Wood, *Continuation*, 27.

13. Wood, *Continuation*, 66.

14. Wood, *Continuation*, 67.

15. Wood, *Continuation*, 66.

16. *The Account of the Willughby's of Wollaton, taken out of the Pedigree, old Letters and old Books of Accounts, in my Brother Sir Thomas Willoughby's study, Dec. A.D. 1702*, by Cassandra Willoughby (later Duchess of Chandos) is in two volumes in the Middleton Collection at the University of Nottingham Library, Mi LM 26 and 27. Volume 1 was published, with subtle but significant omissions, in the Historical Manuscripts Commission *Report on Manuscripts of Lord Middleton Preserved at Wollaton Hall, Nottinghamshire*, edited by W. H. Stevenson (London, 1911). Volume 2 was published and edited by A. C. Wood under the title *The Continuation of the History of the Willoughby Family by Cassandra Duchess of Chandos* (Eton, Windsor, 1958). The two variant spellings used in Cassandra's title were adopted by her to distinguish between the two branches of the family. A short biography, *Excellent Cassandra: The Life and Times of the Duchess of Chandos* (Gloucester, 1981) was published by Joan Johnston. For the troubles involving Sir Josiah Child, see Wood, *Continuation*, 117ff, [Mi LM 27, 139ff]. For Francis Willoughby, F.R.S., see Mary A. Welch, "Francis Willoughby of Middleton, Warwickshire and Wollaton, Nottinghamshire: A Seventeenth Century Naturalist," *Transactions of the Thoroton Society*, 70 (1977), 33–40. A date of 1679 on a

drainpipe indicates, however, that some work had been done during Willoughby's minority.

17. Wood, *Continuation*, 125.

18. Wood, *Continuation*, 67. See also Mi 90 (a); J. H. Hodson, "The Wollaton Estate and the Civil War," *Thoroton Society Record Series* 31 (1962): 3–15.

19. Wood, *Continuation*, 129.

20. Wood, *Continuation*, 123, and 134ff.

21. For seventeenth-century greenhouses, see Billie S. Britz, "Environmental Provisions for Plants in Seventeenth-Century Northern Europe," *JSAH* 33 no. 2 (May 1974): 133–44. Letter no. 4 in Cassandra's *Letter Book* at the Shakespeare Birthplace Trust mentions "a pretty little wilderness" in which Cassandra loved to sit and read.

22. See Edward Croft-Murray, *Decorative Painting in England 1537–1827* (London, 1962), vol. 1, 254a, 274a; vol. 2, 70, 269b, 324b. These murals were first mentioned by Throseby in his 1790 edition of Thoroton's *Nottinghamshire* (vol. 2, 214). They were restored by J. F. Rigaud in 1807, by "Mr. Brown" in 1835, and again in 1953 by Mr. Alistair N. Stewart. For Rigaud's description of them, see Mi P 3a D.

23. An extended discussion of this subject is given by Peter Thornton in *Seventeenth-Century Interior Decoration in England, France and Holland* (New Haven and London, 1978).

24. Wood, *Continuation*, 138.

25. For women's status in this period, see Derek Jarret, *England in the Age of Hogarth* (London, 1974), 114–43, and Katharine M. Rogers, *Feminism in Eighteenth-Century England* (Hagerstown, MD, 1982).

26. See Wood, *Continuation*, 103–16. Cassandra also used her father's notes on family history, which survive in the Middleton Collection (Mi LM 13). Among the correspondents in contact with Cassandra and her brother in the 1690s was Sir Hans Sloane. His papers in the British Library include a number of relevant letters: see Sloane 4062, ff. 11, 12, 15, 17, 19, 22, 24, 25, and 242; Sloane 4068, f. 12. Sloane was the secretary of the Royal Society. The brother and sister also corresponded with John Ray, their father's collaborator and friend.

27. Wood, *Continuation*, 137. This collecton is now missing, although a seventeenth-century cabinet of specimens now in Lord Middleton's collection at Birdsall may have been a part of the original collection sorted by Cassandra and her brother.

28. Wood, *Continuation*, 136–37.

29. Cassandra's journal, "An Account of the journeys I have taken and where I have been since March 1695," covers the period up to May 1718. It is now in the Shakespeare Birthplace Trust, Stoneleigh Mss.

30. The draft of this history, which includes Cassandra's notes on individual documents, is among the Stowe Mss. at the Huntington Library, STB Box 2(1).

31. *Middleton*, 504–9. For antiquarianism, see Michael Maclagan, "Genealogy and History in the Sixteenth and Seventeenth Centuries," and Stuart Piggott, "Antiquarian Thought in the Sixteenth and Seventeenth Centuries," in *English Historical Scholarship in the Sixteenth and Seventeenth Centuries*, edited by Levi Fox (London, 1956), 31–48 and 93–114. See also John Pocock, "England," in *National Consciousness, History and Political Cul-*

ture in Early-Modern Europe, edited by Orest Ranum (Baltimore, 1975), chap. 4. Cassandra's research spanned some twenty years: Wood, *Continuation,* 100 mentions that it had been twenty-five years since her aunt's death in 1696, i.e., 1721.

32. Wood, *Continuation,* 138 [Mi LM 27, 152]. Cassandra later assembled a collection of early costumes that is now part of the Museum of Costume and Textiles in Nottingham. For the distinctive contributions of women historians, see Natalie Zemon Davis, "Gender and Genre: Women as Historical Writers 1400–1820," in *Beyond Their Sex: Learned Women of the European Past,* edited by P. Labalme (New York, 1980), 153–82.

33. *Middleton,* 565–66.

34. Robert Thoroton, *Antiquities of Nottinghamshire* (London, 1677), 223.

35. For Canons, see Girouard, *Life in the English Country House,* 139, and C. H. C. Baker, *The Life and Circumstances of James Brydges, First Duke of Chandos* (Oxford, 1949), chaps. 6 and 7. The *Canons Household Regulations* (1721) are in the Huntington Library (ST 44).

36. *Middleton,* 584.

37. *Middleton,* 594.

38. For Shaw Hall, see Baker, *Chandos,* chap. 15.

39. Uvedale Price, *Essay on the Picturesque,* vol. 2 (London, 1810), 210 n.1.

40. John Britton, *The Architectural Antiquities of Great Britain,* vol. 2 (London, 1809), 108–10.

41. See also Derek Linstrum, *Sir Jeffry Wyatville: Architect to the King* (Oxford, 1972), 60–67. The architect is referred to as Wyatt, Wyatville, and Wyattville at various times during his career.

42. For the construction of the stables, see F. C. Laird, *The Beauties of England and Wales,* vol. 12 (London, 1813), part 1, 166–76, esp. 174–76.

43. Middleton to Wyatville, 2 February 1832. In the Collection of Mrs. J. M. Dom (cited by Linstrum).

44. Mi P 3A. Lord Middleton's notes are written directly onto the drawing.

45. See note 22 above.

46. The authenticity of the ceiling in the great hall has been disputed in the literature. In *The Builder,* 13 April 1889, 278, P. K. Allen refers to the hammer beam roof "said to have been added by Wyatt," but such a roof was probably in existence much earlier. In his notes on the Wollaton estate (Mi LM 36), the seventh Lord makes an entry in August 1841 recording the placement of oak and brick in the wall for the hall ceiling to rest on (this was done in the 1790s) and the construction and leading of a new roof in 1794. The present decoration of the Prospect Room appears to date from Wyatville's period; Linstrum (as in note 41), 65, suggests that he may have added the shields and the pierced panels, but it is probable that these are also original. Mi P 3A includes records of alterations to the windows, to the hall ceiling (1830), and to the chimney (1831). The steel truss currently in place dates from the 1950s.

47. These projects are mentioned by P. K. Allen (as in note 46 above). The flying buttress scheme was recorded in drawings which are now lost; Allen says he saw a sketch for it by J. J. Johnson dated 8 December 1775 in the estate office at Wollaton. According to one source, the screen was also painted in the nineteenth century: see John Murray, *Handbook for Travellers*

in *Derbyshire, Nottinghamshire, Leicestershire and Staffordshire*, 2d ed. (London, 1874), 69.

48. The gardens were improved throughout the period. The Camellia House at Wollaton was built in 1823 by the firm of Thomas Clark of Birmingham: see John Hix, *The Glass House* (London, 1974), 105.

49. Girouard, *The Victorian Country House* (New Haven, 1979), 130–37, 412–14.

50. Lady Middleton, "Wollaton Hall," in *Other Famous Homes of Great Britain and Their Stories*, edited by A. H. Malan (London, 1902), 3–33.

51. See Sheila M. Strauss, *A Short History of Wollaton and Wollaton Hall* (Nottinghamshire County Council, 1978).

Conclusion

1. W. G. Hoskins, "The Rebuilding of Rural England," *Past and Present* 4 (1953):44–59.

2. R. Machin, "The Great Rebuilding: A Reassessment," *Past and Present* 77 (1977):33–58.

3. Palliser, *The Age of Elizabeth*, chap. 5.

4. D. Durant, *Bess of Hardwick* (London, 1977), 185.

5. This process is outlined by Girouard in *Life in the English Country House*, chap. 5.

6. The literature on this subject is vast. A full and very useful bibliography is included in Stone, *The Family, Sex and Marriage in England* (London, 1977).

7. Cassandra's travel diary is in the Shakespeare Birthplace Trust.

8. See M. Slater and S. Mendelson, "Debate," *Past and Present* 85 (1979):126–35. See M. Slater, *Family Life in the Seventeenth Century: The Verneys of Claydon House* (London, 1984).

Selected Bibliography

Manuscript Sources

The British Library, London, England
    Additional Mss.
    Lansdowne Mss.
    Sloane Mss.
Folger Shakespeare Library, Washington, D.C.
    Cavendish Mss.
Huntington Library, San Marino, California
    Ellesmere Collection
    Esdaile Papers
    Hastings Collection
    Stowe Collection
      Brydges Papers
      Temple Papers
Public Record Office, London, England
    Wills (Various Collections)
Shakespeare Birthplace Trust
    Stoneleigh Mss.
University of Nottingham
    Middleton Mss. (*Mi*)

Drawings

British Library
    J. C. Buckler, Add. Mss. 37121 (35, 36)
    J. Buckler, Add. Mss. 36372 (79–83)
    S. H. Grimm, Add. Mss. 15545 (110, 111)
    Hatfield Maps and Plans 372, I and II
Royal Institute of British Architects
    Smythson Collection
Sir John Soane's Museum
    Notebooks of John Thorpe
University of Nottingham
    Middleton Mss.
      Anonymous Design for a Wall Monument, 1591
      Volume of Drawings by J. and J. C. Buckler (1822), C. S. Smith (1820) and C. Chouler (1830) for Wollaton renovations (Mi P3a–3af)
      J. Wyatt, 1823: servants wing, plans for gatehouse, plans and elevations for "village lodges" and variants for gatehouse turrets.

Victoria and Albert Museum
> Drawings by S. Farthorn, C. J. Richardson, S. Sparrow, J. Nash, W. and J. Walker, J. Wyatville.

Primary Sources

Anon (I. M.). *A Health to the Gentlemanly Profession of Servingmen.* London, 1598.

Banister, John. *The Historie of Man, sucked from the sappe of the most approved Anathomistes.* London, 1578.

———. *Treatise of Chyrurgerie.* London, 1575.

Banks, Joseph, ed. "A Breviate Touching the Order and Government of a Nobleman's House, etc." *Archaeologia* 12 (1800): 315–89.

Barnard, John. *The Tranquilitie of the Mind.* London, 1570.

Bentley, Thomas. *The Monument of Matrons.* London, 1582.

Boorde, Andrew. *A Compendyous Regyment or a Dyetary of Helth.* London, 1549.

Brathwaite, Richard. *Some Rules and orders for the Government of the House of an Earle.* London, 1821.

Bright, Timothy. *A Treatise on Melancholie,* London, 1586.

Clifford, Lady Anne. *The Diary of Lady Anne Clifford,* edited by Vita Sackville-West. London, 1923.

Dugdale, William. *The Antiquities of Warwickshire.* London, 1656.

Fitzherbert, Sir Anthony. *The Book of Husbandrye.* London, 1555.

Gage, John, ed., *Extracts from the Household Book of Edward Stafford, Duke of Buckingham.* London, 1834.

Gedde, Walter. *A Booke of Sundry Draughtes principally serving for glasiers and not impertinent for plasterers and gardiners: besides sundry other professions.* London, 1615.

Gerbier, Balthazar. *Counsel and advice to all builders for the choice of their surveyors, clerks of their works, bricklayers, masons, carpenters and other workmen therein concerned.* London, 1663.

Gosson, Stephen. *Pleasant Quippes for Upstart, Newfangled Gentlewomen.* London, 1595.

Gosynhill, Edward. *Dialogue betwene the comen Secretary and Jelowsy touchynge the unstablenes of harlottes.* London, 1555.

Jones, John. *The benefit of the auncient Bathes of Buckstones.* London, 1572.

Markham, Gervase. *Country Contentments and The English Huswife.* London, 1615.

Markland, James Heywood. "Instructions of Henry Percy, ninth Earl of Northumberland, to his son Algernon Percy, touching the management of his Estate, Officers etc." *Archaeologia* 27 (1838): 306–58.

Peacham, Henry. *The Art of Drawing with the Pen and Limning in Water Colours.* London, 1606.

Scott, Sibbald David, Bart., ed. "A Booke of Orders and Rules of Anthony Viscount Montague in 1595." *Sussex Archaeological Collections* 7 (1853–54): 173–212.

Shute, John. *First and Chief Groundes of Architecture.* London, 1563.

Smith, Henry. *A Preparative For Marriage.* London, 1591.

Stevenson, William. "Extracts from 'The Booke of howshold Charges and

Other Paiments laid out by the Lord North and his Commandement.'" *Archaeologia* 19 (1821): 283–301.

Stubbes, Philip. *The Anatomie of Abuses.* London, 1583.

Thoroton, Robert. *The Antiquities of the County of Nottingham.* London, 1677.

———. *Thoroton's History of Nottinghamshire,* 3 vols., edited by J. Throsby. London, 1790.

Weever, John. *Ancient Funerall Monuments.* London, 1631.

Wentworth, William. "Advice to His Son." In *Wentworth Papers, 1597–1628,* edited by J. P. Cooper, 9–24. London, 1973.

Secondary Studies

Allen, P. K. "Wollaton Hall." *The Builder,* 13 April 1889.

Aston, Margaret. "English Ruins and English History: The Dissolution and the Sense of the Past." *Journal of the Warburg and Courtauld Institutes* 36 (1973): 231–55.

Auerbach, Erna. "Portraits of Elizabeth I." *The Burlington Magazine* 95 (1957): 197–205.

———. *Tudor Artists.* London, 1954.

Baker, C. H. Collins, and M. I. Baker. *The Life and Circumstances of James Brydges, First Duke of Chandos, Patron of the Liberal Arts.* Oxford, 1949.

Barley, M. W. *The English Farmhouse and Cottage.* London, 1961.

———. "Rural Housing in England." In vol. 4 of *The Agrarian History of England and Wales, 1500–1640,* edited by Joan Thirsk, Part 4, 696–766. Cambridge, 1967.

Bonfield, Lloyd. *Marriage Settlements 1601–1740: The Adoption of the Strict Settlement.* Cambridge, 1983.

Bestall, J. M., and D. V. Folkes, eds., *Chesterfield Wills and Inventories 1521–1603. Derbyshire Record Society,* 1977.

Bossy, John. *The English Catholic Community 1570–1850.* New York, 1975.

Boynton, Lindsay, ed. *The Hardwick Hall Inventories of 1601.* The Furniture History Society. London, 1971.

Britz, Billie S. "Environmental Provisions for Plants in Seventeenth-Century Northern Europe." *Journal of the Society of Architectural Historians* 33, no. 2 (May 1974): 133–44.

Chatwin, Philip. "Monumental Effigies of the County of Warwick." *Birmingham Archaeological Society Transactions* 48 (1922): 136–68.

Chaytor, Miranda. "Household and Kinship: Ryton in the Early 17th Century." *History Workshop* 10 (1980): 25–60.

Coleman, D. C. *Industry in Tudor and Stuart England.* London, 1975.

Colvin, Howard. *The History of the King's Works,* vol. 3 (1485–1660). London, 1975.

Coward, B. "Disputed Inheritances: Some Difficulties of the Nobility in the Late Sixteenth and Early Seventeenth Centuries." *Bulletin of the Institute of Historical Research* 46, no. 110 (1971): 194–215.

Cressy, David. "Describing the Social Order of Elizabethan and Stuart England." *Literature and History* 3 (1976): 29–44.

———. *Education in Tudor and Stuart England.* Southampton, 1975.

———. *Literacy and the Social Order: Reading and Writing in Tudor and Stuart England.* Cambridge, 1980.

Croft-Murray, Edward. *Decorative Painting in England, 1537–1837.* 2 vols. London, 1962.

Cust, Lionel. "Foreign Artists of the Reformed Religion Working in London from about 1560 to 1660." *Proceedings of the Huguenot Society* 7 (1901–4):45–82.

———. "The Lumley Inventories." *The Walpole Society* 6 (1917–18): 15–35.

Davies, Kathleen M. "The Sacred Condition of Equality—How Original Were Puritan Doctrines of Marriage?" *Social History* 5 (1977):563–80.

Durant, David N. *Bess of Hardwick: Portrait of an Elizabethan Dynast.* London, 1977.

———. "Wollaton Hall: A Rejected Plan." *Transactions of the Thoroton Society* 76 (1972):13–17.

Drury, Peter J. "A Fayre House, Buylt by Sir Thomas Smith: The Development of Hill Hall, Essex 1557–81." *Journal of the British Archaeological Association* 136 (1983):98–123.

Englefield, W. A. D. *The History of the Painter-Stainers Company of London.* London, 1923.

Esdaile, Katherine A. "The Interaction of English and Low Country Sculpture in the 16th Century; with a Note on the Works of Joseph Hollemans of Burton-upon-Trent." *Journal of the Warburg and Courtauld Institutes* 6 (1943):80–88.

———. "The Part Played by Refugee Sculptors 1600–1750." *Proceedings of the Huguenot Society* 18, no.3 (1947–52):254ff.

Finch, Mary E. "The Wealth of Five Northamptonshire Families 1540–1640." *Northamptonshire Record Society,* 19 (1956).

Fitz, Linda T. "'What Says the Married Woman': Marriage Theory and Feminism in the English Renaissance." *Mosaic* 12, no.2 (Winter 1980):1–22.

Foister, Susan. "Paintings and Other Works of Art in Sixteenth-Century Inventories." *The Burlington Magazine* 123, no. 938 (May 1981): 273–82.

Gent, Lucy. *Picture and Poetry 1560–1620: Relations Between Literature and the Visual Arts in the English Renaissance.* Leamington Spa, 1981.

Giles, M. F. *Wollaton Handbook: Information on the Church and Village.* Ramsgate, 1962.

Girouard, Mark. "Elizabethan Chatsworth." *Country Life* 154 (22 Nov. 1973):1668–72.

———. "Elizabethan Holdenby." *Country Life* 150 (18 and 25 October 1979):1286–89.

———. *Hardwick Hall, Derbyshire.* London: The National Trust, 1976.

———. *Life in the English Country House: A Social and Architectural History.* London, 1978.

———. *Robert Smythson and the Elizabethan Country House.* London, 1983.

Goodison, J. W. "George Gower Serjeant Painter to Queen Elizabeth." *The Burlington Magazine* 90 (1948):261–64.

Greaves, Richard. *Society and Religion in Elizabethan England.* Minneapolis, 1981.

Halliwell, J. O. *Ancient Inventories . . . of the . . . Sixteenth and Seventeenth Centuries.* London, 1854.

Harris, Barbara J. "Marriage Sixteenth-Century Style: Elizabeth Stafford and the Third Duke of Norfolk." *Journal of Social History* 15, no. 3 (Spring 1982):371–82.

Hart, W. M. "Parliamentary Survey of Richmond, Wimbledon and Nonsuch in the County of Surrey, A.D. 1649." *Surrey Archaeological Collections* 5 (1871):75–156.

Harte, N. B. "State Control of Dress and Social Change in Pre-Industrial England." In *Trade, Government and Economy in Pre-Industrial England: Essays Presented to F. J. Fisher*, edited by D. C. Coleman and A. H. John, 132–65. London, 1976.

Heal, Felicity. "The Idea of Hospitality in Early Modern England." *Past and Present* 102 (Feb. 1984):66–93.

Hexter, J. H. *Reappraisals in History.* 2d ed. Chicago, 1979.

Hitchcock, Henry-Russell. *German Renaissance Architecture.* Princeton, 1981.

Hodson, J. H. "The First Wollaton Hall." *Transactions of the Thoroton Society* 72 (1968):59–67.

———. "The Wollaton Estate and the Civil War, 1643–97." *Thoroton Society Record Series* 31 (1962):3–15.

Hogrefe, Pearl. "Legal Rights of Tudor Women." *Sixteenth Century Journal* 3 (1974):97–105.

Hoskins, W. G. "The Rebuilding of Rural England 1570–1640." *Past and Present* 4 (Nov. 1953):44–59.

Howard, Maurice. *The Early Tudor Country House: Architecture and Politics 1490–1550.* London, 1987.

Hull, Suzanne W. *Chaste, Silent and Obedient: English Books for Women, 1475–1640.* San Marino, 1982.

Hurtig, Judith. "Death in Childbirth: Seventeenth-Century English Tombs and Their Place in Contemporary Thought." *Art Bulletin* 65, no. 4 (December 1983):603–15.

———. "English Shroud Tombs: Classical Revival and Anglican Context." *Art Bulletin* 64 (June 1982):217–39.

Jardine, Lisa. "Humanism and the 16th Century Cambridge Arts Course." *History of Education* 4, no. 1 (1975):16–31.

———. *Still Harping on Daughters: Women and Drama in the Age of Shakespeare.* London, 1983.

Jervis, Simon. *Printed Furniture Designs Before 1650.* The Furniture History Society. London, 1974.

Kelso, Ruth. *Doctrine for the Lady of the Renaissance.* Urbana, 1956.

Kemp, Brian. *English Church Monuments.* London, 1980.

Labalme, Patricia H., ed. *Beyond Their Sex: Learned Women of the European Past.* New York, 1980.

Lowe, A. E. Lawson. "Wollaton and the Willoughby Monuments." *The Genealogist* 1 (1877):169–71.

Llewellyn, Nigel. "John Weever and English Funeral Monuments of the Sixteenth and Seventeenth Centuries." Ph.D. diss., University of London, 1983.

Lloyd, Rachel. *Dorset Elizabethans at Home and Abroad.* London, 1967.

MacCulloch, Diarmaid. "Kett's Rebellion in Context." *Past and Present* 84 (1979):36–59.

MacDonald, Michael. *Mystical Bedlam: Madness, Anxiety and Healing in Seventeenth-Century England.* Cambridge, 1981.

Machin, R. "The Great Rebuilding: A Reassessment." *Past and Present* 77 (1977):33–58.

MacKisack, May. *Mediaeval History in the Tudor Age.* Oxford, 1971.

Maclean, Ian. *The Renaissance Notion of Women.* Cambridge, 1980.

Manners, Lady Victoria. "The Rutland Monuments in Bottesford Church." *The Art Journal* (1903):269–74; 289–95; 335–39.

Mercer, Eric. *English Art 1553–1625.* Oxford, 1962.

———. *Furniture 700–1700.* London, 1969.

———. "The Decoration of the Royal Palaces 1553–1625." *Archaeological Journal* 110 (1953):151ff.

———. "The Houses of the Gentry." *Past and Present* 5 (1954):11–32.

Middleton, Lady. "Wollaton Hall." In *Other Famous Homes of Great Britain and Their Stories,* edited by A. H. Malan, 3–33. London, 1902.

Mowl, Tim and Earnshaw, Brian. *Trumpet at a Distant Gate: The Lodge as Prelude to the Country House.* Boston, 1985.

Nichols, John. *The Progresses of Queen Elizabeth.* 3 vols. London, 1823.

———. *Progresses of James I.* London, 1828.

O'Connell, Laura Stevenson. "The Elizabethan Bourgeois Hero-Tale: Aspects of an Adolescent Social Consciousness." In *After the Reformation: Essays in Honor of J. H. Hexter,* edited by B. C. Malament, 267–90. Philadelphia, 1980.

Oswald, Arthur. "Tudor Outlook Towers." *Country Life Annual* (1957).

Outhwaite, R. B., ed. *Marriage and Society: Studies in the Social History of Marriage.* London, 1981.

Palliser, David M. *The Age of Elizabeth: England Under the Late Tudors.* London, 1983.

Pevsner, Nickolaus. "Double Profile: A Reconsideration of the Elizabethan Style as Seen at Wollaton." *Architectural Review* 107 (March 1950): 147–53.

Power, d'Arcy. "Notes on Early Portraits of John Banister, of William Harvey and the Barber-Surgeons Visceral Lecture in 1581." *Proceedings of the Royal Society of Medicine* 6 (1912):18–27.

Prest, Wilfred R. *The Inns of Court Under Elizabeth and the Early Stuarts.* London, 1972.

———. "Legal Education of the Gentry 1560–1640." *Past and Present* 38 (Dec. 1967):20–39.

———, ed. *Lawyers in Early Modern Europe and America.* London, 1981.

Pugh, R. B. *Old Wardour Castle, Wiltshire.* London, 1968.

Quaife, G. R. *Wanton Wenches and Wayward Wives: Peasants and Illicit Sex in Early Seventeenth-Century England.* New Brunswick, 1979.

Roberts, R. S. "The Personnel and Practice of Medicine in Tudor and Stuart England." *Medical History* 6 (1962).

Rossell, P. E. *The Building of Wollaton Hall 1580–88.* 2 vols. M.A. thesis. University of Sheffield, 1957.

Shammas, Carol. "The Domestic Environment in Early Modern England and America." *Journal of Social History* (Fall 1980):2–25.

Simpson, A. W. B. *An Introduction to the History of the Land Law.* Oxford, 1961.

Slater, Miriam. "The Weightiest Business: Marriage in An Upper-Gentry Family in 17th Century England." *Past and Present* 72 (Aug. 1976): 25–54.

————. *Family Life in the Seventeenth Century: The Verneys of Claydon House.* London, 1984.

Smith, R. S. "A Woad Growing Project at Wollaton in the 1580s." *Transactions of the Thoroton Society* 65 (1961):27–46.

————. "England's First Rails: A Reconsideration." *Renaissance and Modern Studies* 4 (1960):119–34.

————. "Huntingdon Beaumont Adventurer in Coal Mines." *Renaissance and Modern Studies* 1 (1957):115–53.

————. "Sir Francis Willoughby's Ironworks 1570–1610." *Renaissance and Modern Studies* 11 (1967) 90–140.

————. "The Willoughbys of Wollaton 1500–1643: With Special Reference to Mining in Nottinghamshire." Ph.D. diss., University of Nottingham. 1964.

Spiers, Walter Lewis, ed., *The Notebook and Account Book of Nicholas Stone. Walpole Society,* vol. 7 (1918–19).

Stallybrass, Basil. "Bess of Hardwick's Buildings and Building Accounts." *Archaeologia.* 64 (1912–13):347–98.

Stone, Lawrence. "An Elizabethan Coalmine." *Economic History Review,* 2d ser., 3, no. 1 (1950):97–106.

————. "Social Mobility in England, 1500–1700." *Past and Present* 33 (April 1966):16–55.

————. "The Building of Hatfield House," *Archaeological Journal* 112 (1955): 100–128.

————. *The Crisis of the Aristocracy, 1558–1641.* Oxford, 1965.

————. "The Educational Revolution in England 1560–1640." *Past and Present* 28 (1964):40–80.

————. *The Family, Sex and Marriage in England, 1500–1800.* London, 1977.

————. "The Manners Earls of Rutland 1460–1660." In *Family and Fortune: Studies in Aristocratic Finance in the Sixteenth and Seventeenth Centuries.* Oxford, 1973.

Stone, Lawrence, and J. C. F. Stone. *An Open Elite? England 1540–1840.* Oxford, 1984.

Strauss, Sheila M. *A Short History of Wollaton and Wollaton Hall.* Nottingham, 1978.

Strong, Roy. *Artists of the Tudor Court: The Portrait Miniature Rediscovered.* London, 1983.

————. *The Cult of Elizabeth.* London, 1977.

————. *The English Icon: Elizabethan and Jacobean Portraiture.* London, 1969.

————. *Portraits of Queen Elizabeth.* London, 1963.

Summerson, John. *Architecture in Britain 1530–1830.* Harmondsworth, 1970.

————. "The Building of Theobalds." *Archaeologia* 97 (1959):107–27.

————. "Piante palladiane nelle dimore del periodo elisabettiano." *Bolletino del Centro internazionale di storia dell' architettura* 11 (1969):277–86.

————, ed. "The Book of Architecture of John Thorpe." *Walpole Society* 90 (1966).

Tafuri, Manfredo. "Alle origini del palladianesimo: Alessandro Farnese, Jacques Androuet Du Cerceau, Inigo Jones." *Storia dell' Arte* 9/10 (1971):149–61.

Thomas, Keith. "The Double Standard." *Journal of the History of Ideas* 20 (1959):195–216.

Watson, Foster. *Vives and the Renascence Education of Women.* London, 1912.

Webster, Charles, ed. *Health, Medicine and Mortality in the Sixteenth Century.* Cambridge, 1979.

Weigall, Rachel. "An Elizabethan Gentlewoman: The Diary of Lady Mildmay 1570–1617." *Quarterly Review* 215 (1911): 119–38.

Welch, Mary A., ed. "Willoughby Letters of the First Half of the Sixteenth Century." *Thoroton Society Record Series* 24 (1967): 1–98; 153ff.

———. "Francis Willughby of Middleton, Warwickshire and Wollaton, Nottinghamshire: A Seventeenth Century Naturalist." *Transactions of the Thoroton Society* 81 (1977): 33–40.

Wharton, E. R. *The Whartons of Wharton Hall.* Oxford, 1898.

Williams, E. Carleton. *Bess of Hardwick.* London, 1959.

Williams, Elijah. *Early Holborn and the Legal Quarter of London.* 2 vols. London, 1927.

Wilton-Ely, John. "The Professional Architect in England." In *The Architect: Chapters in the History of the Profession,* edited by Spiro Kostoff, 180–208. New York, 1977.

Wood, A. C. *The Continuation of the History of the Willoughby Family by Cassandra Duchess of Chandos.* Eton, Windsor, 1958.

———. *A History of Nottinghamshire.* Nottingham, 1947.

Wrightson, Keith. *English Society 1580–1680.* London, 1982.

Yates, Frances. "Elizabethan Chivalry: The Romance of the Accession Day Tilts." In *Astraea: The Imperial Theme in the Sixteenth Century,* 88–111. London, 1975.

———. *The Rosicrucian Enlightenment.* London, 1972.

———. *Theatre of the World.* London, 1969.

Index

*Account of the Willughby's of Wolla-
ton taken out of the Pedigree, old
Letters, and old Books of Accounts
in my Brother Sir Thomas Willoughby's study, Dec. A.D. 1702,
The* (Cassandra Willoughby), 1,
3, 24, 38–39, 41, 61, 122, 131,
138–39, 158–59, 160, 189 nn.1,
2, 210 n.16

Accres, Thomas, 103, 104, 109,
122, 130

Advice to His Son (ninth Earl of
Northumberland). See *Instructions* (Percy)

Advice to His Son (Wentworth),
60–61

Aldridge, Robert, 155

Anatomy of Melancholy, The (Burton), 70

Antiquities of Nottinghamshire
(Thoroton), 165, 167, 169

Architectural and decorative styles,
5, 6, 34–35, 71–73, 76, 81–
85, 97, 151–54, 189 nn.6–9,
10; continental influences, 75,
76, 79, 81–82, 85, 93, 95, 97,
99–100, 110–12, 122, 125,
130–31, 143, 148

*Architectural Antiquities of Great
Britain* (Britton), 167, 169

Architectural patronage and amateur builders, 33–36

Architectural spaces and women.
See Women

Art and Illusion (Gombrich), 10–11

Arundell, Sir Matthew, 21, 36

Audley, Sir Thomas, 19

Azay-le-Rideau, 95

Banister, John, 31, 45

Barwick, Gabriel, 16

Baxandall, Michael, 10

Beaumont, Nicholas, 25

Bentley, Thomas: *The Monument
of Matrons,* 56

Bess of Hardwick, Elizabeth Talbot, Countess of Shrewsbury,
56–58, 60, 62, 106, 136, 143,
180. *See also* Hardwick Hall

Bottesford, Leics., 108–9

Britton, John: *Architectural Antiquities of Great Britain,* 167, 169

Brydges, James (first Duke of
Chandos), 163, 166

Burghley, Robert Cecil, 33

Burghley, William Cecil, 33–34

Burton, Robert: *The Anatomy of
Melancholy,* 70

Buxton, Derbyshire, 55, 136

Camden, William, 12

Castle Bolton, Yorkshire, 85

Cecil, Robert, first Earl of Salisbury, 33

Cecil, William, Lord Burghley,
33–34, 56

Charlton House (Greenwich),
153, 154

Chatsworth, Derbyshire, 97, 104

Chenonceaux, 95

Child, Sir Josiah, 159

Cludd, Thomas, 42, 44, 62, 67,
137

Coal mining, 25–26

Cock, Hieronymous, 111, 112

Conrados, Francis, 66–67

Country houses, 4–6, 8–9, 11,
36, 71, 82, 85, 88–89, 93–95,
97, 104–5, 112, 143, 148, 151,
154, 166, 167, 177, 179

Coventry, Warwickshire, 25, 62

Crispin, Richard, 107

De Bruyn, Nicholas, 112
De Passe, Crispin van, 125, 128
Details of Elizabethan Architecture
  (Shaw), 106, 107
De Vos, Martin, 112
De Vries, Jan Vredeman, 85, 88,
  112–15, 204n.21
Draycott, Henry, 42, 43, 44, 62
Du Cerceau, Jacques Androuet,
  76, 79–80, 85, 99, 110
Dudley, John, Duke of North-
  umberland, 17, 102
Dudley, John, Earl of Warwick, 14
Dudley, Robert, Earl of Leicester,
  21

Edlin, Edward, 28, 29
Education of gentry, 17–20,
  192n.22, 193n.26
Essay of the Picturesque (Price), 167
Evesham, Epiphanius, 125

*Family, Sex, and Marriage in En-
  gland, 1500–1800, The* (Stone),
  68
*First and Chief Groundes of Architec-
  ture* (Shute), 102
Fisher, Sir Clement, 61, 137
Funerary sculpture. *See* Stone carving and masonry sculpture

Gender and space. *See* Women
Girouard, Mark, 6, 12, 35, 84, 95,
  146, 194n.57, 197n.14, 203n.1,
  204n.16, 209n.41
Gombrich, Ernst: *Art and Illusion*,
  10–11
Gower, George, 28
Greenaway, Thomas, 106
Grey, Henry (Marquis of Dorset
  and Duke of Suffolk), 17, 18
Grey, Lady Jane, 17, 18
Grey, Lord John, 21, 54

Hall, John, 16
Hardwick Hall, Derbyshire, 6, 82,
  94, 104, 105, 130, 143, 144,
  151, 152, 154
Hastings, Henry, 67
Hastings, Henry, third Earl of
  Huntington, 67, 135
Hatfield House, Herts., 154

Hatton, Sir Christopher, 33
Herstmonceaux Castle, Sussex, 85
Hicks, Sir Michael, 64
Hill (Hills), John, 104, 109,
  206n.46
Hoskins, W. G., 179
Household orders, 41–43
Houses of the Gentry, The (Mer-
  cer), 6

Ingatestone (Essex), 143
Instructions (Percy), 50, 60–61
Interpretive history. *See* Meth-
  odology of the study

Jackson (Jaxson), John, 106,
  206n.51
James, Isaac, 124
Jardine, Lisa: *Still Harping on
  Daughters*, 7, 190n.14
Johnson, Garret, 108–10, 111,
  122
Johnson, Nicholas, 122, 124
Jones, Inigo, 72–73

Kenilworth Castle, Warwickshire,
  22–23, 36
Kingsbury Hall, Warwickshire, 14,
  38, 61
Kip, J., 162
Knollys, Lady Elizabeth, 21
Knollys, Sir Francis, 20–21, 24
Knyff, L., 162

Laguerre, Louis, 160
Laneham, Robert, 23, 36
Libraries, scholarly, 30–33
Littleton, Elizabeth (Lady Wil-
  loughby), 3, 21, 22, 28, 45–46,
  55–56, 58–59, 61–65, 70,
  135–37, 166, 199n.6,
  205–6n.40
Littleton, Sir John (of Frankley),
  21, 22, 55
London-based stone carvers,
  119–20
Longleat House, Wiltshire, 36, 71,
  207n.61
Lovell, Christopher, 33, 103, 104,
  109, 122
Lovell, Humphrey, Queen's Master
  Mason, 71

Markham, Sir Gervase, 67
Markham, Sir Thomas, 67, 137
Marmion, Henry, 16
Marmion, William, 42, 44, 60, 67
Matthews, John, 108
Maynard, Allen, 71, 112
Medley, George, 16
Medley, Sir Henry, 17
Medley, Thomas, 17
Mercer, Eric: *The Houses of the Gentry*, 6
Methodology of the study, 8, 10–11
Middleton, Barons. *See* Willoughby, individual entries
Middleton Collection, (University of Nottingham), 5–6, 85, 189 n.8
Middleton Hall, Warwickshire, 14, 23–25, 38, 55, 137–39, 162
Monument of Matrons, The (Bentley), 56
Mount Edgecumb, Cornwall, 85

Nonsuch Palace, Surrey, 96–97
Northumberland, Duke of. *See* Dudley, John, Duke of Northumberland
Northumberland, ninth Earl of. *See* Percy, Henry (ninth Earl of Northumberland): *Instructions*

Paget, William, first Lord, 18
Palladio, Andrea: *Quattro libri dell' architettura*, 73–76, 93–95
Patronage, architectural, 12, 13
Payne, Robert, 26–27
Penne, John, 42, 62
Percy, Henry (ninth Earl of Northumberland): *Instructions*, 50, 60–61
Period eye. *See* Methodology of the study
Petre, William, 143
Preparative to Marriage (Henry Smith), 56–57
Price, Uvedale: *Essay on the Picturesque*, 167
Printing and architectural education, 76–77
Property rights, 57–58, 200 nn.18–20

Quattro libri dell' architettura (Palladio), 73–75, 93–95

Ridgeway, Sir Thomas, 155
Rigaud, J. F., R. A., 168
Rodes (Rhodes), Christopher, 103, 104, 109
Rodes (Rhodes), John, 103, 104, 109
Royley, Gabriel, 122, 123
Royley, Richard, 122, 123

Sculpture. *See* Stone carving and masonry sculpture
Serlio, Sebastiano, 77–79, 85, 89, 99–100, 133, 203 n.10, 204 n.11
Servants, status of, 41–45
Shaw, Henry: *Details of Elizabethan Architecture*, 106, 107
Shrewsbury, George Talbot, fifth Earl of, 55–58, 60, 62. *See also* Bess of Hardwick
Shute, John: *First and Chief Groundes of Architecture*, 102
Siberechts, Jan, 160, 161
Squire, John, 43, 44
Sloane, Sir Hans, 211 n.26
Smith, Abraham, 106
Smith, Sir Henry: *Preparative to Marriage*, 56–57
Smythson, John, 102, 104, 153
Smythson, Robert, 4, 6, 13, 33, 36, 70–72, 75–76, 79, 102–4, 108, 109, 134, 203 n.1; drawings, 5–6, 81–84, 86–87, 118, 130, 139, 146; and Wollaton Hall, 84, 102–4, 183
Society and court, 8, 17, 18, 21–23, 69
Spencer, Robert (Baron Spencer of Wormleighton), 67, 136
Spurre, Cornelius, 107
Stanhope, Sir Thomas, 59
Stevens, Richard, 122, 124, 133
Still Harping on Daughters: Women and Drama in the Age of Shakespeare (Jardine), 7, 190 n.14
Stone, Lawrence: *The Family, Sex, and Marriage in England, 1500–1800*, 68
Stone, Nicholas, 122, 124, 125

Stone carving and masonry sculpture, 109–34, 206n.60
Strong, Roy, 148
Styles, William, 103, 109, 206n.41
Summerson, John, 6, 189n.9

Tamworth, Dorothy (Lady Willoughby), 137, 139, 141, 208n.14
Thornhill, Sir James, 160
Thoroton, Robert: *Antiquities of Nottinghamshire*, 165, 167, 169
Thorpe, John, 95, 96, 97, 139, 140
Thurland House (Nottingham), 26
Thynne, Sir John, 36, 71
Tilty, Essex, 17
Tresham, Sir Thomas, 34, 35
Trussell, Henry, 43, 44, 135
Tyler, John, 25

Wardour Castle, Wiltshire, 36, 71, 95, 98, 112, 117–19
Wentworth, Sir William: *Advice to His Son*, 60–61
Willoughby, Abagail, 67
Willoughby, Lady Bridget, 66–67, 136–38, 155–58
Willoughby, Cassandra (Duchess of Chandos): *The Accounts of the Willughby's of Wollaton . . .* , 1, 3, 24, 38–39, 41, 61, 122, 131, 138–39, 158–59, 160, 189nn.1–2, 210n.16; education, 160, 162–63; as a historian, 1, 3, 29, 38, 41, 44, 45, 61–62, 90, 122, 133, 157, 163–66, 211nn.26, 29, 212nn.31, 32; marriage, 163, 181; as mistress of Wollaton, 1–3, 130, 157–60, 162, 163, 165, 181, 211n.21
Willoughby, Dorothy, 67, 135
Willoughby, Edward, 67, 202n.58
Willoughby, Lady Elizabeth. *See* Littleton, Elizabeth (Lady Willoughby)
Willoughby, Frances, 67
Willoughby, Sir Francis (b. 1546–d. 1596): and architecture, 32–33, 35–37, 71–72; business ventures and political activities, 25–27, 50–51, 138, 194nn.62, 63, 199n.46; correspondence, 3, 22–23, 54, 58, 60, 63, 66, 135, 189n.3; and the Court, 22–24, 28, 69; death, 104, 138–39; education and learning, 18–20, 23, 29, 30; heritage, 16; lawsuits, 27; library, 29–33, 196n.91; marriage, first, 21–22, 54–55, 63–64, 135–36; marriage, second, 137, 139, 141; patronage of arts, 28–29, 106; personality, 21, 24–25, 27, 37, 59, 62–63, 70, 136, 137, 166; portrait of, 28; tastes and interests, 13, 19, 24–27, 28, 30–33, 35, 72; wardship, 20, 21; wealth, investments, and property, 12, 24, 28, 38, 179–80, 194nn.62–63
Willoughby, Francis, F. R. S., (d. 1672, Cassandra's father), 160, 162
Willoughby, Sir Francis (b. 1668–d. 1688, Cassandra's brother), 1, 159
Willoughby, George, 21, 24
Willoughby, Sir Henry (d. 1528), 14
Willoughby, Sir Henry (d. 1549), 14
Willoughby, Henry, sixth Lord Middleton (d. 1835), 167–68
Willoughby, Sir Hugh (d. 1553), 14, 191n.10
Willoughby, Sir John (d. 1548), 14
Willoughby, Margaret, Lady Arundell, (b. 1544, sister of Francis), 16, 17, 18, 21, 36, 54
Willoughby, Margaret (daughter of Francis), 67
Willoughby, Sir Percival (d. 1643), 66–67, 136, 138–39, 141, 155, 156, 158, 209n.14
Willoughby, Sir Richard (d. 1471), 197n.5
Willoughby, Thomas (b. 1540–d. 1559), 16, 17, 18, 21, 192n.18
Willoughby, Thomas, first Lord Middleton (b. 1673), 30, 159–63, 189n.8
Willoughby, Sir Thomas (of Chiddingstone), 59, 66

Willoughby, Winifred, 67, 202 n. 58

Willoughby family: and coal mining, 25–26, 51; correspondence, 3, 22–24, 37, 42, 43, 51, 58–60, 63–64, 135–38, 155–58, 189 n. 3; genealogical tree, 15; history, 13–15, 16–27, 191 n. 7, 197 n. 5; kinship, marriage ties, and service bonds, 43–45, 64, 67, 136–38, 198 nn. 15, 19, 201 n. 46, 202 n. 58; landholdings and other property, 14, 25–27, 38, 66, 68, 136; problems and disputes, 9, 16, 21–22, 45, 53–55, 58, 60–63, 66–68, 135–39, 166; rank and power, 14, 17, 44; residences other than Wollaton Hall, 5, 38–40, 55, 135, 155; in Wollaton Hall, 155–56, 158

Wimbledon House, 90, 91, 148

Woad, 26–27

Worksop, Nottinghamshire, 97, 104

Wollaton Hall, building: appearance and size, 9, 12, 39, 69–70, 72, 85–86, 90, 99, 101, 164; builders and craftsmen, 103, 104, 106–9, 112, 119, 122, 125, 130, 131, 134, 205–6 n. 40, 206 nn. 50–51; Camellia House, 177; construction, techniques, and materials, 27, 106–8; cost of construction and decoration, 12, 106–9, 164–65, 206 n. 59; decoration and ornamentation, 33, 85, 87, 105 n. 7, 109, 112, 130–31, 133, 142, 160, 168; exterior sculpture and carvings, 108–9, 112, 115, 116, 119–22, 125–32; fire, 125, 131, 158; furnishings, 139, 141–44, 146, 160, 165; gardens and terraces, 1, 90, 147–49, 160, 167; interior, 90–91, 99, 139–47, 149,

151; origin of the new Hall, 5, 25, 35, 36–38, 40, 67; plan and design, 36–37, 51–52, 54, 67–70, 71, 72, 84–86, 90–99, 148–49; renovations and remodelling, 1, 106, 125, 130, 139, 144, 145, 147, 158, 159, 160, 166–68, 177, 212 n. 47; sale of the Hall, 177, 189 n. 8; social and cultural significance, 4–5, 13, 35, 46, 51, 69, 72, 99, 102, 135, 149, 166, 167, 181–83; spatial characteristics and their social implications, 8, 13, 69–70, 91, 93, 96, 136, 149–51, 168; vacant, 125, 141, 158, 159

Wollaton Hall, household: entertainment and visitors, 28, 29, 42, 47, 70, 135, 136, 155, 158, 163–64; expenses, 28, 30, 51, 195 n. 79; general characteristics, 27–29, 39–40, 41–52, 136, 156, 180; protocol, order, and ceremony, 29, 41–43, 47–49, 185–87, 198 n. 16; staff, officers, and servants, 41–45, 59–60, 66–68, 103–4, 137, 141, 157, 159, 165, 185–87, 198 n. 15; women in, 45–50, 62, 68, 147, 148, 156–58, 180

Wollaton Hall, Old (Manor house), 38–41, 197 n. 3

Wollaton, St. Leonard's Church, 102, 131

Women: in households, 45–50, 160, 182, 199 nn. 39, 41, 202 n. 60; and psychology of property rights, 56–59, 60–61, 181–82; in social structure, 6–7, 64–65, 68–69, 163, 190 nn. 12, 13, 202 n. 50, 210 n. 4, 211 n. 25; treatment and punishment of, 61, 62, 202 nn. 49, 51

Wyatville, Sir Jeffry, 144, 168